Books of the Apocrypha:

The Books of Enoch and the Gnostic Gospels

Micah Williams; Grapevine Press

Published by

GRAPEVINE INDIA PUBLISHERS PVT LTD

www.grapevineindia.com
Delhi | Mumbai
email: grapevineindiapublishers@gmail.com

Ordering Information:
Quantity sales: Special discounts are available on quantity purchases by corporations, associations, and others.
For details, reach out to the publisher.

First published by Grapevine India 2023

CONTENTS

BOOK OF 1 ENOCH

SECTION I. INTRODUCTION

CHAPTER 1

1 The words of the blessing of Enoch, wherewith he blessed the elect and righteous,
who will be 2 living in the day of tribulation, when all the wicked and godless are to
be removed. And he took up his parable and said Enoch a righteous man, whose eyes
were opened by God, saw the vision of the Holy One in the heavens, which the angels
showed me, and from them I heard everything, and from them I understood as I saw,
but not for this generation, but for a remote one which is 3 for to come. Concerning the
elect I said, and took up my parable concerning them:

The Holy Great One will come forth from His dwelling,

4 And the eternal God will tread upon the earth, (even) on Mount Sinai,

[And appear from His camp]

And appear in the strength of His might from the heaven of heavens.

5 And all shall be smitten with fear.

And the Watchers shall quake,

And great fear and trembling shall seize them unto the ends of the earth.

6 And the high mountains shall be shaken,

And the high hills shall be made low,

And shall melt like wax before the flame.

7 And the earth shall be wholly rent in sunder,

And all that is upon the earth shall perish,

And there shall be a judgement upon all (men).

8 But with the righteous He will make peace.

And will protect the elect,

And mercy shall be upon them.

And they shall all belong to God,

And they shall be prospered,

And they shall all be blessed.

And He will help them all,

And light shall appear unto them,

And He will make peace with them'.

9 And behold! He cometh with ten thousand of His holy ones

To execute judgement upon all,

And to destroy all the ungodly:

And to convict all flesh

Of all the works of their ungodliness which they have ungodly committed,

And of all the hard things which ungodly sinners have spoken against Him.

CHAPTER 2

Observe ye everything that takes place in the heaven, how they do not change their orbits, and the luminaries which are in the heaven, how they all rise and set in order each in its season, and transgress not against their appointed order. Behold ye the earth and give heed to the things which take place upon it from first to last, how steadfast they are, how none of the things upon earth change, but all the works of God appear to you. Behold the summer and the winter, how the whole earth is filled with water, and clouds and dew and rain lie upon it.

CHAPTER 3

Observe and see how (in the winter) all the trees seem as though they had withered and shed all their leaves, except fourteen trees, which do not lose their foliage but retain the old foliage from two to three years till the new comes.

CHAPTER 4

And again, observe ye the days of summer how the sun is above the earth over against it. And you seek shade and shelter by reason of the heat of the sun, and the earth also burns with growing heat, and so you cannot tread on the earth, or on a rock by reason of its heat.

CHAPTER 5

1 Observe ye how the trees cover themselves with green leaves and bear fruit: wherefore give ye heed and know with regard to all His works and recognize how He that liveth for ever hath made them so. 2 And all His works go on thus from year to year for ever, and all the tasks which they accomplish for Him, and their tasks change not, but according as God hath ordained so is it done. 3 And behold how the sea and the rivers in like manner accomplish and change not their tasks from His commandments'.

4 But ye -ye have not been steadfast, nor done the commandments of the Lord,

But ye have turned away and spoken proud and hard words.

With your impure mouths against His greatness.

Oh, ye hard-hearted, ye shall find no peace.

5 Therefore shall ye execrate your days,

And the years of your life shall perish,

And the years of your destruction shall be multiplied in eternal execration,

And ye shall find no mercy.

6a In those days ye shall make your names an eternal execration unto all the righteous,

b And by you shall all who curse, curse,

And all the sinners and godless shall imprecate by you,

7c And for you the godless there shall be a curse.

6d And all the . . . shall rejoice,

e And there shall be forgiveness of sins,

f And every mercy and peace and forbearance:

g There shall be salvation unto them, a goodly light.

i And for all of you sinners there shall be no salvation,

j But on you all shall abide a curse.

7a But for the elect there shall be light and joy and peace,

b And they shall inherit the earth.

8 And then there shall be bestowed upon the elect wisdom,

And they shall all live and never again sin,

Either through ungodliness or through pride:

But they who are wise shall be humble.

9 And they shall not again transgress,

Nor shall they sin all the days of their life,

Nor shall they die of (the divine) anger or wrath,

But they shall complete the number of the days of their life.

And their lives shall be increased in peace,

And the years of their joy shall be multiplied,

In eternal gladness and peace,

All the days of their life

CHAPTER 6

1 And it came to pass when the children of men had multiplied that in those days were born unto 2 them beautiful and comely daughters. And the angels, the children of the heaven, saw and lusted after them, and said to one another: 'Come, let us choose us wives from among the children of men 3 and beget us children.' And Semjaza, who was their leader, said unto them: 'I fear ye will not 4 indeed agree to do this deed, and I alone shall have to pay the penalty of a great sin.' And they all answered him and said: 'Let us all swear an oath, and all bind ourselves by mutual imprecations 5 not to abandon this plan but to do this thing.' Then sware they all together and bound themselves 6 by mutual imprecations upon it. And they were in all two hundred, who descended in the days of Jared on the summit of Mount Hermon, and they called it Mount Hermon, because they had sworn 7 and bound themselves by mutual imprecations upon it. And these are the names of their leaders: Samlazaz, their leader, Araklba, Rameel, Kokablel, Tamlel, Ramlel, Danel, Ezeqeel, Baraqijal, 8 Asael, Armaros, Batarel, Ananel, Zaqiel, Samsapeel, Satarel, Turel, Jomjael, Sariel. These are their chiefs of tens.

CHAPTER 7

1 And all the others together with them took unto themselves wives, and each chose for himself one, and they began to go in unto them and to defile themselves with them, and they taught them charms 2 and enchantments, and the cutting of roots, and made them acquainted with plants. And they 3 became pregnant, and they bare great giants, whose height was three thousand ells: Who consumed 4 all the acquisitions of

men. And when men could no longer sustain them, the giants turned against 5 them
and devoured mankind. And they began to sin against birds, and beasts, and reptiles,
and 6 fish, and to devour one another's flesh, and drink the blood. Then the earth laid
accusation against the lawless ones.

CHAPTER 8

1 And Azazel taught men to make swords, and knives, and shields, and breastplates,
and made known to them the metals of the earth and the art of working them, and
bracelets, and ornaments, and the use of antimony, and the beautifying of the eyelids,
and all kinds of costly stones, and all 2 colouring tinctures. And there arose much
godlessness, and they committed fornication, and they 3 were led astray, and became
corrupt in all their ways. Semjaza taught enchantments, and root-cuttings, 'Armaros the
resolving of enchantments, Baraqijal (taught) astrology, Kokabel the constellations,
Ezeqeel the knowledge of the clouds, Araqiel the signs of the earth, Shamsiel the signs
of the sun, and Sariel the course of the moon. And as men perished, they cried, and
their cry went up to heaven . . .

CHAPTER 9

1 And then Michael, Uriel, Raphael, and Gabriel looked down from heaven and saw
much blood being 2 shed upon the earth, and all lawlessness being wrought upon the
earth. And they said one to another: 'The earth made without inhabitant cries the voice
of their cryingst up to the gates of heaven. 3 And now to you, the holy ones of heaven,
the souls of men make their suit, saying, "Bring our cause 4 before the Highest."' And
they said to the Lord of the ages: 'Lord of lords, God of gods, King of kings, and God
of the ages, the throne of Thy glory (standeth) unto all the generations of the 5 ages,
and Thy name holy and glorious and blessed unto all the ages! Thou hast made all
things, and power over all things hast Thou: and all things are naked and open in Thy
sight, and Thou seest all 6 things, and nothing can hide itself from Thee. Thou seest
what Azazel hath done, who hath taught all unrighteousness on earth and revealed the
eternal secrets which were (preserved) in heaven, which 7 men were striving to learn:
And Semjaza, to whom Thou hast given authority to bear rule over his associates.
And they have gone to the daughters of men upon the earth, and have slept with the 9
women, and have defiled themselves, and revealed to them all kinds of sins. And the
women have 10 borne giants, and the whole earth has thereby been filled with blood
and unrighteousness. And now, behold, the souls of those who have died are crying
and making their suit to the gates of heaven, and their lamentations have ascended:
and cannot cease because of the lawless deeds which are 11 wrought on the earth. And
Thou knows all things before they come to pass, and Thou seest these things and Thou
dost suffer them, and Thou dost not say to us what we are to do to them in regard to
these.'

CHAPTER 10

1 Then said the Most High, the Holy and Great One spake, and sent Uriel to the son
of Lamech, 2 and said to him: 'Go to Noah and tell him in my name "Hide thyself!"
and reveal to him the end that is approaching: that the whole earth will be destroyed,
and a deluge is about to come 3 upon the whole earth, and will destroy all that is on it.
And now instruct him that he may escape 4 and his seed may be preserved for all the
generations of the world.' And again, the Lord said to Raphael: 'Bind Azazel hand and
foot and cast him into the darkness: and make an opening 5 in the desert, which is in
Dudael, and cast him therein. And place upon him rough and jagged rocks, and cover
him with darkness, and let him abide there for ever, and cover his face that he may not
see light. And on the day of the great judgement, he shall be cast into the fire. And heal
the earth which the angels have corrupted, and proclaim the healing of the earth, that
they may heal the plague, and that all the children of men may not perish through all
the secret things that the 8 Watchers have disclosed and have taught their sons. And
the whole earth has been corrupted 9 through the works that were taught by Azazel:
to him ascribe all sin.' And to Gabriel said the Lord: 'Proceed against the bastards and
the reprobates, and against the children of fornication: and destroy [the children of
fornication and] the children of the Watchers from amongst men [and cause them to
go forth]: send them one against the other that they may destroy each other in battle:
for length of days shall they not have. And no request that they (i.e., their fathers)
make of thee shall be granted unto their fathers on their behalf; for they hope to live
an eternal life, and that each one of them will live five hundred years.' And the Lord
said unto Michael: 'Go, bind Semjaza and his associates who have united themselves
with women to have defiled themselves with them in all their uncleanness. And when
their sons have slain one another, and they have seen the destruction of their beloved
ones, bind them fast for seventy generations in the valleys of the earth, till the day
of their judgement and of their consummation, till the judgement that is for ever and
ever is consummated. In those days they shall be led off to the abyss of fire: and to the
torment and the prison in which they shall be confined for ever. And whosoever shall
be condemned and destroyed will from thenceforth be bound together with them to
the end of all generations. And destroy all the spirits of the reprobate and the children
of the Watchers, because 16 they have wronged mankind. Destroy all wrong from
the face of the earth and let every evil work come to an end: and let the plant of
righteousness and truth appear and it shall prove a blessing; the works of righteousness
and truth' shall be planted in truth and joy for evermore.

17 And then shall all the righteous escape,

And shall live till they beget thousands of children.

And all the days of their youth and their old age

Shall they complete in peace.

18 And then shall the whole earth be tilled in righteousness and shall all be planted
with trees and 19 be full of blessing. And all desirable trees shall be planted on it, and
they shall plant vines on it: and the vine which they plant thereon shall yield wine in
abundance, and as for all the seed which is sown thereon each measure (of it) shall bear

a thousand, and each measure of olives shall yield 20 ten presses of oil. And cleanse thou the earth from all oppression, and from all unrighteousness, and from all sin, and from all godlessness: and all the uncleanness that is wrought upon the earth 21 destroy from off the earth. And all the children of men shall become righteous, and all nations 22 shall offer adoration and shall praise Me, and all shall worship Me. And the earth shall be cleansed from all defilement, and from all sin, and from all punishment, and from all torment, and I will never again send (them) upon it from generation to generation and for ever.

CHAPTER 11

1 And in those days, I will open the store chambers of blessing which are in the heaven, so as to send 2 them down upon the earth over the work and labour of the children of men. And truth and peace shall be associated together throughout all the days of the world and throughout all the generations of men.'

CHAPTER 12

1 Before these things Enoch was hidden, and no one of the children of men knew where he was 2 hidden, and where he abode, and what had become of him. And his activities had to do with the Watchers, and his days were with the holy ones. 3 And I Enoch was blessing the Lord of majesty and the King of the ages, and lo! the Watchers 4 called me -Enoch the scribe- and said to me: 'Enoch, thou scribe of righteousness, go, declare to the Watchers of the heaven who have left the high heaven, the holy eternal place, and have defiled themselves with women, and have done as the children of earth do, and have taken unto themselves 5 wives: "Ye have wrought great destruction on the earth: And ye shall have no peace nor forgiveness 6 of sin: and inasmuch as they delight themselves in their children, The murder of their beloved ones shall they see, and over the destruction of their children shall they lament, and shall make supplication unto eternity, but mercy and peace shall ye not attain."'

CHAPTER 13

1 And Enoch went and said: 'Azazel, thou shalt have no peace: a severe sentence has gone forth 2 against thee to put thee in bonds: And thou shalt not have toleration nor request granted to thee, because of the unrighteousness which thou hast taught, and because of all the works of godlessness 3 and unrighteousness and sin which thou hast shown to men.' Then I went and spoke to them all 4 together, and they were all afraid, and fear and trembling seized them. And they besought me to draw up a petition for

them that they might find forgiveness, and to read their petition in the presence 5 of the Lord of heaven. For from thenceforward they could not speak (with Him) nor lift their 6 eyes to heaven for shame of their sins for which they had been condemned. Then I wrote out their petition, and the prayer regarding their spirits and their deeds individually and in regard to their 7 requests that they should have forgiveness and length. And I went off and sat down at the waters of Dan, in the land of Dan, to the south of the west of Hermon: I read their petition till I fell 8 asleep. And behold a dream came to me, and visions fell down upon me, and I saw visions of chastisement, and a voice came bidding (me) I to tell it to the sons of heaven and reprimand them. 9 And when I awaked, I came unto them, and they were all sitting gathered, weeping in 10 'Abelsjail, which is between Lebanon and Seneser, with their faces covered. And I recounted before them all the visions which I had seen in sleep, and I began to speak the words of righteousness, and to reprimand the heavenly Watchers.

CHAPTER 14

The book of the words of righteousness, and of the reprimand of the eternal Watchers in accordance with the command of the Holy Great One in that vision. I saw in my sleep what I will now say with a tongue of flesh and with the breath of my mouth: which the Great One has given to men to converses therewith and understand with the heart. As He has created and given to man the power of understanding the word of wisdom, so hath He created me also and given me the power of reprimanding the Watchers, the children of heaven. I wrote out your petition, and in my vision, it appeared thus, that your petition will not be granted unto you throughout all the days of eternity, and that judgement has been finally passed upon you: yea (your petition) will not be granted unto you. And from henceforth you shall not ascend into heaven unto all eternity, and in bonds of the earth the decree has gone forth to bind you for all the days of the world. And (that) previously you shall have seen the destruction of your beloved sons and ye shall have no pleasure in them, but they shall fall before you by the sword. And your petition on their behalf shall not be granted, nor yet on your own: even though you weep and pray and speak all the words contained in the writing which I have written. And the vision was shown to me thus: Behold, in the vision clouds invited me and a mist summoned me, and the course of the stars and the lightnings sped and hastened me, and the winds in the vision caused me to fly and lifted me upward and bore me into heaven. And I went in till I drew nigh to a wall which is built of crystals and surrounded by tongues of fire: and it began to affright 10 me. And I went into the tongues of fire and drew nigh to a large house which was built of crystals: and the walls of the house were like a tessellated floor (made) of crystals, and its groundwork was of crystal. Its ceiling was like the path of the stars and the lightnings, and between them were fiery cherubim, and their heaven was (clear as) water. A flaming fire surrounded the walls, and its portals blazed with fire. And I entered that house, and it was hot as fire and cold as ice: there were no delights of life therein: fear covered me, and trembling got hold upon me. And as I quaked and trembled, I fell upon my face. And I beheld a vision, and lo! there was a second house, greater than the former, and the entire portal stood open before me, and it was built of flames of fire. And in every respect, it so excelled in splendour and magnificence and extent that I cannot describe to you its splendour and its extent. And its floor was of fire, and above it was lightninging and the path of the stars, and its ceiling also was flaming fire. And I looked and saw therein a lofty throne: its appearance was as crystal, and the wheels thereof as the shining sun, and there was the vision of cherubim. And from underneath the throne came streams of flaming fire so that I could not look thereon. And the Great Glory sat thereon, and His raiment shone more brightly than the sun and was whiter than any snow. None of the angels could enter and could behold His face by reason of the magnificence and glory and no flesh could behold Him. The flaming fire was round about Him, and a great fire stood before Him, and none around could draw nigh Him: ten thousand times ten thousand (stood) before Him, yet He needed no counsellor. And the most holy ones who were nigh to Him did not leave by night nor depart from Him. And until then I had been prostrated on my face, trembling: and the Lord called me with His own mouth, and said to me: ' Come hither, Enoch, and hear my word.' And one of the holy ones came to me and waked me, and He made me rise up and approach the door: and I bowed my face downwards.

CHAPTER 15

And He answered and said to me, and I heard His voice: 'Fear not, Enoch, thou righteous man and scribe of righteousness: approach hither and hear my voice. And go, say to the Watchers of heaven, who have sent thee to intercede for them: "You should intercede" for men, and not men for you: Wherefore have ye left the high, holy, and eternal heaven, and lain with women, and defiled yourselves with the daughters of men and taken to yourselves wives, and done like the children of earth, and begotten giants (as your) sons? And though ye were holy, spiritual, living the eternal life, you have defiled yourselves with the blood of women, and have begotten (children) with the blood of flesh, and, as the children of men, have lusted after flesh and blood as those also do who die and perish. Therefore, have I given them wives also that they might impregnate them, and beget children by them, that thus nothing might be wanting to them on earth. But you were formerly spirituals, living the eternal life, and immortal for all generations of the world. And therefore, I have not appointed wives for you; for as for the spiritual ones of the heaven, in heaven is their dwelling. And now, the giants, who are produced from the spirits and flesh, shall be called evil spirits upon the earth, and on the earth shall be their dwelling. Evil spirits have proceeded from their bodies; because they are born from men and from the holy Watchers is their beginning and primal origin; 10 they shall be evil spirits on earth, and evil spirits shall they be called. [As for the spirits of heaven, in heaven shall be their dwelling, but as for the spirits of the earth which were born upon the earth, on the earth shall be their dwelling.] And the spirits of the giants afflict, oppress, destroy, attack, do battle, and work destruction on the earth, and cause trouble: they take no food, but nevertheless hunger and thirst, and cause offences. And these spirits shall rise up against the children of men and against the women, because they have proceeded from them.

CHAPTER 16

1 From the days of the slaughter and destruction and death of the giants, from the souls of whose flesh the spirits, having gone forth, shall destroy without incurring judgement -thus shall they destroy until the day of the consummation, the great judgement in which the age shall be 2 consummated, over the Watchers and the godless, yea, shall be wholly consummated." And now as to the watchers who have sent thee to intercede for them, who had been a foretime in heaven, (say 3 to them): "You have been in heaven, but all the mysteries had not yet been revealed to you, and you knew worthless ones, and these in the hardness of your hearts you have made known to the women, and through these mysteries women and men work much evil on earth." 4 Say to them therefore: " You have no peace."'

CHAPTER 17

1 And they took and brought me to a place in which those who were there were like flaming fire, 2 and, when they wished, they appeared as men. And they brought me to the place of darkness, and to a mountain the point of whose summit reached to heaven. And I saw the places of the luminaries and the treasuries of the stars and of the thunder and in the uttermost depths, where were 4 a fiery bow and arrows and their quiver, and a fiery sword and all the lightnings. And they took 5 me to the living waters, and to the fire of the west, which receives every setting of the sun. And I came to a river of fire in which the fire flows like water and discharges itself into the great sea towards 6 the west. I saw the great rivers and came to the great river and to the great darkness and went 7 to the place where no flesh walks. I saw the mountains of the darkness of winter and the place 8 whence all the waters of the deep flow. I saw the mouths of all the rivers of the earth and the mouth of the deep.

CHAPTER 18

I saw the treasuries of all the winds: I saw how He had furnished with them the whole creation and the firm foundations of the earth. And I saw the cornerstone of the earth: I saw the four winds which bear [the earth and] the firmament of the heaven. And I saw how the winds stretch out the vaults of heaven and have their station between heaven and earth: these are the pillars of the heaven. I saw the winds of heaven which turn and bring the circumference of the sun and all the stars to their setting. I saw the winds on the earth carrying the clouds: I saw the paths of the angels. I saw at the end of the earth the firmament of the heaven above. And I proceeded and saw a place which burns day and night, where there are seven mountains of magnificent stones, three towards the east, and three towards the south. And as for those towards the east, was of coloured stone, and one of pearl, and one of jacinth, and those towards the south of red stone. But the middle one reached to heaven like the throne of God, of alabaster, and the summit of the ,0 throne was of sapphire. And I saw a flaming fire. And beyond these mountains Is a region the end of the great earth: there the heavens were completed. And I saw a deep abyss, with columns of heavenly fire, and among them I saw columns of fire fall, which were beyond measure alike towards the height and towards the depth. And beyond that abyss I saw a place which had no firmament of the heaven above, and no firmly founded earth beneath it: there was no water upon it, and no birds, but it was a waste and horrible place. I saw there seven stars like great burning mountains, and to me, when I inquired regarding them, the angel said: 'This place is the end of heaven and earth: this has become a prison for the stars and the host of heaven. And the stars which roll over the fire are they which have transgressed the commandment of the Lord in the beginning of their rising, because they did not come forth at their appointed times. And He was wroth with them and bound them till the time when their guilt should be consummated (even) for ten thousand years.'

CHAPTER 19

1 And Uriel said to me: 'Here shall stand the angels who have connected themselves with women, and their spirits assuming many different forms are defiling mankind and shall lead them astray into sacrificing to demons as gods, (here shall they stand,) till the day of the great judgement in 2 which they shall be judged till they are made an end of. And the women also of the angels who 3 went astray shall become sirens.' And I, Enoch, alone saw the vision, the ends of all things: and no man shall see as I have seen.

CHAPTER 20

1,2 And these are the names of the holy angels who watch. Uriel, one of the holy angels, who is 3 over the world and over Tartarus. Raphael, one of the holy angels, who is over the spirits of men. 4,5 Raguel, one of the holy angels who takes vengeance on the world of the luminaries. Michael, one 6 of the holy angels, to wit, he that is set over the best part of mankind and over chaos. Saraqael, 7 one of the holy angels, who is set over the spirits, who sin in the spirit. Gabriel, one of the holy 8 angels, who is over Paradise and the serpents and the Cherubim. Remiel, one of the holy angels, whom God set over those who rise.

CHAPTER 21

, And I proceeded to where things were chaotic. And I saw there something horrible: I saw neither a heaven above nor a firmly founded earth, but a place chaotic and horrible. And there I saw seven stars of the heaven bound together in it, like great mountains and burning with fire. Then I said: 'For what sin are they bound, and on what account have they been cast in hither?' Then said Uriel, one of the holy angels, who was with me, and was chief over them, and said: 'Enoch, why dost thou ask, and why art thou eager for the truth? These are of the number of the stars of heaven, which have transgressed the commandment of the Lord, and are bound here till ten thousand years, the time entailed by their sins, are consummated.' And from thence I went to another place, which was still more horrible than the former, and I saw a horrible thing: a great fire there which burnt and blazed, and the place was cleft as far as the abyss, being full of great descending columns of fire: neither its extent or magnitude could I see, nor could I conjecture. Then I said: 'How fearful is the place and how terrible to look upon!' Then Uriel answered me, one of the holy angels who was with me, and said unto me: 'Enoch, why hast thou such fear and affright?' And I answered: 'Because of this fearful place, and because of the spectacle of the pain.' And he said unto me: 'This place is the prison of the angels, and here they will be imprisoned for ever.'

CHAPTER 22

And thence I went to another place, and he mountain [and] of hard rock. And there was in it four hollow places, deep and wide and very smooth. How smooth are the hollow places and deep and dark to look at. Then Raphael answered, one of the holy angels who was with me, and said unto me: 'These hollow places have been created for this very purpose, that the spirits of the souls of the dead should assemble therein, yea that all the souls of the children of men should assemble here. And these places have been made to receive them till the day of their judgement and till their appointed period [till the period appointed], till the great judgement (comes) upon them.' I saw (the spirit of) a dead man making suit, and his voice went forth to heaven and made suit. And I asked Raphael the angel who was with me, and I said unto him: 'This spirit which make suit, whose is it, whose voice goes forth and make suit to heaven?' And he answered me saying: 'This is the spirit which went forth from Abel, whom his brother Cain slew, and he makes his suit against him till his seed is destroyed from the face of the earth, and his seed is annihilated from amongst the seed of men.' The I asked regarding it, and regarding all the hollow places: 'Why is one separated from the other?' And he answered me and said unto me: 'These three have been made that the spirits of the dead might be separated. And such a division has been making (for) the spirits of the righteous, in which there is the bright spring of water. And such has been made for sinners when they die and are buried in the earth and judgement has not been executed on them in their lifetimes. Here their spirits shall be set apart in this great pain till the great day of judgement and punishment and torment of those who curse for ever and retribution for their spirits. There He shall bind them for ever. And such a division has been made for the spirits of those who make their suit, who make disclosures concerning their destruction, when they were slain in the days of the sinners. Such has been made for the spirits of men who were not righteous but sinners, who were complete in transgression, and of the transgressors they shall be companions: but their spirits shall not be slain in the day of judgement, nor shall they be raised from thence.' The I blessed the Lord of glory and said: 'Blessed be my Lord, the Lord of righteousness, who ruleth for ever.'

CHAPTER 23

, From thence I went to another place to the west of the ends of the earth. And I saw a burning fire which ran without resting and paused not from its course day or night but (ran) regularly. And I asked saying: 'What is this which rests not?' Then Raguel, one of the holy angels who was with me, answered me and said unto me: 'This course of fire which thou hast seen is the fire in the west which persecutes all the luminaries of heaven.'

CHAPTER 24

And from thence I went to another place of the earth, and he showed me a mountain range of fire which burnt day and night. And I went beyond it and saw seven magnificent mountains all differing each from the other, and the stones (thereof) were magnificent and beautiful, magnificent, of glorious appearance and fair exterior: three towards the east, one founded on the other, and three towards the south, one upon the other, and deep rough ravines, no one of which joined with any other. And the seventh mountain was in the midst of these, and it excelled them in height, resembling the seat of a throne: and fragrant trees encircled the throne. And amongst them was a tree such as I had never yet smelt, neither was any amongst them nor were others like it: it had a fragrance beyond all fragrance, and its leaves and blooms and wood wither not for ever: and its fruit is beautiful, and its fruit n resembles the dates of a palm. Then I said: 'How beautiful is this tree, and fragrant, and its leaves are fair, and its blooms very delightful in appearance.' Then answered Michael, one of the holy and honoured angels who was with me and was their leader.

CHAPTER 25

And he said unto me: 'Enoch, why dost thou ask me regarding the fragrance of the tree, and why dost thou wish to learn the truth?' Then I answered him saying: 'I wish to know about everything, but especially about this tree.' And he answered saying: 'This high mountain which thou hast seen, whose summit is like the throne of God, is His throne, where the Holy Great One, the Lord of Glory, the Eternal King, will sit, when He shall come down to visit the earth with goodness. And as for this fragrant tree no mortal is permitted to touch it till the great judgement, when He shall take vengeance on all and bring (everything) to its consummation for ever. It shall then be given to the righteous and holy. Its fruit shall be for food to the elect: it shall be transplanted to the holy place, to the temple of the Lord, the Eternal King.

6 Then shall they rejoice with joy and be glad,

And into the holy place shall they enter.

And its fragrance shall be in their bones,

And they shall live a long life on earth,

Such as thy fathers lived:

And in their days shall no sorrow or plague

Or torment or calamity touch them.'

7 Then blessed I the God of Glory, the Eternal King, who hath prepared such things for the righteous, and hath created them and promised to give to them.

CHAPTER 26

And I went from thence to the middle of the earth, and I saw a blessed place in which there were trees with branches abiding and blooming [of a dismembered tree]. And there I saw a holy mountain, and underneath the mountain to the east there was a stream and it flowed towards the south. And I saw towards the east another mountain higher than this, and between them a deep and narrow ravine: in it also ran a stream underneath the mountain. And to the west thereof there was another mountain, lower than the former and of small elevation, and a ravine deep and dry between them: and another deep and dry ravine was at the extremities of the three mountains. And all the ravines were deep and narrow, (being formed) of hard rock, and trees were not planted upon them. And I marvelled at the rocks, and I marvelled at the ravine, yea, I marvelled very much.

CHAPTER 27

1 Then said I: 'For what object is this blessed land, which is entirely filled with trees, and these 2 accursed valleys between?' Then Uriel, one of the holy angels who was with me, answered and said: 'This accursed valley is for those who are accursed for ever: Here shall all the accursed be gathered who utter with their lips against the Lord unseemly words and of His glory speak hard things. Here shall they be gathered, and here 3 shall be their place of judgement. In the last days there shall be upon them the spectacle of righteous judgement in the presence of the righteous for ever: here shall the merciful bless the Lord of glory, the Eternal King. 4 In the days of judgement over the former, they shall bless Him for the mercy in accordance with 5 which He has assigned them (their lot).' Then I blessed the Lord of Glory and set forth His glory and lauded Him gloriously.

CHAPTER 28

And thence I went towards the east, into the midst of the mountain range of the desert, and I saw a wilderness and it was solitary, full of trees and plants. And water gushed forth from above. Rushing like a copious watercourse [which flowed] towards the north-west it caused clouds and dew to ascend on every side.

CHAPTER 29

And thence I went to another place in the desert and approached to the east of this mountain range. And there I saw aromatic trees exhaling the fragrance of frankincense and myrrh, and the trees also were like the almond tree.

CHAPTER 30

, And beyond these, I went afar to the east, and I saw another place, a valley (full) of water. And therein there was a tree, the colour (?) of fragrant trees such as the mastic. And on the sides of those valleys, I saw fragrant cinnamon. And beyond these I proceeded to the east.

CHAPTER 31

And I saw other mountains, and amongst them were groves of trees, and there flowed forth from them nectar, which is named sarara and galbanum. And beyond these mountains I saw another mountain to the east of the ends of the earth, whereon were aloe-trees, and all the trees were full of state, being like almond-trees. And when one burnt it, it smelt sweeter than any fragrant odour.

CHAPTER 32

And after these fragrant odours, as I looked towards the north over the mountains, I saw seven mountains full of choice nard and fragrant trees and cinnamon and pepper. And thence I went over the summits of all these mountains, far towards the east of the earth, and passed above the Erythraean sea and went far from it and passed over the angel Zotiel. And I came to the Garden of Righteousness, I and from afar off trees more numerous than I these trees and great-two trees there, very great, beautiful, and glorious, and magnificent, and the tree of knowledge, whose holy fruit they eat and know great wisdom. That tree is in height like the fir, and its leaves are like (those of) the Carob tree: and its fruit is like the clusters of the vine, very beautiful: and the fragrance of the tree penetrates afar. Then I said: 'How beautiful is the tree, and how attractive is its look!' Then Raphael the holy angel, who was with me, answered me and said: 'This is the tree of wisdom, of which thy father old (in years) and thy aged mother, who were before thee, have eaten, and they learnt wisdom and their eyes were opened, and they knew that they were naked, and they were driven out of the garden.'

CHAPTER 33

And from thence I went to the ends of the earth and saw their great beasts, and each differed from the other; and (I saw) birds also differing in appearance and beauty and voice, the one differing from the other. And to the east of those beasts, I saw the ends of the earth whereon the heaven rests, and the portals of the heaven open. And I saw how the stars of heaven come forth, and I counted the portals out of which they proceed, and wrote down all their outlets, of each individual star by itself, according to their number and their names, their courses and their positions, and their times and their months, as Uriel the holy angel who was with me showed me. He showed all things to me and wrote them down for me: also their names he wrote for me, and their laws and their companies.

CHAPTER 34

And from thence I went towards the north to the ends of the earth, and there I saw a great and glorious device at the ends of the whole earth. And here I saw three portals of heaven open in the heaven: through each of them proceed north winds: when they blow there is cold, hail, frost, snow, dew, and rain. And out of one portal they blow for good: but when they blow through the other two portals, it is with violence and affliction on the earth, and they blow with violence.

CHAPTER 35

And from thence I went towards the west to the ends of the earth and saw there three portals of the heaven open such as I had seen in the east, the same number of portals, and the same number of outlets.

CHAPTER 36

And from thence I went to the south to the ends of the earth and saw there three open portals of the heaven: and thence there come dew, rain, and wind. And from thence I went to the east to the ends of the heaven and saw here the three eastern portals of heaven open and small portals above them. Through each of these small portals pass the stars of heaven and run their course to the west on the path which is shown to them. And as often as I saw I blessed always the Lord of Glory, and I continued to bless the Lord of Glory who has wrought great and glorious wonders, to show the greatness of His work to the angels and to spirits and to men, that they might praise His work and all His creation: that they might see the work of His might and praise the great work of His hands and bless Him for ever.

SECTION II. CHAPTERS XXXVII-LXXI

THE PARABLES

CHAPTER 37

The second vision which he saw, the vision of wisdom -which Enoch the son of Jared, the son of Mahalalel, the son of Cainan, the son of Enos, the son of Seth, the son of Adam, saw. And this is the beginning of the words of wisdom which I lifted up my voice to speak and say to those which dwells on earth: Hear, ye men of old time, and see, ye that come after, the words of the Holy One which I will speak before the Lord of Spirits. It was better to declare (them only) to the men of old time, but even from those that come after we will not withhold the beginning of wisdom. Till the present day such wisdom has never been given by the Lord of Spirits as I have received according to my insight, according to the good pleasure of the Lord of Spirits by whom the lot of eternal life has been given to me. Now three Parables were imparted to me, and I lifted up my voice and recounted them to those that dwell on the earth.

CHAPTER 38

1 The first Parable.

When the congregation of the righteous shall appear,

And sinners shall be judged for their sins,

And shall be driven from the face of the earth:

2 And when the Righteous One shall appear before the eyes of the righteous,

Whose elect works hang upon the Lord of Spirits,

And light shall appear to the righteous and the elect who dwell on the earth,

Where then will be the dwelling of the sinners,

And where the resting-place of those who have denied the Lord of Spirits?

It had been good for them if they had not been born.

3 When the secrets of the righteous shall be revealed and the sinners judged,

And the godless driven from the presence of the righteous and elect,

4 From that time those that possess the earth shall no longer be powerful and exalted:

And they shall not be able to behold the face of the holy,

For the Lord of Spirits has caused His light to appear

On the face of the holy, righteous, and elect.

5 Then shall the kings and the mighty perish.

And be given into the hands of the righteous and holy.

6 And thenceforward none shall seek for themselves mercy from the Lord of Spirits

For their life is at an end.

CHAPTER 39

1 [And it shall come to pass in those days that elect and holy children will descend from the 2 high heaven, and their seed will become one with the children of men. And in those days Enoch received books of zeal and wrath, and books of disquiet and expulsion.]

And mercy shall not be accorded to them, saith the Lord of Spirits.

3 And in those days a whirlwind carried me off from the earth,

And set me down at the end of the heavens.

4 And there I saw another vision, the dwelling-places of the holy,

And the resting-places of the righteous.

5 Here mine eyes saw their dwellings with His righteous angels,

And their resting-places with the holy.

And they petitioned and interceded and prayed for the children of men,

And righteousness flowed before them as water,

And mercy like dew upon the earth:

Thus, it is amongst them for ever and ever.

6a And in that place mine eyes saw the Elect One of righteousness and of faith,

7a And I saw his dwelling-place under the wings of the Lord of Spirits.

6b And righteousness shall prevail in his days,

And the righteous and elect shall be without number before Him for ever and ever.

7b And all the righteous and elect before Him shall be strong as fiery lights,

And their mouth shall be full of blessing,

And their lips extol the name of the Lord of Spirits,

And righteousness before Him shall never fail,

[And uprightness shall never fail before Him.]

8 There I wished to dwell,

And my spirit longed for that dwelling-place:

And there heretofore hath been my portion,

For so has it been established concerning me before the Lord of Spirits.

9 In those days I praised and extolled the name of the Lord of Spirits with blessings and praises, because He hath destined me for blessing and glory according to the good pleasure of the Lord of Spirits. For a long time, my eyes regarded that place, and I blessed Him and praised Him, saying: 'Blessed is He, and may He be blessed from the beginning and for evermore. And before Him there is no ceasing. He knows before the world was created what is for ever and what will be from generation unto generation. Those who sleep not bless Thee: they stand before Thy glory and bless, praise, and extol, saying: "Holy, holy, holy, is the Lord of Spirits: He fillet the earth with spirits."' And here my eyes saw all those who sleep not: they stand before Him and bless and say: 'Blessed be Thou and blessed be the name of the Lord for ever and ever.' And my face was changed; for I could no longer behold.

CHAPTER 40

And after that I saw thousands of thousands and ten thousand times ten thousand, I saw a multitude beyond number and reckoning, who stood before the Lord of Spirits. And on the four sides of the Lord of Spirits I saw four presences, different from those that sleep not, and I learnt their names: for the angel that went with me made known to me their names and showed me all the hidden things. And I heard the voices of those four presences as they uttered praises before the Lord of glory. , The first voice blesses the Lord of Spirits for ever and ever. And the second voice I heard blessing the Elect One and the elect ones who hang upon the Lord of Spirits. And the third voice I heard pray and intercede for those who dwell on the earth and supplicate in the name of the Lord of Spirits. And I heard the fourth voice fending off the Satans and forbidding them to come before the Lord of Spirits to accuse them who dwell on the earth. After that I asked the angel of peace who went with me, who showed me everything that is hidden: 'Who are these four presences which I have seen and whose words I have heard and written down?' And he said to me: 'This first is Michael, the merciful and long-suffering: and the second, who is set over all the diseases and all the wounds of the children of men, is Raphael: and the third, who is set over all the powers, is Gabriel: and the fourth, who is set over the repentance unto hope of those who inherit eternal life, is named Phanuel.' And these are the four angels of the Lord of Spirits and the four voices I heard in those days.

CHAPTER 41

1 And after that I saw all the secrets of the heavens, and how the kingdom is divided, and how the 2 actions of men are weighed in the balance. And there I saw the mansions of the elect and the mansions of the holy, and mine eyes saw there all the sinners being driven from thence which deny the name of the Lord of Spirits and being dragged off: and they could not abide because of the punishment which proceeds from the Lord of Spirits. 3 And there mine eyes saw the secrets of the lightning and of the thunder, and the secrets of the winds, how they are divided to blow over the earth, and the secrets of the clouds and dew, and there 4 I saw from whence they proceed in that place and from whence they saturate the dusty earth. And there I saw closed chambers out of which the winds are divided, the chamber of the hail and winds, the chamber of the mist, and of the clouds, and the cloud thereof hovers over the earth from the 5 beginning of the world. And I saw the chambers of the sun and moon, whence they proceed and whither they come again, and their glorious return, and how one is superior to the other, and their stately orbit, and how they do not leave their orbit, and they add nothing to their orbit and they take nothing from it, and they keep faith with each other, in accordance with the oath by which they 6 are bound together. And first the sun goes forth and traverses his path according to the commandment 7 of the Lord of Spirits, and mighty is His name for ever and ever. And after that I saw the hidden and the visible path of the moon, and she accomplishes the course of her path in that place by day and by night-the one holding a position opposite to the other before the Lord of Spirits.

And they give thanks and praise and rest not.

For unto them is their thanksgiving rest.

8 For the sun changes oft for a blessing or a curse,

And the course of the path of the moon is light to the righteous

And darkness to the sinners in the name of the Lord,

Who made a separation between the light and the darkness,

And divided the spirits of men,

And strengthened the spirits of the righteous,

In the name of His righteousness.

9 For no angel hinders and no power is able to hinder; for He appoints a judge for them all and He judges them all before Him.

CHAPTER 42

1 Wisdom found no place where she might dwell.

Then a dwelling-place had assigned her in the heavens.

2 Wisdom went forth to make her dwelling among the children of men,

And found no dwelling-place:

Wisdom returned to her place,

And took her seat among the angels.

3 And unrighteousness went forth from her chambers:

Whom she sought not she found,

And dwelt with them,

As rain in a desert

And dew on a thirsty land.

CHAPTER 43

1 And I saw other lightnings and the stars of heaven, and I saw how He called them all by their 2 names and they hearkened unto Him. And I saw how they are weighed in a righteous balance according to their proportions of light: (I saw) the width of their spaces and the day of their appearing, and how their revolution produces lightning: and (I saw) their revolution according to the 3 number of the angels, and (how) they keep faith with each other. And I asked the angel who went 4 with me who showed me what was hidden: 'What are these?' And he said to me: 'The Lord of Spirits hath showed thee their parabolic meaning (lit. 'their parable'): these are the names of the holy who dwell on the earth and believe in the name of the Lord of Spirits for ever and ever.'

CHAPTER 44

Also, another phenomenon I saw in regard to the lightnings: how some of the stars arise and become lightnings and cannot part with their new form.

CHAPTER 45

1 And this is the second Parable concerning those who deny the name of the dwelling of the holy ones and the Lord of Spirits.

2 And into the heaven they shall not ascend,

And on the earth, they shall not come:

Such shall be the lot of the sinners.

Who have denied the name of the Lord of Spirits,

Who are thus preserved for the day of suffering and tribulation.

3 On that day Mine Elect One shall sit on the throne of glory.

And shall try their works,

And their places of rest shall be innumerable.

And their souls shall grow strong within them when they see Mine Elect Ones,

And those who have called upon My glorious name:

4 Then will I cause Mine Elect One to dwell among them.

And I will transform the heaven and make it an eternal blessing and light.

5 And I will transform the earth and make it a blessing:

And I will cause Mine elect ones to dwell upon it:

But the sinners and evil doers shall not set foot thereon.

6 For I have provided and satisfied with peace My righteous ones.

And have caused them to dwell before Me:

But for the sinners there is judgement impending with Me,

So that I shall destroy them from the face of the earth.

CHAPTER 46

1 And there I saw One who had a head of days,

And His head was white like wool,

And with Him was another being whose countenance had the appearance of a man,

And his face was full of graciousness, like one of the holy angels.

2 And I asked the angel who went with me and showed me all the hidden things,
concerning that.

3 Son of Man, who he was, and whence he was, (and) why he went with the Head of
Days? And he answered and said unto me:

This is the son of Man who hath righteousness,

With whom dwelleth righteousness,

And who revealeth all the treasures of that which is hidden,

Because the Lord of Spirits hath chosen him,

And whose lot hath the pre-eminence before the Lord of Spirits in uprightness for ever.

4 And this Son of Man whom thou hast seen.

Shall raise up the kings and the mighty from their seats,

[And the strong from their thrones]

And shall loosen the reins of the strong,

And break the teeth of the sinners.

5 [And he shall put down the kings from their thrones and kingdoms]

Because they do not extol and praise Him,

Nor humbly acknowledge whence the kingdom was bestowed upon them.

6 And he shall put down the countenance of the strong,

And shall fill them with shame.

And darkness shall be their dwelling,

And worms shall be their bed,

And they shall have no hope of rising from their beds,

Because they do not extol the name of the Lord of Spirits.

[And raise their hands against the Highest],

And tread upon the earth and dwell upon it.

And all their deeds manifest unrighteousness,

And their power rests upon their riches,

And their faith is in the gods which they have made with their hands,

And they deny the name of the Lord of Spirits,

8 And they persecute the houses of His congregations,

And the faithful who hang upon the name of the Lord of Spirits.

CHAPTER 47

1 And in those days shall have ascended the prayer of the righteous,

And the blood of the righteous from the earth before the Lord of Spirits.

2 In those days the holy ones who dwell above in the heavens.

Shall unite with one voice.

And supplicate and pray [and praise,

And give thanks and bless the name of the Lord of Spirits

On behalf of the blood of the righteous which has been shed,

And that the prayer of the righteous may not be in vain before the Lord of Spirits,

That judgement may be done unto them,

And that they may not have to suffer for ever.

3 In those days I saw the Head of Days when He seated himself upon the throne of His glory,

And the books of the living were opened before Him:

And all His host which is in heaven above and His counsellors stood before Him,

4 And the hearts of the holy were filled with joy;

Because the number of the righteous had been offered,

And the prayer of the righteous had been heard,

And the blood of the righteous been required before the Lord of Spirits.

CHAPTER 48

1 And in that place, I saw the fountain of righteousness.

Which was inexhaustible:

And around it was many fountains of wisdom:

And all the thirsty drank of them,

And were filled with wisdom,

And their dwellings were with the righteous and holy and elect.

2 And at that hour that Son of Man was named in the presence of the Lord of Spirits,

And his name before the Head of Days.

3 Yea, before the sun and the signs were created,

Before the stars of the heaven were made,

His name was named before the Lord of Spirits.

4 He shall be a staff to the righteous whereon to stay themselves and not fall,

And he shall be the light of the Gentiles,

And the hope of those who are troubled of heart.

5 All who dwell on earth shall fall and worship before him,

And will praise and bless and celebrate with song the Lord of Spirits.

6 And for this reason hath he been chosen and hidden before Him,

Before the creation of the world and for evermore.

7 And the wisdom of the Lord of Spirits hath revealed him to the holy and righteous.

For he hath preserved the lot of the righteous,

Because they have hated and despised this world of unrighteousness,

And have hated all its works and ways in the name of the Lord of Spirits:

For in his name they are saved,

And according to his good pleasure hath it been in regard to their life.

8 In these days downcast in countenance shall the kings of the earth have become,

And the strong who possess the land because of the works of their hands,

For on the day of their anguish and affliction they shall not (be able to) save themselves.

And I will give them over into the hands of My elect:

9As straw in the fire so shall they burn before the face of the holy:

As lead in the water shall they sink before the face of the righteous,

And no trace of them shall any more be found.

10 And on the day of their affliction there shall be rest on the earth,

And before them they shall fall and not rise again:

And there shall be no one to take them with his hands and raise them:

For they have denied the Lord of Spirits and His Anointed.

The name of the Lord of Spirits be blessed.

CHAPTER 49

1 For wisdom is poured out like water,

And glory faileth not before him for evermore.

2 For he is mighty in all the secrets of righteousness,

And unrighteousness shall disappear as a shadow,

And have no continuance.

Because the Elect One standeth before the Lord of Spirits,

And his glory is for ever and ever,

And his might unto all generations.

3 And in him dwells the spirit of wisdom,

And the spirit which gives insight,

And the spirit of understanding and of might,

And the spirit of those who have fallen asleep in righteousness.

4 And he shall judge the secret things,

And none shall be able to utter a lying word before him.

For he is the Elect One before the Lord of Spirits according to His good pleasure.

CHAPTER 50

1 And in those days a change shall take place for the holy and elect,

And the light of days shall abide upon them,

And glory and honour shall turn to the holy,

2 On the day of affliction on which evil shall have been treasured up against the sinners.

And the righteous shall be victorious in the name of the Lord of Spirits:

And He will cause the others to witness (this)

That they may repent

And forgo the works of their hands.

3 They shall have no honour through the name of the Lord of Spirits,

Yet through His name shall they be saved,

And the Lord of Spirits will have compassion on them,

For His compassion is great.

4 And He is righteous also in His judgement,

And in the presence of His glory unrighteousness also shall not maintain itself:

At His judgement the unrepentant shall perish before Him.

5 And from henceforth I will have no mercy on them, saith the Lord of Spirits.

CHAPTER 51

1 And in those days shall the earth also give back that which has been entrusted to it,

And Sheol also shall give back that which it has received,

And hell shall give back that which it owes.

5a For in those days the Elect One shall arise,

2 And he shall choose the righteous and holy from among them:

For the day has drawn nigh that they should be saved.

3 And the Elect One shall in those days sit on My throne,

And his mouth shall pour forth all the secrets of wisdom and counsel:

For the Lord of Spirits hath given (them) to him and hath glorified him.

4 And in those days shall the mountains leap like rams,

And the hills also shall skip like lambs satisfied with milk,

And the faces of [all] the angels in heaven shall be lighted up with joy.

5b And the earth shall rejoice,

c And the righteous shall dwell upon it,

d And the elect shall walk thereon.

CHAPTER 52

1 And after those days in that place where I had seen all the visions of that which is
hidden -for 2 I had been carried off in a whirlwind and they had borne me towards the
west-There mine eyes saw all the secret things of heaven that shall be, a mountain of
iron, and a mountain of copper, and a mountain of silver, and a mountain of gold, and a
mountain of soft metal, and a mountain of lead. 3 And I asked the angel who went with
me, saying, 'What things are these which I have seen in 4 secrets?' And he said unto
me: 'All these things which thou hast seen shall serve the dominion of His Anointed
that he may be potent and mighty on the earth.' 5 And that angel of peace answered,
saying unto me: 'Wait a little, and there shall be revealed unto thee all the secret things
which surround the Lord of Spirits.

6 And these mountains which thine eyes have seen,

The mountain of iron, and the mountain of copper, and the mountain of silver,

And the mountain of gold, and the mountain of soft metal, and the mountain of lead,

All these shall be in the presence of the Elect One

As wax: before the fire,

And like the water which streams down from above [upon those mountains],

And they shall become powerless before his feet.

7 And it shall come to pass in those days that none shall be saved,

Either by gold or by silver,

And none be able to escape.

8 And there shall be no iron for war,

Nor shall one clothe oneself with a breastplate.

Bronze shall be of no service,

And tin [shall be of no service and] shall not be esteemed,

And lead shall not be desired.

9 And all these things shall be [denied and] destroyed from the surface of the earth,

When the Elect One shall appear before the face of the Lord of Spirits.'

CHAPTER 53

1 There mine eyes saw a deep valley with open mouths, and all who dwell on the earth and sea and islands shall bring to him gifts and presents and tokens of homage, but that deep valley shall not become full.

2 And their hands commit lawless deeds,

And the sinners devour all whom they lawlessly oppress:

Yet the sinners shall be destroyed before the face of the Lord of Spirits,

And they shall be banished from off the face of His earth,

And they shall perish for ever and ever.

3 For I saw all the angels of punishment abiding (there) and preparing all the instruments
of Satan. 4 And I asked the angel of peace who went with me: ' For whom are they
preparing these Instruments?' 5 And he said unto me: ' They prepare these for the
kings and the mighty of this earth, that they may thereby be destroyed. 6 And after
this the Righteous and Elect One shall cause the house of his congregation to appear:
henceforth they shall be no more hindered in the name of the Lord of Spirits.

7 And these mountains shall not stand as the earth before his righteousness,

But the hills shall be as a fountain of water,

And the righteous shall have rest from the oppression of sinners.'

CHAPTER 54

1 And I looked and turned to another part of the earth and saw there a deep valley with

burning 2 fires. And they brought the kings and the mighty and began to cast them into
this deep valley. 3 And there mine eyes saw how they made these their instruments,
iron chains of immeasurable weight. 4 And I asked the angel of peace who went with
me, saying: ' For whom are these chains being prepared? ' And he said unto me: ' These
are being prepared for the hosts of Azazel, so that they may take them and cast them
into the abyss of complete condemnation, and they shall cover their jaws with rough
stones as the Lord of Spirits commanded. 6 And Michael, and Gabriel, and Raphael,
and Phanuel shall take hold of them on that great day, and cast them on that day into
the burning furnace, that the Lord of Spirits may take vengeance on them for their
unrighteousness in becoming subject to Satan and leading astray those who dwell on
the earth.' 7 And in those days shall punishment come from the Lord of Spirits, and he
will open all the chambers of waters which are above the heavens, and of the fountains
which are beneath the earth. 8 And all the waters shall be joined with the waters:
that which is above the heavens is the masculine, 9 and the water which is beneath
the earth is the feminine. And they shall destroy all who dwell 10 on the earth and
those who dwell under the ends of the heaven. And when they have recognized their
unrighteousness which they have wrought on the earth, then by these shall they perish.

CHAPTER 55

1 And after that the Head of Days repented and said: ' In vain have I destroyed all who
dwell 2 on the earth.' And He swear by His great name: ' Henceforth I will not do so to
all who dwell on the earth, and I will set a sign in the heaven: and this shall be a pledge
of good faith between Me and them for ever, so long as heaven is above the earth. And
this is in accordance with My command. 3 When I have desired to take hold of them
by the hand of the angels on the day of tribulation and pain because of this, I will cause
My chastisement and My wrath to abide upon them, saith 4 God, the Lord of Spirits.
Ye mighty kings who dwell on the earth, ye shall have to behold Mine Elect One, how
he sits on the throne of glory and judges Azazel, and all his associates, and all his hosts
in the name of the Lord of Spirits.'

CHAPTER 56

1 And I saw there the hosts of the angels of punishment going, and they held scourges
and chains 2 of iron and bronze. And I asked the angel of peace who went with me,
saying: ' To whom are 3 these who hold the scourges going? ' And he said unto me: '
To their elect and beloved ones, that they may be cast into the chasm of the abyss of
the valley.

4 And then that valley shall be filled with their elect and beloved,

And the days of their lives shall be at an end,

And the days of their leading astray shall not thenceforward be reckoned.

5 And in those days the angels shall return.

And hurl themselves to the east upon the Parthians and Medes:

They shall stir up the kings, so that a spirit of unrest shall come upon them,

And they shall rouse them from their thrones,

That they may break forth as lions from their lairs,

And as hungry wolves among their flocks.

6 And they shall go up and tread underfoot the land of His elect ones.

[And the land of His elect ones shall be before them a threshing-floor and a highway:]

7 But the city of my righteous shall be a hindrance to their horses.

And they shall begin to fight among themselves,

And their right hand shall be strong against themselves,

And a man shall not know his brother,

Nor a son his father or his mother,

Till there be no number of the corpses through their slaughter,

And their punishment be not in vain.

8 In those days Sheol shall open its jaws,

And they shall be swallowed up therein.

And their destruction shall be at an end.

Sheol shall devour the sinners in the presence of the elect.'

CHAPTER 57

1 And it came to pass after this that I saw another host of wagons, and men riding
thereon, and 2 coming on the winds from the east, and from the west to the south. And
the noise of their wagons was heard, and when this turmoil took place the holy ones
from heaven remarked it, and the pillars of the earth were moved from their place, and
the sound thereof was heard from the one end of heaven 3 to the other, in one day. And
they shall all fall and worship the Lord of Spirits. And this is the end of the second
Parable.

CHAPTER 58

1 And I began to speak the third Parable concerning the righteous and elect.

2 Blessed are ye, ye righteous and elect,

For glorious shall be your lot.

3 And the righteous shall be in the light of the sun.

And the elect in the light of eternal life:

The days of their life shall be unending,

And the days of the holy without number.

4 And they shall seek the light and find righteousness with the Lord of Spirits:

There shall be peace to the righteous in the name of the Eternal Lord.

5 And after this it shall be said to the holy in heaven.

That they should seek out the secrets of righteousness, the heritage of faith:

For it has become bright as the sun upon earth,

And the darkness is past.

6 And there shall be a light that never ended,

And to a limit (lit. ' number ') of days they shall not come,

For the darkness shall first have been destroyed,

[And the light established before the Lord of Spirits]

And the light of uprightness established for ever before the Lord of Spirits.

CHAPTER 59

1 [In those days mine eyes saw the secrets of the lightnings, and of the lights, and the judgements they execute (lit. ' their judgement '): and they lighten for a blessing or a curse as the Lord of 2 Spirits willeth. And there I saw the secrets of the thunder, and how when it resounds above in the heaven, the sound thereof is heard, and he caused me to see the judgements executed on the earth, whether they be for well-being and blessing, or for a curse according to the word of the Lord of Spirits. 3 And after that all the secrets of the lights and lightnings were shown to me, and they lighten for blessing and for satisfying.]

CHAPTER 60 A FRAGMENT OF THE BOOK OF NOAH

1 In the year 500, in the seventh month, on the fourteenth day of the month in the life of Enoch. In that Parable I saw how a mighty quaking made the heaven of heavens to quake, and the host of the Highest, and the angels, a thousand thousands and ten thousand times ten thousand, were 2 disquieted with a great disquiet. And the Head of Days sat on the throne of His glory, and the angels and the righteous stood around Him.

3 And a great trembling seized me,

And fear took hold of me,

And my loins gave way,

And dissolved were my reins,

And I fell upon my face.

4 And Michael sent another angel from among the holy ones and he raised me up, and when he had raised me up my spirit returned; for I had not been able to endure the look of this host, and the 5 commotion and the quaking of the heaven. And Michael said unto me: ' Why art thou disquieted with such a vision? Until this day lasted the day of His mercy; and He hath been merciful and 6 long-suffering towards those who dwell on the earth. And when the day, and the power, and the punishment, and the judgement come, which the Lord of Spirits hath prepared for those who worship not the righteous law, and for those who deny the righteous judgement, and for those who take His name in vain-that day is prepared, for the elect a covenant, but for sinners an inquisition. When the punishment of the Lord of Spirits shall rest upon them, it shall rest in order that the punishment of the Lord of Spirits may not come, in vain, and it shall slay the children with their mothers and the children with their fathers. Afterwards the judgement shall take place according to His mercy and His patience.' 7 And on that day were two monsters parted, a female monster named Leviathan, to dwell in the 8 abysses of the ocean over the fountains of the waters. But the male is named Behemoth, who occupied with his breast a waste wilderness named Duidain, on the east of the garden where the elect and righteous dwell, where my grandfather was taken up, the seventh from Adam, the first 9 man whom the Lord of Spirits created. And I besought the other angel that he should show me the might of those monsters, how they were parted on one day and cast, the one into the abysses of the sea, and the other unto the dry land of the wilderness. And he said to me: ' Thou son of man, herein thou dost seek to know what is hidden.' And the other angel who went with me and showed me what was hidden told me what is first and last in the heaven in the height, and beneath the earth in the depth, and at the ends of the heaven, and on the foundation of the heaven. And the chambers of the winds, and how the winds are divided, and how they are weighed, and (how) the portals of the winds are reckoned, each according to the power of the wind, and the power of the lights of the moon, and according to the power that is fitting: and the divisions of the stars according to their names, and how all the divisions are divided. And the thunders according to the places

where they fall, and all the divisions that are made among the lightnings that it may lighten, and their host that they may at once obey. For the thunder has places of rest (which) are assigned (to it) while it is waiting for its peal; and the thunder and lightning are inseparable, and although not one and undivided, they both go together through the spirit and separate not. For when the lightning lightens, the thunder utters its voice, and the spirit enforces a pause during the peal, and divides equally between them; for the treasury of their peals is like the sand, and each one of them as it peals is held in with a bridle, and turned back by the power of the spirit, and pushed forward according to the many quarters of the earth. And the spirit of the sea is masculine and strong, and according to the might of his strength he draws it back with a rein, and in like manner it is driven forward and disperses amid all the mountains of the earth. And the spirit of the hoar frost is his own angel, and the spirit of the hail is a good angel. And the spirit of the snow has forsaken his chambers on account of his strength -There is a special spirit therein, and that which ascends from it is like smoke, and its name is frost. And the spirit of the mist is not united with them in their chambers, but it has a special chamber; for its course is glorious both in light and in darkness, and in winter and in summer, and in its chamber is an angel. And the spirit of the dew has its dwelling at the ends of the heaven, and is connected with the chambers of the rain, and its course is in winter and summer: and its clouds and the clouds of the mist are connected, and the one gives to the other. And when the spirit of the rain goes forth from its chamber, the angels come and open the chamber and lead it out, and when it is diffused over the whole earth it unites with the water on the earth. And whensoever it unites with the water on the earth . . . For the waters are for those who dwell on the earth; for they are nourishment for the earth from the Highest who is in heaven: therefore, there is a measure for the rain, , and the angels take it in charge. And these things I saw towards the Garden of the Righteous. And the angel of peace who was with me said to me: ' These two monsters, prepared conformably to the greatness of God, shall feed . . .

CHAPTER 61

1 And I saw in those days how long cords were given to those angels, and they took to themselves wings and flew, and they went towards the north. 2 And I asked the angel, saying unto him: ' Why have those (angels) taken these cords and gone off? ' And he said unto me: ' They have gone to measure.'

3 And the angel who went with me said unto me:

' These shall bring the measures of the righteous,

And the ropes of the righteous to the righteous,

That they may stay themselves on the name of the Lord of Spirits for ever and ever.

4 The elect shall begin to dwell with the elect,

And those are the measures which shall be given to faith.

And which shall strengthen righteousness.

5 And these measures shall reveal all the secrets of the depths of the earth,

And those who have been destroyed by the desert,

And those who have been devoured by the beasts,

And those who have been devoured by the fish of the sea,

That they may return and stay themselves

On the day of the Elect One.

For none shall be destroyed before the Lord of Spirits,

And none can be destroyed.

6 And all who dwell above in the heaven received a command and power and one voice and one light like unto fire.

7 And that One (with) their first words they blessed,

And extolled and lauded with wisdom,

And they were wise in utterance and in the spirit of life.

8 And the Lord of Spirits placed the Elect one on the throne of glory.

And he shall judge all the works of the holy above in the heaven,

And in the balance shall their deeds be weighed

9 And when he shall lift his countenance.

To judge their secret ways according to the word of the name of the Lord of Spirits,

And their path according to the way of the righteous judgement of the Lord of Spirits,

Then shall they all with one voice speak and bless,

And glorify and extol and sanctify the name of the Lord of Spirits.

10 And He will summon all the host of the heavens, and all the holy ones above, and the host of God, the Cherubic, Seraphin and Ophannin, and all the angels of power, and all the angels of principalities, and the Elect One, and the other powers on the earth (and) over the water On that day shall raise one voice, and bless and glorify and exalt in the spirit of faith, and in the spirit of wisdom, and in the spirit of patience, and in the spirit of mercy, and in the spirit of judgement and of peace, and in the spirit of goodness, and shall all say with one voice: " Blessed is He, and may the name of the Lord of Spirits be blessed for ever and ever."

12 All who sleep not above in heaven shall bless Him:

All the holy ones who are in heaven shall bless Him,

And all the elect who dwell in the garden of life:

And every spirit of light who can bless, and glorify, and extol, and hallow Thy blessed name,

And all flesh shall beyond measure glorify and bless Thy name for ever and ever.

13 For great is the mercy of the Lord of Spirits, and He is long-suffering,

And all His works and all that He has created He has revealed to the righteous and elect.

In the name of the Lord of Spirits.

CHAPTER 62

1 And thus the Lord commanded the kings and the mighty and the exalted, and those who dwell on the earth, and said:

' Open your eyes and lift your horns if ye are able to recognize the Elect One.'

2 And the Lord of Spirits seated him on the throne of His glory,

And the spirit of righteousness was poured out upon him,

And the word of his mouth slays all the sinners,

And all the unrighteous are destroyed from before his face.

3 And there shall stand up in that day all the kings and the mighty,

And the exalted and those who hold the earth,

And they shall see and recognize How he sits on the throne of his glory,

And righteousness is judged before him,

And no lying word is spoken before him.

4 Then shall pain come upon them as on a woman in travail,

[And she has pain in bringing forth]

When her child enters the mouth of the womb,

And she has pain in bringing forth.

5 And one portion of them shall look on the other,

And they shall be terrified,

And they shall be downcast of countenance,

And pain shall seize them,

When they see that Son of Man Sitting on the throne of his glory.

6 And the kings and the mighty and all who possess the earth shall bless and glorify and extol him who rules overall, who was hidden.

7 For from the beginning the Son of Man was hidden,

And the Highest preserved him in the presence of His might,

And revealed him to the elect.

8 And the congregation of the elect and holy shall be sown,

And all the elects shall stand before him on that day.

9 And all the kings and the mighty and the exalted and those who rule the earth.

Shall fall before him on their faces,

And worship and set their hope upon that Son of Man,

And petition him and supplicate for mercy at his hands.

10 Nevertheless that Lord of Spirits will so press them.

That they shall hastily go forth from His presence,

And their faces shall be filled with shame,

And the darkness grows deeper on their faces.

11 And He will deliver them to the angels for punishment,

To execute vengeance on them because they have oppressed His children and His elect.

12 And they shall be a spectacle for the righteous and for His elect:

They shall rejoice over them,

Because the wrath of the Lord of Spirits rested upon them,

And His sword is drunk with their blood.

13 And the righteous and elect shall be saved on that day,

And they shall never thenceforward see the face of the sinners and unrighteous.

14 And the Lord of Spirits will abide over them,

And with that Son of Man shall they eat

And lie down and rise up for ever and ever.

15 And the righteous and elect shall have risen from the earth,

And ceased to be of downcast countenance.

And they shall have been clothed with garments of glory,

16 And these shall be the garments of life from the Lord of Spirits:

And your garments shall not grow old,

Nor your glory pass away before the Lord of Spirits.

CHAPTER 63

1 In those days shall the mighty and the kings who possess the earth implore (Him) to grant them a little respite from His angels of punishment to whom they were delivered, that they might fall 2 down and worship before the Lord of Spirits and confess their sins before Him. And they shall bless and glorify the Lord of Spirits, and say:

' Blessed is the Lord of Spirits and the Lord of kings,

And the Lord of the mighty and the Lord of the rich,

And the Lord of glory and the Lord of wisdom,

3 And splendid in every secret thing is Thy power from generation to generation,

And Thy glory for ever and ever:

Deep are all Thy secrets and innumerable,

And Thy righteousness is beyond reckoning.

4 We have now learnt that we should glorify.

And bless the Lord of kings and Him who is king over all kings.'

5 And they shall say:

' Would that we had rest to glorify and give thanks.

And confess our faith before His glory!

6 And now we long for a little rest but find it not:

We follow hard upon and obtain (it) not:

And light has vanished from before us,

And darkness is our dwelling-place for ever and ever:

7 For we have not believed before Him.

Nor glorified the name of the Lord of Spirits, [nor glorified our Lord]

But our hope was in the sceptre of our kingdom,

And in our glory.

8 And in the day of our suffering and tribulation He saves us not,

And we find no respite for confession.

That our Lord is true in all His works, and in His judgements and His justice,

And His judgements have no respect of persons.

And we pass away from before His face on account of our works,

And all our sins are reckoned up in righteousness.'

10 Now they shall say unto themselves: ' Our souls are full of unrighteous gain, but it does not prevent us from descending from the midst thereof into the burden of Sheol.'

11 And after that their faces shall be filled with darkness.

And shame before that Son of Man,

And they shall be driven from his presence,

And the sword shall abide before his face in their midst.

12 Thus spoke the Lord of Spirits: ' This is the ordinance and judgement with respect to the mighty and the kings and the exalted and those who possess the earth before the Lord of Spirits.'

CHAPTER 64

1,2 And other forms I saw hidden in that place. I heard the voice of the angel saying: ' These are the angels who descended to the earth, and revealed what was hidden to the children of men and seduced the children of men into committing sin.'

CHAPTER 65

1, 2 And in those days, Noah saw the earth that it had sunk down and its destruction
was nigh. And he arose from thence and went to the ends of the earth and cried aloud
to his grandfather Enoch: 3 and Noah said three times with an embittered voice: Hear
me, hear me, hear me.' And I said unto him: ' tell me what it is that is falling out on the
earth that the earth is in such evil plight 4 and shaken, lest perchance I shall perish with
it? ' And thereupon there was a great commotion, on the earth, and a voice was heard
from heaven, and I fell on my face. And Enoch my grandfather came and stood by me,
and said unto me: ' Why hast thou cried unto me with a bitter cry and weeping 6 And
a command has gone forth from the presence of the Lord concerning those who dwell
on the earth that their ruin is accomplished because they have learnt all the secrets
of the angels, and all the violence of the Satans, and all their powers -the most secret
ones- and all the power of those who practice sorcery, and the power of witchcraft, and
the power of those who make molten images 7 for the whole earth: And how silver is
produced from the dust of the earth, and how soft metal 8 originates in the earth. For
lead and tin are not produced from the earth like the first: it is a fountain 9 that produces
them, and an angel stands therein, and that angel is pre-eminent.' And after that my
grandfather Enoch took hold of me by my hand and raised me up, and said unto me:
' Go, for I have 10 asked the Lord of Spirits as touching this commotion on the earth.
And He said unto me: " Because of their unrighteousness their judgement has been
determined upon and shall not be withheld by Me for ever. Because of the sorceries
which they have searched out and learnt, the earth and those 11 who dwell upon it
shall be destroyed." And these-they have no place of repentance for ever because they
have shown them what was hidden, and they are the damned: but as for thee, my son,
the Lord of Spirits knows that thou art pure, and guiltless of this reproach concerning
the secrets.

12 And He has destined thy name to be among the holy,

And will preserve thee amongst those who dwell on the earth,

And has destined thy righteous seed both for kingship and for great honours,

And from thy seed shall proceed a fountain of the righteous and holy without number for ever.

CHAPTER 66

1 And after that he showed me the angels of punishment who are prepared to come and
let lose all the powers of the waters which are beneath in the earth to bring judgement
and destruction 2 on all who [abide and] dwell on the earth. And the Lord of Spirits
gave commandment to the angels who were going forth, that they should not cause the
waters to rise but should hold them 3 in check; for those angels were over the powers
of the waters. And I went away from the presence of Enoch.

CHAPTER 67

1 And in those days the word of God came unto me, and He said unto me: ' Noah, thy lot has come Up before Me, a lot without blame, a lot of love and uprightness. And now the angels are making a wooden (building), and when they have completed that task, I will place My hand upon it and preserve it, and there shall come forth from it the seed of life, and a change shall set in so that the earth will not remain without inhabitant. And I will make fast thy sed before me for ever and ever, and I will spread abroad those who dwell with thee: it shall not be unfruitful on the face of the earth, but it shall be blessed and multiply on the earth in the name of the Lord.' And He will imprison those angels, who have shown unrighteousness, in that burning valley which my grandfather Enoch had formerly shown to me in the west among the mountains of gold and silver and iron and soft metal and tin. And I saw that valley in which there was a great 6 convulsion and a convulsion of the waters. And when all this took place, from that fiery molten metal and from the convulsion thereof in that place, there was produced a smell of sulphur, and it related to those waters, and that valley of the angels who had led astray (mankind) burned 7 beneath that land. And through its valleys proceed streams of fire, where these angels are punished who had led astray those who dwell upon the earth. But those waters shall in those days serve for the kings and the mighty and the exalted, and those who dwell on the earth, for the healing of the body, but for the punishment of the spirit; now their spirit is full of lust, that they may be punished in their body, for they have denied the Lord of Spirits and see their punishment daily, and yet believe not in His name. And in proportion as the burning of their bodies becomes severe, a corresponding change shall take place in their spirit for ever and ever; for before the Lord of Spirits none shall utter an idle word. For the judgement shall come upon them because they believe in the lust of their body and deny the Spirit of the Lord. And those same waters will undergo a change in those days; for when those angels are punished in these waters, these water-springs shall change their temperature, and when the angels ascend, this water of the springs shall change and become cold. And I heard Michael answering and saying: ' This judgement wherewith the angels are judged is a testimony for the kings and the mighty who possess the earth.' Because these waters of judgement minister to the healing of the body of the kings and the lust of their body; therefore, they will not see and will not believe that those waters will change and become a fire which burns for ever.

CHAPTER 68

And after that my grandfather Enoch gave me the teaching of all the secrets in the book in the Parables which had been given to him, and he put them together for me in the words of the book of the Parables. And on that day Michael answered Raphael and said: ' The power of the spirit transports and makes me to tremble because of the severity of the judgement of the secrets, the judgement of the angels: who can endure the severe judgement which has been executed, and before which they melt away?

' And Michael answered again, and said to Raphael: ' Who is he whose heart is not
softened concerning it, and whose reins are not troubled by this word of judgement 4
(that) has gone forth upon them because of those who have thus led them out? ' And it
came to pass when he stood before the Lord of Spirits, Michael said thus to Raphael: ' I
will not take their part under the eye of the Lord; for the Lord of Spirits has been angry
with them because they do as if they were the Lord. Therefore, all that is hidden shall
come upon them for ever and ever; for neither angel nor man shall have his portion (in
it), but alone they have received their judgement for ever and ever.

CHAPTER 69

1 And after this judgement they shall terrify and make them to tremble because they
have shown this to those who dwell on the earth. 2 And behold the names of those
angels [and these are their names: the first of them is Samjaza, the second Artaqifa,
and the third Armen, the fourth Kokabel, the fifth Turael, the sixth Rumjal, the seventh
Danjal, the eighth Neqael, the ninth Baraqel, the tenth Azazel, the eleventh Armaros,
the twelfth Batarjal, the thirteenth Busasejal, the fourteenth Hananel, the fifteenth
Turel, and the sixteenth Simapesiel, the seventeenth Jetrel, the eighteenth Tumael,
the nineteenth Turel, 3 the twentieth Rumael, the twenty-first Azazel. And these are
the chiefs of their angels and their names, and their chief ones over hundreds and over
fifties and over tens]. 4 The name of the first Jeqon: that is, the one who led astray [all]
the sons of God, and brought them 5 down to the earth, and led them astray through
the daughters of men. And the second was named Asbeel: he imparted to the holy sons
of God evil counsel and led them astray so that they defiled 6 their bodies with the
daughters of men. And the third was named Gadreel: he it is who showed the children
of men all the blows of death, and he led astray Eve, and showed [the weapons of death
to the sons of men] the shield and the coat of mail, and the sword for battle, and all the
weapons 7 of death to the children of men. And from his hand they have proceeded
against those who dwell 8 on the earth from that day and for evermore. And the fourth
was named Penemue: he taught the 9 children of men the bitter and the sweet, and he
taught them all the secrets of their wisdom. And he instructed mankind in writing with
ink and paper, and thereby many sinned from eternity to 10 eternity and until this day.
For men were not created for such a purpose, to give confirmation 11 to their good
faith with pen and ink. For men were created exactly like the angels, to the intent that
they should continue pure and righteous, and death, which destroys everything, could
not have taken hold of them, but through this their knowledge they are perishing, and
through this power 12 it is consuming me. And the fifth was named Kasdeja: this is he
who showed the children of men all the wicked smitings of spirits and demons, and the
smitings of the embryo in the womb, that it may pass away, and [the smitings of the
soul] the bites of the serpent, and the smitings 13 which befall through the noontide
heat, the son of the serpent named Taba'et. And this is the task of Kasbeel, the chief of
the oath which he showed to the holy ones when he dwelt high 14 above in glory, and
its name is Biqa. This (angel) requested Michael to show him the hidden name, that
he might enunciate it in the oath, so that those might quake before that name and oath
who revealed all that was in secret to the children of men. And this is the power of this

oath, for it is powerful and strong, and he placed this oath Akae in the hand of Michael.

16 And these are the secrets of this oath

And they are strong through his oath:

And the heaven was suspended before the world was created,

And for ever

17 And through it the earth was founded upon the water,

And from the secret recesses of the mountains come beautiful waters,

From the creation of the world and unto eternity.

18 And through that oath the sea was created,

And as its foundation He set for it the sand against the time of (its) anger,

And it dares not pass beyond it from the creation of the world unto eternity.

19 And through that oath are the depths made fast,

And abide and stir not from their place from eternity to eternity.

20 And through that oath the sun and moon complete their course,

And deviate not from their ordinance from eternity to eternity.

21 And through that oath the stars complete their course,

And He calls them by their names,

And they answer Him from eternity to eternity.

22 [And in like manner the spirits of the water, and of the winds, and of all zephyrs, and (their) paths from all the quarters of the winds. And there are preserved the voices of the thunder and the light of the lightnings: and there are preserved the chambers of the hail and the chambers of the hoarfrost, and the chambers of the mist, and the chambers of the rain and the dew. And all these believe and give thanks before the Lord of Spirits, and glorify (Him) with all their power, and their food is in every act of thanksgiving: they thank and glorify and extol the name of the Lord of Spirits for ever and ever.]

25 And this oath is mighty over them.

And through it [they are preserved and] their paths are preserved,

And their course is not destroyed.

26 And there was great joy amongst them,

And they blessed and glorified and extolled.

Because the name of that Son of Man had been revealed unto them.

27 And he sat on the throne of his glory,

And the sum of judgement was given unto the Son of Man,

And he caused the sinners to pass away and be destroyed from off the face of the earth,

And those who have led the world astray.

28 With chains shall they be bound,

And in their assemblage-place of destruction shall they be imprisoned,

And all their works vanish from the face of the earth.

29 And from henceforth there shall be nothing corruptible.

For that Son of Man has appeared,

And has seated himself on the throne of his glory,

And all evil shall pass away before his face,

And the word of that Son of Man shall go forth.

And be strong before the Lord of Spirits.

CHAPTER 70

1 And it came to pass after this that his name during his lifetime was raised aloft to that
Son of 2 Man and to the Lord of Spirits from amongst those who dwell on the earth.
And he was raised aloft 3 on the chariots of the spirit and his name vanished among
them. And from that day I was no longer numbered amongst them: and he set me
between the two winds, between the North and the 4 West, where the angels took the
cords to measure for me the place for the elect and righteous. And there I saw the first
fathers and the righteous who from the beginning dwell in that place.

CHAPTER 71

1 And it came to pass after this that my spirit was translated.

And it ascended into the heavens:

And I saw the holy sons of God.

They were stepping on flames of fire:

Their garments were white [and their raiment],

And their faces shone like snow.

2 And I saw two streams of fire,

And the light of that fire shone like hyacinth,

And I fell on my face before the Lord of Spirits.

3 And the angel Michael [one of the archangels] seized me by my right hand,

And lifted me up and led me forth into all the secrets,

And he showed me all the secrets of righteousness.

4 And he showed me all the secrets of the ends of the heaven,

And all the chambers of all the stars, and all the luminaries,

Whence they proceed before the face of the holy ones.

5 And he translated my spirit into the heaven of heavens,

And I saw there as it were a structure built of crystals,

And between those crystals' tongues of living fire.

6 And my spirit saw the girdle which girt that house of fire,

And on its four sides were streams full of living fire,

And they girt that house.

7 And roundabout was Seraphin, Cherubic, and Ophannin:

And these are they who sleep not.

And guard the throne of His glory.

8 And I saw angels who could not be counted,

A thousand thousand, and ten thousand times ten thousand,

Encircling that house.

And Michael, and Raphael, and Gabriel, and Phanuel,

And the holy angels who are above the heavens,

Go in and out of that house.

9 And they came forth from that house,

And Michael and Gabriel, Raphael and Phanuel,

And many holy angels without number.

10 And with them the Head of Days,

His head white and pure as wool,

And His raiment indescribable.

11 And I fell on my face,

And my whole body became relaxed,

And my spirit was transfigured.

And I cried with a loud voice, . . .

with the spirit of power,

And blessed and glorified and extolled.

12 And these blessings which went forth out of my mouth were well pleasing before that Head of Days. And that Head of Days came with Michael and Gabriel, Raphael and Phanuel, thousands and ten thousand of angels without number.

[Lost passage wherein the Son of Man was described as accompanying the Head of Days, and Enoch asked one of the angels (as in xlvi. 3) concerning the Son of Man as to who he was.]

14 And he (i.e., the angel) came to me and greeted me with His voice, and said unto me'.

This is the Son of Man who is born unto righteousness,

And righteousness abides over him,

And the righteousness of the Head of Days forsakes him not.'

15 And he said unto me:

' He proclaims unto thee peace in the name of the world to come.

For from hence has proceeded peace since the creation of the world,

And so shall it be unto thee for ever and for ever and ever.

16 And all shall walk in his ways since righteousness never forsakes him:

With him will be their dwelling-places, and with him their heritage,

And they shall not be separated from him for ever and ever and ever.

And so there shall be length of days with that Son of Man,

And the righteous shall have peace and an upright way.

In the name of the Lord of Spirits for ever and ever.'

SECTION III.

THE BOOK OF THE HEAVENLY LUMINARIES

CHAPTER 72

1 The book of the courses of the luminaries of the heaven, the relations of each, according to their classes, their dominion and their seasons, according to their names and places of origin, and according to their months, which Uriel, the holy angel, who was with me, who is their guide, showed me; and he showed me all their laws exactly as they are, and how it is with regard to all the years of the world and unto eternity, till the new creation is accomplished which dureth till eternity. And this is the first law of the luminaries: the luminary the Sun has its rising in the eastern portals of the heaven, and its setting in the western portals of the heaven. And I saw six portals in which the sun rises, and six portals in which the sun sets and the moon rises and sets in these portals, and the leaders of the stars and those whom they lead: six in the east and six in the west, and all following each other in accurately corresponding order: also many windows to the right and left of these portals. And first there goes forth the great luminary, named the Sun, and his circumference is like the circumferences of the heaven, and he is quite filled with illuminating and heating fire. The chariot on which he ascends, the wind drives, and the sun goes down from the heaven and returns through the north in order to reach the east and is so guided that he comes to the appropriate (lit. ' that ') portal and shines in the face of the heaven. In this way he rises in the first month in the great portal, which is the fourth [those six portals in the cast]. And in that fourth portal from which the sun rises in the first month are twelve window-openings, from which proceed a flame when they are opened in their season. When the sun rises in the heaven, he comes forth through that fourth portal thirty, mornings in succession, and sets accurately in the fourth portal in the west of the heaven. And during this period the day becomes daily longer and the night nightly shorter to the thirtieth morning. On that day the day is longer than the night by a ninth part, and the day amounts exactly to ten parts and the night to eight parts. And the sun rises from that fourth portal and sets in the fourth and returns to the fifth portal of the east thirty mornings and rises from it and sets in the fifth portal. And then the day becomes longer by two parts and amounts to eleven parts, and the night becomes shorter and amounts to seven parts. And it returns to the east and enters the sixth portal and rises and sets in the sixth portal one-and-thirty mornings on account of its sign. On that day the day becomes longer than the night, and the day becomes double the night, and the day becomes twelve parts, and the night is shortened and becomes six parts. And the sun mounts up to make the day shorter and the night longer, and the sun returns to the east and enters into the sixth portal and rises from it and sets thirty mornings. And when thirty mornings are accomplished, the day decreases by exactly one part, and becomes eleven parts, and the night seven. And the sun goes forth from that sixth portal in the west and goes to the east and rises in the fifth portal for thirty mornings and sets in the west again in the fifth western portal. On that day the day decreases by two part and amounts to ten parts and the night to eight parts. And the sun goes forth from that fifth portal and sets in the fifth portal of the east and rises in the fourth portal for one- and-thirty mornings

on account of its sign and sets in the west. On that day the day is equalized with the night, [and becomes of equal length], and the night amounts to nine parts and the day to nine parts. And the sun rises from that portal and sets in the west and returns to the east and rises thirty mornings in the third portal and sets in the west in the third portal. And on that day the night becomes longer than the day, and night becomes longer than night, and day shorter than day till the thirtieth morning, and the night amounts exactly to ten parts and the day to eight parts. And the sun rises from that third portal and sets in the third portal in the west and returns to the east, and for thirty mornings rises in the second portal in the east, and in like manner sets in the second portal in the west of the heaven. And on that day the night amounts to eleven parts and the day to seven parts. And the sun rises on that day from that second portal and sets in the west in the second portal and returns to the east into the first portal for one-and-thirty mornings and sets in the first portal in the west of the heaven. And on that day the night becomes longer and amounts to the double of the day: and the night amounts exactly to twelve parts and the day to six. And the sun has (therewith) traversed the divisions of his orbit and turns again on those divisions of his orbit and enters that portal thirty mornings and sets also in the west opposite to it. And on that night has the night decreased in length by a ninth part, and the night has become eleven parts and the day seven parts. And the sun has returned and entered into the second portal in the east and returns on those his divisions of his orbit for thirty mornings, rising and setting. And on that day the night decreases in length, and the night amounts to ten parts and the day to eight. And on that day the sun rises from that portal, and sets in the west, and returns to the east, and rises in the third portal for one-and-thirty mornings and sets in the west of the heaven. On that day the night decreases and amounts to nine parts, and the day to nine parts, and the night is equal to the day and the year is exactly as to its days three hundred and sixty-four. And the length of the day and of the night, and the shortness of the day and of the night arise-through the course of the sun these distinctions are made (lit. ' they are separated '). So, it comes that its course becomes daily longer, and its course nightly shorter. And this is the law and the course of the sun, and his return as often as he returns sixty times and rises, i.e., the great luminary, which is named the sun, for ever and ever. And that which (thus) rises is the great luminary, and is so named according to its appearance, according as the Lord commanded. As he rises, so he sets and decreases not, and rests not, but runs day and night, and his light is sevenfold brighter than that of the moon; but as regards size they are both equal.

CHAPTER 73

1 And after this law I saw another law dealing with the smaller luminary, which is named the Moon. And her circumference is like the circumference of the heaven, and her chariot in which she rides is driven by the wind, and light is given to her in (definite) measure. And her rising and setting change every month: and her days are like the days of the sun, and when her light is uniform (i.e., full) it amounts to the seventh part of the light of the sun. And thus, she rises. And her first phase in the east comes forth on the thirtieth morning: and on that day she becomes visible and constitutes for you the first phase of the moon on the thirtieth day together with the

sun in the portal where the sun rises. And the one half of her goes forth by a seventh part, and her whole circumference is empty, without light, with the exception of one-seventh part of it, (and) the fourteenth part of her light. And when she receives one-seventh part of the half of her light, her light amounts to one-seventh part and the half thereof. And she sets with the sun, and when the sun rises the moon rises with him and receives the half of one part of light, and in that night in the beginning of her morning [in the commencement of the lunar day] the moon sets with the sun, and is invisible that night with the fourteen parts and the half of one of them. And she rises on that day with exactly a seventh part and comes forth and recedes from the rising of the sun, and in her remaining days she becomes bright in the (remaining) thirteen parts.

CHAPTER 74

And I saw another course, a law for her, (and) how according to that law she performs her monthly revolution. And all these Uriel, the holy angel who is the leader of them all, showed to me, and their positions, and I wrote down their positions as he showed them to me, and I wrote down their months as they were, and the appearance of their lights till fifteen days were accomplished. In single seventh parts she accomplishes all her light in the east, and in single seventh parts accomplish all her 4 darkness in the west. And in certain months she alters her settings, and in certain months she pursues her own peculiar course. In two months, the moon sets with the sun: in those two middle portals the third and the fourth. She goes forth for seven days and turns about and returns again through the portal where the sun rises and accomplishes all her light: and she recedes from the sun, and in eight days enters the sixth portal from which the sun goes forth. And when the sun goes forth from the fourth portal, she goes forth seven days, until she goes forth from the fifth and turns back again in seven days into the fourth portal and accomplishes all her light: and she recedes and enters into the first portal in eight days. And she returns again in seven days into the fourth portal from which the sun goes forth. Thus, I saw their position -how the moons rose, and the sun set in those days. And if five years are added together the sun has an overplus of thirty days, and all the days which accrue to it for one of those five years, when they are full, amount to 364 days. And the overplus of the sun and of the stars amounts to six days: in 5 years 6 days every year come to 30 days: and the moon falls behind the sun and stars to the number of 30 days. And the sun and the stars bring in all the years exactly, so that they do not advance or delay their position by a single day unto eternity; but complete the years with perfect justice in 364 days. In 3 years, there are 1,092 days, and in 5 years 1,820 days, so that in 8 years there are 2,912 days. For the moon alone the days amount in 3 years to 1,062 days, and in 5 years she falls 50 days behind: [i.e., to the sum (of 1,770) there is 5 to be added (1,000 and) 62 days.] And in 5 years there are 1,770 days, so that for the moon the days 6 in 8 years amount to 21,832 days. [For in 8 years she falls behind to the amount of 80 days], all the 17 days she falls behind in 8 years are 80. And the year is accurately completed in conformity with their world-stations and the stations of the sun, which rise from the portals through which it (the sun) rises and sets 30 days.

CHAPTER 75

And the leaders of the heads of the thousands, who are placed over the whole creation and over all the stars, have also to do with the four intercalary days, being inseparable from their office, according to the reckoning of the year, and these render service on the four days which are not reckoned in the reckoning of the year. And owing to them men go wrong therein, for those luminaries truly render service on the world-stations, one in the first portal, one in the third portal of the heaven, one in the fourth portal, and one in the sixth portal, and the exactness of the year is accomplished through its separate three hundred and sixty-four stations. For the signs and the times and the years and the days the angel Uriel showed to me, whom the Lord of glory hath set for ever over all the luminaries of the heaven, in the heaven and in the world, that they should rule on the face of the heaven and be seen on the earth, and be leaders for the day and the night, i.e. the sun, moon, and stars, and all the ministering creatures which make their revolution in all the chariots of the heaven. In like manner twelve doors Uriel showed me, open in the circumference of the sun's chariot in the heaven, through which the rays of the sun break forth: and from them is warmth diffused over the earth, when they are opened at their appointed seasons. [And for the winds and the spirit of the dew when they are opened, standing open in the heavens at the ends.] As for the twelve portals in the heaven, at the ends of the earth, out of which go forth the sun, moon, and stars, and all the works of heaven in the east and in the west, There are many windows open to the left and right of them, and one window at its (appointed) season produces warmth, corresponding (as these do) to those doors from which the stars come forth according as He has commanded them, 8 and wherein they set corresponding to their number. And I saw chariots in the heaven, running 9 in the world, above those portals in which revolve the stars that never set. And one is larger than all the rest, and it is that that makes its course through the entire world.

CHAPTER 76

And at the ends of the earth, I saw twelve portals open to all the quarters (of the heaven), from which the winds go forth and blow over the earth. Three of them are open on the face (i.e., the east) of the heavens, and three in the west, and three on the right (i.e. the south) of the heaven, and three on the left (i.e. the north). And the three first are those of the east, and three are of the north, and three [after those on the left] of the south, and three of the wests. Through four of these come winds of blessing and prosperity, and from those eight come hurtful winds: when they are sent, they bring destruction on all the earth and on the water upon it, and on all who dwell thereon, and on everything which is in the water and on the land. And the first wind from those portals, called the east wind, comes forth through the first portal which is in the east, inclining towards the south: from it come forth desolation, drought, heat, and destruction. And through the second portal in the middle comes what is fitting, and from it there come rain and fruitfulness and prosperity and dew; and through the third portal which lies toward the north come cold and drought. And after these come forth the south winds through three portals: through the first portal of them inclining to the east comes forth a hot wind. And through the middle portal next to it there come forth fragrant smells, and dew and rain, and prosperity and health. And through the third portal lying to the west come forth dew and rain, locusts, and desolation. And after these the north winds: from the seventh portal in the east come dew and rain, locusts, and desolation. And from the middle portal come in a direct direction health and rain and dew and prosperity; and through the third portal in the west come cloud and hoar-frost, and snow and rain, and dew and locusts. And after these [four] are the west winds: through the first portal adjoining the north come forth dew and hoar-frost, and cold and snow and frost. And from the middle portal come forth dew and rain, and prosperity and blessing; and through the last portal which adjoins the south come forth drought and desolation and burning and destruction. And the twelve portals of the four quarters of the heaven are therewith completed, and all their laws and all their plagues and all their benefactions have I shown to thee, my son Methuselah.

CHAPTER 77

And the first quarter is called the east, because it is the first: and the second, the south, because the Highest will descend there, yea, there in quite a special sense will He who is blessed for every descend. And the west quarter is named the diminished because there all the luminaries of the heaven wane and go down. And the fourth quarter, named the north, is divided into three parts: the first of them is for the dwelling of men: and the second contains seas of water, and the abysses and forests and rivers, and darkness and clouds; and the third part contains the garden of righteousness. I saw seven high mountains, higher than all the mountains which are on the earth: and thence comes forth hoar-frost, and days, seasons, and years pass away. I saw seven rivers on the earth larger than all the rivers: one of them coming from the west pours its waters into the Great Sea. And these two come from the north to the sea and pour their waters into the Erythraean Sea in the east. And the remaining, four come forth on the side of the north to their own sea, two of them to the Erythraean Sea, and two into the Great Sea and discharge themselves there [and some say into the desert]. Seven great islands I saw in the sea and in the mainland: two in the mainland and five in the Great Sea.

CHAPTER 78

And the names of the sun are the following: the first Orjares, and the second Tomas. And the moon has four names: the first name is Asonja, the second Ebla, the third Benase, and the fourth Erae. These are the two great luminaries: their circumference is like the circumference of the heaven, and the size of the circumference of both is alike. In the circumference of the sun there are seven portions of light which are added to it more than to the moon, and in definite measures it is s transferred till the seventh portion of the sun is exhausted. And they set and enter the portals of the west, and make their revolution by the north, and come forth through the eastern portals on the face of the heaven. And when the moon rises one-fourteenth part appears in the heaven [the light becomes full in her]: on the fourteenth day she accomplishes her light. And fifteen parts of light are transferred to her till the fifteenth day (when) her light is accomplished, according to the sign of the year, and she becomes fifteen parts, and the moon grows by (the addition of) fourteenth parts. And in her waning (the moon) decreases on the first day to fourteen parts of her light, on the second to thirteen parts of light, on the third to twelve, on the fourth to eleven, on the fifth to ten, on the sixth to nine, on the seventh to eight, on the eighth to seven, on the ninth to six, on the tenth to five, on the eleventh to four, on the twelfth to three, on the thirteenth to two, on the fourteenth to the half of a seventh, and all her remaining light disappears wholly on the fifteenth. And 10 in certain months the month has twenty-nine days and once twenty-eight. And Uriel showed me another law: when light is transferred to the moon, and on which side it is transferred to her by the sun. During all the period during which the moon is growing in her light, she is transferring it to herself when opposite to the sun for fourteen days [her light is accomplished in the heaven, and when she is illumined throughout, her light is accomplished full in the heaven. And on the first 13 day she is called the new moon, for on that day the light rises upon her. She becomes full moon exactly on the day when the sun sets in the west, and from the east she rises at night, and the moon shines the whole night through till the sun rises over against her and the moon is seen over against the sun. On the side whence the light of the moon comes forth, there again she wanes till all the light vanishes and all the days of the month are at an end, and her circumference is empty, void of light. And three months she makes of thirty days, and at her time she makes three months of twenty- nine days each, in which she accomplishes her waning in the first period of time, and in the first portal for one hundred and seventy-seven days. And in the time of her going out she appears for three months (of) thirty days each, and for three months she appears (of) twenty-nine each. At night she appears like a man for twenty days each time, and by day she appears like the heaven, and there is nothing else in her save her light.

CHAPTER 79

1 And now, my son, I have shown thee everything, and the law of all the stars of the heaven is 2 completed. And he showed me all the laws of these for every day, and for every season of bearing rule, and for every year, and for its going forth, and for the order prescribed to it every month 3 and every week: And the waning of the moon which takes place in the sixth portal: for in this 4 sixth portal her light is accomplished, and after that there is the beginning of the waning: (And the waning) which takes place in the first portal in its season, till one hundred and seventy-seven 5 days are accomplished: reckoned according to weeks, twenty-five (weeks) and two days. She falls behind the sun and the order of the stars exactly five days in the course of one period, and when 6 this place which thou seest has been traversed. Such is the picture and sketch of every luminary which Uriel the archangel, who is their leader, showed unto me.

CHAPTER 80

1 And in those days the angel Uriel answered and said to me: ' Behold, I have shown thee everything, Enoch, and I have revealed everything to thee that thou shouldst see this sun and this moon, and the leaders of the stars of the heaven and all those who turn them, their tasks and times and departures.

2 And in the days of the sinners the years shall be shortened,

And their seed shall be tardy on their lands and fields,

And all things on the earth shall alter,

And shall not appear in their time:

And the rain shall be kept back

And the heaven shall withhold (it).

3 And in those times the fruits of the earth shall be backward,

And shall not grow in their time,

And the fruits of the trees shall be withheld in their time.

4 And the moon shall alter her order,

And not appear at her time.

5 [And in those days the sun shall be seen and he shall journey in the evening on the extremity of the great chariot in the west]

And shall shine more brightly than accords with the order of light.

6 And many chiefs of the stars shall transgress the order (prescribed).

And these shall alter their orbits and tasks,

And not appear at the seasons prescribed to them.

7 And the whole order of the stars shall be concealed from the sinners,

And the thoughts of those on the earth shall err concerning them,

[And they shall be altered from all their ways],

Yea, they shall err and take them to be gods.

8 And evil shall be multiplied upon them,

And punishment shall come upon them So as to destroy all.'

CHAPTER 81

1 And he said unto me:

' Observe, Enoch, these heavenly tablets,

And read what is written thereon,

And mark every individual fact.'

2 And I observed the heavenly tablets and read everything which was written (thereon) and understood everything, and read the book of all the deeds of mankind, and of all
the children of flesh 3 that shall be upon the earth to the remotest generations. And forthwith I blessed the great Lord the King of glory for ever, in that He has made all the works of the world,

And I extolled the Lord because of His patience,

And blessed Him because of the children of men.

4 And after that I said:

' Blessed is the man who dies in righteousness and goodness,

Concerning whom there is no book of unrighteousness written,

And against whom no day of judgement shall be found.'

5 And those seven holy ones brought me and placed me on the earth before the door of my house and said to me: ' Declare everything to thy son Methuselah, and show to all thy children that no flesh is righteous in the sight of the Lord, for He is their Creator. One year we will leave thee with thy son, till thou givest thy (last) commands, that thou mayest teach thy children and record (it) for them and testify to all thy children; and in the second year they shall take thee from their midst.

7 Let thy heart be strong,

For the good shall announce righteousness to the good;

The righteous with the righteous shall rejoice,

And shall offer congratulation to one another.

8 But the sinners shall die with the sinners,

And the apostate go down with the apostate.

9 And those who practice righteousness shall die on account of the deeds of men,

And be taken away on account of the doings of the godless.'

10 And in those days they ceased to speak to me, and I came to my people, blessing the Lord of the world.

CHAPTER 82

1 And now, my son Methuselah, all these things I am recounting to thee and writing down for thee! and I have revealed to thee everything, and given thee books concerning all these: so preserve, my son Methuselah, the books from thy father's hand, and (see) that thou deliver them to the generations of the world.

2 I have given Wisdom to thee and to thy children,

[And thy children that shall be to thee],

That they may give it to their children for generations,

This wisdom (namely) that passeth their thought.

3 And those who understand it shall not sleep,

But shall listen with the ear that they may learn this wisdom,

And it shall please those that eat thereof better than good food.

4 Blessed are all the righteous, blessed are all those who walk In the way of righteousness and sin not as the sinners, in the reckoning of all their days in which the sun traverses the heaven, entering into and departing from the portals for thirty days with the heads of thousands of the order of the stars, together with the four which are intercalated which divide the four portions of the year, which lead them and enter with them four days. Owing to them men shall be at fault and not reckon them in the whole reckoning of the year: yea, men shall be at fault, and not recognize them accurately. For they belong to the reckoning of the year and are truly recorded (thereon) for ever, one in the first portal and one in the third, and one in the fourth and one in the sixth, and the year is completed in three hundred and sixty-four days. And the account thereof is accurate and the recorded reckoning thereof exact; for the luminaries, and months and festivals, and years and days, has Uriel shown and revealed to me, to whom the Lord of the whole creation of the world hath subjected the host of heaven. And he has power over night and day in the heaven to cause the light to give light to men -sun, moon, and stars, and all the powers of the heaven which revolve in their circular chariots. And these are the orders of the stars, which set in their places, and in their seasons and festivals and months. And these are the names of those who lead them, who watch that they enter at their times, in their orders, in their seasons, in their months, in their periods of dominion, and in their positions. Their four leaders who divide the four parts of the year enter first; and after them the twelve leaders of the orders who divide the months; and for the three hundred and sixty (days) there are heads over thousands who divide the days; and for the four intercalary days there are the leaders which sunder the four parts of the year. And these heads over thousands are intercalated between leader and leader, each behind a station, but their leaders make the division. And these are the names of the leaders who divide the four parts of the year which are ordained: Milki'el, Hel'emmelek, and Mel'ejal, 14 and Narel. And the names of those who lead them: Adnar'el, and Ijasusa'el, and 'Elome'el- these three follow the leaders of the orders, and there is one that follows the three leaders of the orders which follow those leaders of stations that divide the four parts of the year. In the beginning of the

year Melkejal rises first and rules, who is named Tam'aini and sun, and all the days of his dominion whilst he bears rule are ninety-one days. And these are the signs of the days which are to be seen on earth in the days of his dominion: sweat, and heat, and calms; and all the trees bear fruit, and leaves are produced on all the trees, and the harvest of wheat, and the rose-flowers, and all the flowers which come forth in the field, but the trees of the winter season become withered. And these are the names of the leaders which are under them: Berka'el, Zelebs'el, and another who is added a head of a thousand, called Hilujaseph: and the days of the dominion of this (leader) are at an end. The next leader after him is Hel'emmelek, whom one names the shining sun, and all the days of his light are ninety-one days. And these are the signs of (his) days on the earth: glowing heat and dryness, and the trees ripen their fruits and produce all their fruits ripe and ready, and the sheep pair and become pregnant, and all the fruits of the earth are gathered in, and everything that is in the fields, and the winepress: these things take place in the days of his dominion. These are the names, and the orders, and the leaders of those heads of thousands: Gida'ljal, Ke'el, and He'el, and the name of the head of a thousand which is added to them, Asfa'el: and the days of his dominion are at an end.

SECTION IV. CHAPTERS LXXXIII-XC.

THE DREAM-VISIONS

CHAPTER 83

1 And now, my son Methuselah, I will show thee all my visions which I have seen,
recounting them before thee. Two visions I saw before I took a wife, and the one was
quite unlike the other: the first when I was learning to write: the second before I took
thy mother, (when) I saw a terrible vision. And regarding them I prayed to the Lord. I
had laid me down in the house of my grandfather Mahalalel, (when) I saw in a vision
how the heaven collapsed and was borne off and fell to the earth. And when it fell to
the earth, I saw how the earth was swallowed up in a great abyss, and mountains were
suspended on mountains, and hills sank down on hills, and high trees were rent 5 from
their stems, and hurled down and sunk in the abyss. And thereupon a word fell into my
mouth, and I lifted (my voice) to cry aloud and said: ' The earth is destroyed.' And my
grandfather Mahalalel waked me as I lay near him, and said unto me: ' Why dost thou
cry so, my son, and why dost thou make such lamentation?' And I recounted to him the
whole vision which I had seen, and he said unto me: ' A terrible thing hast thou seen,
my son, and of grave moment is thy dream- vision as to the secrets of all the sin of
the earth: it must sink into the abyss and be destroyed with 8 a great destruction. And
now, my son, arise and make petition to the Lord of glory, since thou art a believer,
that a remnant may remain on the earth, and that He may not destroy the whole earth.
My son, from heaven all this will come upon the earth, and upon the earth there will be
great destruction. After that I arose and prayed and implored and besought and wrote
down my prayer for the generations of the world, and I will show everything to thee,
my son Methuselah. And when I had gone forth below and seen the heaven, and the
sun rising in the east, and the moon setting in the west, and a few stars, and the whole
earth, and everything as He had known it in the beginning, then I blessed the Lord
of judgement and extolled Him because He had made the sun to go forth from the
windows of the east, and he ascended and rose on the face of the heaven, and set out
and kept traversing the path shown unto him.

CHAPTER 84

1 And I lifted up my hands in righteousness and blessed the Holy and Great One, and spoke with the breath of my mouth, and with the tongue of flesh, which God has made for the children of the flesh of men, that they should speak therewith, and He gave them breath and a tongue and a mouth that they should speak therewith:

2 Blessed be Thou, O Lord, King,

Great and mighty in Thy greatness,

Lord of the whole creation of the heaven,

King of kings and God of the whole world.

And Thy power and kingship and greatness abide for ever and ever,

And throughout all generations Thy dominion.

And all the heavens are Thy throne for ever,

And the whole earth Thy footstool for ever and ever.

3 For Thou hast made and Thou rulest all things,

And nothing is too hard for Thee,

Wisdom departs not from the place of Thy throne,

Nor turns away from Thy presence.

And Thou knows and sees and hears everything,

And there is nothing hidden from Thee [for Thou sees everything]

4 And now the angels of Thy heavens are guilty of trespass,

And upon the flesh of men abideth Thy wrath until the great day of judgement.

5 And now, O God and Lord and Great King,

I implore and beseech Thee to fulfil my prayer,

To leave me a posterity on earth,

And not destroy all the flesh of man,

And make the earth without inhabitant,

So that there should be an eternal destruction.

6 And now, my Lord, destroy from the earth the flesh which has aroused Thy wrath,

But the flesh of righteousness and uprightness establish as a plant of the eternal seed,

And hide not Thy face from the prayer of Thy servant, O Lord.'

CHAPTER 85

1,2 And after this I saw another dream, and I will show the whole dream to thee, my son. And Enoch lifted up (his voice) and spoke to his son Methuselah: ' To thee, my son, will I speak: hear my words-incline thine ear to the dream-vision of thy father. Before I took thy mother Edna, I saw in a vision on my bed, and behold a bull came forth from the earth, and that bull was white; and after it came forth a heifer, and along with this (latter) came forth two bulls, one of them black and 4 the other red. And that black bull gored the red one and pursued him over the earth, and thereupon I could no longer see that red bull. But that black bull grew, and that heifer went with him, and I saw that many oxen proceeded from him which resembled and followed him. And that cow, that first one, went from the presence of that first bull in order to seek that red one, but found him not, and lamented with a great lamentation over him and sought him. And I looked till that first bulls came to her and quieted her, and from that time onward she cried no more. And after that she bore another white bull, and after him she bore many bulls and black cows. And I saw in my sleep that white bull likewise grow and become a great white bull, and from Him proceeded many white bulls, and they resembled him. And they began to beget many white bulls, which resembled them, one following the other, (even) many.

CHAPTER 86

And again, I saw with mine eyes as I slept, and I saw the heaven above, and behold a star fell from heaven, and it arose and eat and pastured amongst those oxen. And after that I saw the large and the black oxen and behold, they all changed their stalls and pastures and their cattle and began to live with each other. And again, I saw in the vision, and looked towards the heaven, and behold I saw many stars descend and cast themselves down from heaven to that first star, and they became bulls amongst those cattle and pastured with them [amongst them]. And I looked at them and saw, and behold they all let out their privy members, like horses, and began to cover the cows of the oxen, and they all became pregnant and bare elephants, camels, and asses. And all the oxen feared them and were affrighted at them and began to bite with their teeth and to devour, and to gore with their horns. And they began, moreover, to devour those oxen; and behold all the children of the earth began to tremble and quake before them and to flee from them.

CHAPTER 87

And again I saw how they began to gore each other and to devour each other, and the earth began to cry aloud. And I raised mine eyes again to heaven, and I saw in the vision, and behold there came forth from heaven beings who were like white men: and four went forth from that place and three with them. And those three that had last come forth grasped me by my hand and took me up, away from the generations of the earth, and raised me up to a lofty place, and showed me a tower raised high above the earth, and all the hills were lower. And one said unto me: ' Remain here till thou sees everything that befalls those elephants, camels, and asses, and the stars and the oxen, and all of them.'

CHAPTER 88

And I saw one of those four who had come forth first, and he seized that first star which had fallen from the heaven, and bound it hand and foot and cast it into an abyss: now that abyss was narrow and deep, and horrible and dark. And one of them drew a sword and gave it to those elephants and camels and asses: then they began to smite each other, and the whole earth quaked because of them. And as I was beholding in the vision, lo, one of those four who had come forth stoned (them) from heaven and gathered and took all the great stars whose privy members were like those of horses, and bound them all hand and foot, and cast them in an abyss of the earth.

CHAPTER 89

And one of those four went to that white bull and instructed him in a secret, without his being terrified: he was born a bull and became a man, and built for himself a great vessel and dwelt thereon; and three bulls dwelt with him in that vessel, and they were covered in. And again, I raised mine eyes towards heaven and saw a lofty roof, with seven water torrents thereon, and those torrents flowed with much water into an enclosure. And I saw again, and behold fountains were opened on the surface of that great enclosure, and that water began to swell and rise upon the surface, and I saw that enclosure till all its surface was covered with water. And the water, the darkness, and mist increased upon it; and as I looked at the height of that water, that water had risen above the height of that enclosure, and was streaming over that enclosure, and it stood upon the earth. And all the cattle of that enclosure were gathered until I saw how they sank and were swallowed up and perished in that water. But that vessel floated on the water, while all the oxen and elephants and camels and asses sank to the bottom with all the animals, so that I could no longer see them, and they were not able to escape, (but) perished and sank into the depths. And again, I saw in the vision till those water torrents were removed from that high roof, and the chasms of the earth were levelled up and other abysses were opened. Then the water began to run down into these, till the earth became visible; but that vessel settled on the earth, and the darkness retired, and light appeared. But that white bull which had become a man came out of that vessel, and the three bulls with him, and one of those three was white like that bull, and one of them was red as blood, and one black: and that white bull departed from them. And they began to bring forth beasts of the field and birds, so that there arose different genera: lions, tigers, wolves, dogs, hyenas, wild boars, foxes, squirrels, swine, falcons, vultures, kites, eagles, and ravens; and among them was born a white bull. And they began to bite one another; but that white bull which was born amongst them begat a wild ass and a white bull with it, and the wild asses multiplied. But that bull which was born from him begat a black wild boar and a white sheep; and the former begat many boars, but that sheep begat twelve sheep. And when those twelve sheep had grown, they gave up one of them to the asses, and those asses again gave up that sheep to the wolves, and that sheep grew up among the wolves. And the Lord brought the eleven sheep to live with it and to pasture with it among the wolves: and they multiplied and became many flocks of sheep. And the wolves began to fear them, and they oppressed them until they destroyed their little ones, and they cast their young into a river of much water: but those sheep began to cry aloud on account of their little ones, and to complain unto their Lord. And a sheep which had been saved from the wolves fled and escaped to the wild asses; and I saw the sheep how they lamented and cried, and besought their Lord with all their might, till that Lord of the sheep descended at the voice of the sheep from a lofty abode and came to them and pastured them. And He called that sheep which had escaped the wolves and spoke with it concerning the wolves that it should admonish them not to touch the sheep. And the sheep went to the wolves according to the word of the Lord, and another sheep met it and went with it, and the two went and entered together into the assembly of those wolves and spoke with them and admonished them not to touch the sheep from henceforth. And thereupon I saw the wolves, and how they oppressed the sheep exceedingly with all their power; and the sheep cried aloud. And the Lord came to the sheep, and they began to smite those wolves: and the wolves began to make lamentation; but the sheep became quiet and forthwith ceased to cry out. And I saw the sheep till they departed from amongst the wolves; but the eyes of the wolves were blinded, and those wolves departed in pursuit of the sheep with all their power. And the Lord of the sheep went with them, as their leader, and all His sheep followed Him: and his face was dazzling and glorious and terrible to behold. But the wolves began to pursue those sheep till they reached a sea of water. And that sea was divided, and the water stood on this side and on that before their face, and their Lord led them and placed Himself between them and the wolves. And as those wolves did not yet see the sheep, they proceeded into the midst of that sea, and the wolves followed the sheep, and [those wolves] ran after them into that sea. And when they saw the Lord of the sheep, they turned to flee before His face, but that sea gathered itself together, and became as it had been created, and the water swelled and rose till it covered those wolves. And I saw till all the wolves who pursued those sheep perished and were drowned. But the sheep escaped from that water and went forth into a wilderness, where there was no water and no grass; and they began to open their eyes and to see; and I saw the Lord of the sheep pasturing them and giving them water and grass, and that sheep going and leading them. And that sheep ascended to the summit of that lofty rock, and the Lord of the sheep sent it to them. And after that I saw the Lord of the sheep who stood before them, and His appearance was great and terrible and majestic, and all those sheep saw Him and were afraid before His face. And they all feared and trembled because of Him, and they cried to that sheep with them [which was amongst them]: ' We are not able to stand before our Lord or to behold Him.' And that sheep which led them again ascended to the summit of that rock, but the sheep began to be blinded and to wander from the way which he had showed them, but that sheep wot not thereof. And the Lord of the sheep was wrathful exceedingly against them, and that sheep discovered it, and went down from the summit of the rock, and came to the sheep, and found the greatest part of them blinded and fallen away. And when they saw it they feared and trembled at its presence, and desired to return to their folds. And that sheep took other sheep with it, and came to those sheep which had fallen away, and began to slay them; and the sheep feared its presence, and thus that sheep brought back those sheep that had fallen away, and they returned to their folds. And I saw in this vision till that sheep became a man and built a house for the Lord of the sheep and placed all the sheep in that house. And I saw till this sheep which had met that sheep which led them fell asleep: and I saw till all the great sheep perished and little ones arose in their place, and they came to a pasture, and approached a stream of water. Then that sheep, their leader which had become a man, withdrew from them and fell asleep, and all the sheep sought it and cried over it with a great crying. And I saw till they left off crying for that sheep and crossed that stream of water, and there arose the two sheep as leaders in the place of those which had led them and fallen asleep (lit. ' had fallen asleep and led them '). And I saw till the sheep came to a goodly place, and a pleasant and glorious land, and I saw till those sheep were satisfied; and that house stood amongst them in the pleasant land. And sometimes their eyes were opened, and sometimes blinded, till another sheep arose and led them and brought them all back, and their eyes were opened. And the dogs and the foxes and the wild boars began to devour those sheep till the Lord of the sheep raised up [another sheep] a ram from their midst, which led them. And that ram began to butt on either side those dogs, foxes, and wild boars till he had destroyed them all. And that sheep whose eyes were opened saw that ram, which was amongst the sheep, till it forsook its glory and began to butt those sheep, and trampled upon them, and behaved itself unseemly. And the Lord of the sheep sent the lamb to another lamb and raised it to being a ram and leader of the sheep instead of that ram which had forsaken its glory. And it went to it and spoke to it alone, and raised it to being a ram, and made it the prince and leader of the sheep; but during all these things those dogs oppressed the sheep. And the first ram pursued that second ram, and that second ram arose and fled before it; and I saw till those dogs pulled 48 down the first ram. And that second ram arose and led the [little] sheep. And those sheep grew and multiplied; but all the dogs, and foxes, and wild boars feared and fled before it, and that ram butted and killed the wild beasts, and those wild beasts had no longer any power among the sheep and robbed them no more of nought. And that ram begat many sheep and fell asleep; and a little sheep became ram in its stead and became prince and leader of those sheep. And that house became great and broad, and it was built for those sheep: (and) a tower lofty and great was built on the house for the Lord of the sheep, and that house was low, but the tower was elevated and lofty, and the Lord of the sheep stood on that tower, and they offered a full table before Him. And again I saw those sheep that they again erred and went many ways, and forsook that their house, and the Lord of the sheep called some from amongst the sheep and sent them to the sheep, but the sheep began to slay them. And one of them was saved and was not slain, and it sped away and cried aloud over the sheep; and they sought to slay it, but the Lord of the sheep saved it from the sheep, and brought it up to me, and caused it to dwell there. And many other sheep He sent to those sheep to testify unto them and lament over them. And after that I saw that when they forsook the house of the Lord and His tower they fell away entirely, and their eyes were blinded; and I saw the Lord of the sheep how He wrought much slaughter amongst them in their herds until those sheep invited that slaughter and betrayed His place. And He gave them over into the hands of the lions and tigers, and wolves and hyenas, and into the hand of the foxes, and to all the wild beasts, and those wild beasts began to tear in pieces those sheep. And I saw that He forsook that their house and their tower and gave them all into the hand of the lions, to tear and devour them, into the hand of all the wild beasts. And I began to cry aloud with all my power, and to appeal to the Lord of the sheep, and to represent to Him regarding the sheep that they were devoured by all the wild beasts. But He remained unmoved, though He saw it, and rejoiced that they were devoured and swallowed and robbed and left them to be devoured in the hand of all the beasts. And He called seventy shepherds and cast those sheep to them that they might pasture them, and He spoke to the shepherds and their companions: ' Let everyone of you pasture the sheep henceforward, and everything that I shall command you that do ye. And I will deliver them over unto you duly numbered and tell you which of them are to be destroyed-and them destroy ye.' And He gave over unto them those sheep. And He called another and spoke unto him: ' Observe and mark everything that the shepherds will do to those sheep; for they will destroy more of them than I have commanded them. And every excess and the destruction which will be wrought through the shepherds, record (namely) how many they destroy according to my command, and how many according to their own caprice: record against every individual shepherd all the destruction he effects. And read out before me by number how many they destroy, and how many they deliver over for destruction, that I may have this as a testimony against them, and know every deed of the shepherds, that I may comprehend and see what they do, whether or not they abide by my command which I have commanded them. But they shall not know it, and thou shalt not declare it to them, nor admonish them, but only record against each individual all the destruction which the shepherd's effect each in his time and lay it all before me.' And I saw till those shepherds pastured in their season, and they began to slay and to destroy more than they were bidden, and they delivered those sheep into the hand of the lions. And the lions and tigers eat and devoured the greater part of those sheep, and the wild boars eat along with them; and they burnt that tower and demolished that house. And I became exceedingly sorrowful over that tower because that house of the sheep was demolished, and afterwards I was unable to see if those sheep entered that house. 68 And the shepherds and their associates delivered over those sheep to all the wild beasts, to devour them, and each one of them received in his time a definite number: it was written by the other in a book how many each one of them destroyed of them. And each one slew and destroyed many more than was prescribed; and I began to weep and lament on account of those sheep. And thus in the vision I saw that one who wrote, how he wrote down every one that was destroyed by those shepherds, day by day, and carried up and laid down and showed actually the whole book to the Lord of the sheep-(even) everything that they had done, and all that each one of them had made away with, and all that they had given over to destruction. And the book was read before the Lord of the sheep, and He took the book from his hand and read it and sealed it and laid it down. And forthwith I saw how the shepherds pastured for twelve hours and behold three of those sheep turned back and came and entered and began to build up all that had fallen down of that house; but the wild boars tried to hinder them, but they were not able. And they began again to build as before, and they reared up that tower, and it was named the high tower; and they began again to place a table before the tower, but all the bread on it was polluted and not pure. And as touching all this the eyes of those sheep were blinded so that they saw not, and (the eyes of) their shepherds likewise; and they delivered them in large numbers to their shepherds for destruction, and they trampled the sheep with their feet and devoured them. And the Lord of the sheep remained unmoved till all the sheep were dispersed over the field and mingled with them (i.e., the 76 beasts), and they (i.e. the shepherds) did not save them out of the hand of the beasts. And this one who wrote the book carried it up and showed it and read it before the Lord of the sheep, and implored Him on their account, and besought Him on their account as he showed Him all the doings of the shepherds, and gave testimony before Him against all the shepherds. And he took the actual book and laid it down beside Him and departed.

CHAPTER 90

And I saw till that in this manner thirty-five shepherds undertook the pasturing (of the sheep), and they severally completed their periods as did the first; and others received them into their hands, to pasture them for their period, each shepherd in his own period. And after that I saw in my vision all the birds of heaven coming, the eagles, the vultures, the kites, the ravens; but the eagles led all the birds; and they began to devour those sheep, and to pick out their eyes and to devour their flesh. And the sheep cried out because their flesh was being devoured by the birds, and as for me I looked and lamented in my sleep over that shepherd who pastured the sheep. And I saw until those sheep were devoured by the dogs and eagles and kites, and they left neither flesh nor skin nor sinew remaining on them till only their bones stood there: and their bones too fell to the earth and the sheep became few. And I saw until that twenty-three had undertaken the pasturing and completed in their several periods fifty-eight times. But behold lambs were borne by those white sheep, and they began to open their eyes and to see, and to cry to the sheep. Yea, they cried to them, but they did not hearken to what they said to them, but were exceedingly deaf, and their eyes were very exceedingly blinded. And I saw in the vision how the ravens flew upon those lambs and took one of those lambs, and dashed the sheep in pieces and devoured them. And I saw till horns grew upon those lambs, and the ravens cast down their horns; and I saw till there sprouted a great horn of one of those sheep, and their eyes were opened. And it looked at them [and their eyes opened], and it cried to the sheep, and the rams saw it and all ran to it. And notwithstanding all this those eagles and vultures and ravens and kites still kept tearing the sheep and swooping down upon them and devouring them: still the sheep remained silent, but the rams lamented and cried out. And those ravens fought and battled with it and sought to lay low its horn, but they had no power over it. All the eagles and vultures and ravens and kites were gathered together, and there came with them all the sheep of the field, yea, they all came together, and helped each other to break that horn of the ram. And I saw till a great sword was given to the sheep, and the sheep proceeded against all the beasts of the field to slay them, and all the beasts and the birds of the heaven fled before their face. And I saw that man, who wrote the book according to the command of the Lord, till he opened that book concerning the destruction which those twelve last shepherds had wrought and showed that they had destroyed much more than their predecessors, before the Lord of the sheep. And I saw till the Lord of the sheep came unto them and took in His hand the staff of His wrath, and smote the earth, and the earth clave asunder, and all the beasts and all the birds of the heaven fell from among those sheep and were swallowed up in the earth and it covered them. And I saw till a throne was erected in the pleasant land, and the Lord of the sheep sat Himself thereon, and the other took the sealed books and opened those books before the Lord of the sheep. And the Lord called those men the seven first white ones, and commanded that they should bring before Him, beginning with the first star which led the way, all the stars whose privy members were like those of horses, and they brought them all before Him. And He said to that man who wrote before Him, being one of those seven white ones, and said unto him: ' Take those seventy shepherds to whom I delivered the sheep, and who taking them on their own authority slew more than I commanded them.' And behold they were all bound, I saw, and they all stood before Him. And the judgement was held first over the stars, and they were judged and found guilty, and went to the place of condemnation, and they were cast into an abyss, full of fire and flaming, and full 25 of pillars of fire. And those seventy shepherds were judged and found guilty, and they were cast into that fiery abyss. And I saw at that time how a like abyss was opened in the midst of the earth, full of fire, and they brought those blinded sheep, and they were all judged and found guilty and cast into this fiery abyss, and they burned; now this abyss was to the right of that house. And I saw those sheep burning and their bones burning. And I stood up to see till they folded up that old house; and carried off all the pillars, and all the beams and ornaments of the house were at the same time folded up with it, and they carried it off and laid it in a place in the south of the land. And I saw till the Lord of the sheep brought a new house greater and loftier than that first and set it up in the place of the first which had beer folded up: all its pillars were new, and its ornaments were new and larger than those of the first, the old one which He had taken away, and all the sheep were within it. And I saw all the sheep which had been left, and all the beasts on the earth, and all the birds of the heaven, falling and doing homage to those sheep and making petition to and obeying them in everything. And thereafter those three who were clothed in white and had seized me by my hand [who had taken me up before], and the hand of that ram also seizing hold of me, they took me up and set me down in the midst of those sheep before the judgement took place. And those sheep were all white, and their wool was abundant and clean. And all that had been destroyed and dispersed, and all the beasts of the field, and all the birds of the heaven, assembled in that house, and the Lord of the sheep rejoiced with great joy because they were all good and had returned to His house. And I saw till they laid down that sword, which had been given to the sheep, and they brought it back into the house, and it was sealed before the presence of the Lord, and all the sheep were invited into that house, but it held them not. And the eyes of them all were opened, and they saw the good, and there was not one among them that did not see. And I saw that that house was large and broad and very full. And I saw that a white bull was born, with large horns and all the beasts of the field and all the birds of the air feared him and made petition to him all the time. And I saw till all their generations were transformed, and they all became white bulls; and the first among them became a lamb, and that lamb became a great animal and had great black horns on its head; and the Lord of the sheep rejoiced over it and over all the oxen. And I slept in their midst: and I awoke and saw everything. This is the vision which I saw while I slept, and I awoke and blessed the Lord of righteousness and gave Him glory. Then I wept with a great weeping and my tears stayed not till I could no longer endure it: when I saw, they flowed on account of what I had seen; for everything shall come and be fulfilled, and all the deeds of men in their order were shown to me. On that night I remembered the first dream, and because of it I wept and was troubled-because I had seen that vision.

SECTION V

A BOOK OF EXHORTATION AND PROMISED BLESSING FOR THE RIGHTEOUS AND OF MALEDICTION AND WOE FOR THE SINNERS

CHAPTER 92

1 The book written by Enoch-[Enoch indeed wrote this complete doctrine of wisdom, (which is) praised of all men and a judge of all the earth] for all my children who shall dwell on the earth. And for the future generations who shall observe uprightness and peace.

2 Let not your spirit be troubled on account of the times.

For the Holy and Great One has appointed days for all things.

3 And the righteous one shall arise from sleep,

[Shall arise] and walk in the paths of righteousness,

And all his path and conversation shall be in eternal goodness and grace.

4 He will be gracious to the righteous and give him eternal uprightness,

And He will give him power so that he shall be (endowed) with goodness and righteousness.

And he shall walk in eternal light.

5 And sin shall perish in darkness for ever,

And shall no more be seen from that day for evermore.

CHAPTER 91

1 And now, my son Methuselah, call to me all thy brothers.

And gather together to me all the sons of thy mother.

For the word calls me,

And the spirit is poured out upon me,

That I may show you everything

That shall befall you for ever.'

2 And there upon Methuselah went and summoned to him all his brothers and assembled his relatives.

3 And he spoke unto all the children of righteousness and said:

'Hear, ye sons of Enoch, all the words of your father,

And hearken a right to the voice of my mouth.

For I exhort you and say unto you, beloved:

4 Love uprightness and walk therein.

And draw not nigh to uprightness with a double heart,

And associate not with those of a double heart,

But walk in righteousness, my sons.

And it shall guide you on good paths,

And righteousness shall be your companion.

5 For I know that violence must increase on the earth,

And a great chastisement be executed on the earth,

Yea, it shall be cut off from its roots,

And its whole structure be destroyed.

6 And unrighteousness shall again be consummated on the earth,

And all the deeds of unrighteousness and of violence

And transgression shall prevail in a twofold degree.

7 And when sin and unrighteousness and blasphemy

And violence in all kinds of deeds increase,

And apostasy and transgression and uncleanness increase,

A great chastisement shall come from heaven upon all these,

And the holy Lord will come forth with wrath and chastisement.

To execute judgement on earth.

8 In those days' violence shall be cut off from its roots,

And the roots of unrighteousness together with deceit,

And they shall be destroyed from under heaven.

9 And all the idols of the heathen shall be abandoned,

And the temples burned with fire,

And they shall remove them from the whole earth,

And they (i.e., the heathen) shall be cast into the judgement of fire,

And shall perish in wrath and in grievous judgement for ever.

10 And the righteous shall arise from their sleep,

And wisdom shall arise and be given unto them.

[And after that the roots of unrighteousness shall be cut off, and the sinners shall be destroyed by the sword . . . shall be cut off from the blasphemers in every place, and those who plan violence and those who commit blasphemy shall perish by the sword.]

18 And now I tell you, my sons, and show you.

The paths of righteousness and the paths of violence.

Yea, I will show them to you again.

That ye may know what will come to pass.

19 And now, hearken unto me, my sons,

And walk in the paths of righteousness,

And walk not in the paths of violence.

For all who walk in the paths of unrighteousness shall perish for ever.'

CHAPTER 93

1,2 And after that Enoch both gave and began to recount from the books. And Enoch said:

' Concerning the children of righteousness and concerning the elect of the world,

And concerning the plant of uprightness, I will speak these things,

Yea, I Enoch will declare (them) unto you, my sons:

According to that which appeared to me in the heavenly vision,

And which I have known through the word of the holy angels,

And have learnt from the heavenly tablets.'

3 And Enoch began to recount from the books and said:

' I was born the seventh in the first week,

While judgement and righteousness still endured.

4 And after me there shall arise in the second week great wickedness,

And deceit shall have sprung up.

And in it there shall be the first end.

And in it a man shall be saved.

And after it is ended unrighteousness shall grow up,

And a law shall be made for the sinners.

And after that in the third week at its close

A man shall be elected as the plant of righteous judgement,

And his posterity shall become the plant of righteousness for evermore.

6 And after that in the fourth week, at its close,

Visions of the holy and righteous shall be seen,

And a law for all generations and an enclosure shall be made for them.

7 And after that in the fifth week, at its close,

The house of glory and dominion shall be built for ever.

8 And after that in the sixth week all who live in it shall be blinded,

And the hearts of all of them shall godlessly forsake wisdom.

And in it a man shall ascend.

And at its close the house of dominion shall be burnt with fire,

And the whole race of the chosen root shall be dispersed.

9 And after that in the seventh week shall an apostate generation arise,

And many shall be its deeds,

And all its deeds shall be apostate.

10 And at its close shall be elected.

The elect righteous of the eternal plant of righteousness,

To receive sevenfold instruction concerning all His creation.

11 [For who is there of all the children of men that is able to hear the voice of the Holy One without being troubled? And who can think His thoughts? and who is there that can behold all the works 12 of heaven? And how should there be one who could behold the heaven, and who is there that could understand the things of heaven and see a soul or a spirit and could tell thereof, or ascend and see 13 all their ends and think them or do like them? And who is there of all men that could know what is the breadth and the length of the earth, and to whom has been shown the measure of all of them? 14 Or is there anyone who could discern the length of the heaven and how great is its height, and upon what it is founded, and how great is the number of the stars, and where all the luminaries rest?]

CHAPTER 91

12 And after that there shall be another, the eighth week, that of righteousness,

And a sword shall be given to it that a righteous judgement may be executed on the oppressors,

And sinners shall be delivered into the hands of the righteous.

13 And at its close they shall acquire houses through their righteousness,

And a house shall be built for the Great King in glory for evermore,

14d And all mankind shall look to the path of uprightness.

14a And after that, in the ninth week, the righteous judgement shall be revealed to the whole world,

b And all the works of the godless shall vanish from all the earth,

c And the world shall be written down for destruction.

15 And after this, in the tenth week in the seventh part,

There shall be the great eternal judgement,

In which He will execute vengeance amongst the angels.

16 And the first heaven shall depart and pass away,

And a new heaven shall appear,

And all the powers of the heavens shall give sevenfold light.

17 And after that there will be many weeks without number for ever,

And all shall be in goodness and righteousness,

And sin shall no more be mentioned for ever.

CHAPTER 94

1 And now I say unto you, my sons, love righteousness and walk therein.

For the paths of righteousness are worthy of acceptation,

But the paths of unrighteousness shall suddenly be destroyed and vanish.

2 And to certain men of a generation shall the paths of violence and of death be revealed,

And they shall hold themselves afar from them,

And shall not follow them.

3 And now I say unto you the righteous:

Walk not in the paths of wickedness, nor in the paths of death,

And draw not nigh to them, lest ye be destroyed.

4 But seek and choose for yourselves righteousness and an elect life,

And walk in the paths of peace,

And ye shall live and prosper.

5 And hold fast my words in the thoughts of your hearts,

And suffer them not to be effaced from your hearts.

For I know that sinners will tempt men to evilly-entreat wisdom,

So that no place may be found for her,

And no manner of temptation may minish.

6 Woe to those who build unrighteousness and oppression.

And lay deceit as a foundation.

For they shall be suddenly overthrown,

And they shall have no peace.

7 Woe to those who build their houses with sin.

For from all their foundations shall they be overthrown,

And by the sword shall they fall.

[And those who acquire gold and silver in judgement suddenly shall perish.]

8 Woe to you, ye rich, for ye have trusted in your riches,

And from your riches shall ye depart,

Because ye have not remembered the Highest in the days of your riches.

9 Ye have committed blasphemy and unrighteousness,

And have become ready for the day of slaughter,

And the day of darkness and the day of the great judgement.

10 Thus I speak and declare unto you:

He who hath created you will overthrow you,

And for your fall there shall be no compassion,

And your Creator will rejoice at your destruction.

11 And your righteous ones in those days shall be

A reproach to the sinners and the godless.

CHAPTER 95

1 Oh that mine eyes were [a cloud of] waters.

That I might weep over you,

And pour down my tears as a cloud of waters:

That so I might rest from my trouble of heart!

2 who has permitted you to practice reproaches and wickedness?

And so, judgement shall overtake you, sinners.

3 Fear not the sinners, ye righteous.

For again will the Lord deliver them into your hands,

That ye may execute judgement upon them according to your desires.

4 Woe to you who fulminate anathemas which cannot be reversed:

Healing shall therefore be far from you because of your sins.

5 Woe to you who requite your neighbour with evil.

For ye shall be requited according to your works.

6 Woe to you, lying witnesses,

And to those who weigh out injustice,

For suddenly shall ye perish.

7 Woe to you, sinners, for ye persecute the righteous.

For ye shall be delivered up and persecuted because of injustice,

And heavy shall its yoke be upon you.

CHAPTER 96

1 Be hopeful, ye righteous; for suddenly shall the sinners perish before you,

And ye shall have lordship over them according to your desires.

2 [And in the day of the tribulation of the sinners,

Your children shall mount and rise as eagles,

And higher than the vultures will be your nest,

And ye shall ascend and enter the crevices of the earth,

And the clefts of the rock for ever as coneys before the unrighteous,

And the sirens shall sigh because of you-and weep.]

3 Wherefore fear not, ye that have suffered.

For healing shall be your portion,

And a bright light shall enlighten you,

And the voice of rest ye shall hear from heaven.

4 Woe unto you, ye sinners, for your riches make you appear like the righteous,

But your hearts convict you of being sinners,

And this fact shall be a testimony against you for a memorial of (your) evil deeds.

5 Woe to you who devour the finest of the wheat,

And drink wine in large bowls,

And tread underfoot the lowly with you might.

6 Woe to you who drink water from every fountain,

For suddenly shall ye be consumed and wither away,

Because ye have forsaken the fountain of life.

7 Woe to you who work unrighteousness.

And deceit and blasphemy:

It shall be a memorial against you for evil.

8 Woe to you, ye mighty,

Who with might oppress the righteous.

For the day of your destruction is coming.

In those days many and good days shall come to the righteous-in the day of your judgement.

CHAPTER 97

1 Believe, ye righteous, that the sinners will become a shame.

And perish in the day of unrighteousness.

2 Be it known unto you (ye sinners) that the Highest is mindful of your destruction,

And the angels of heaven rejoice over your destruction.

3 What will ye do, ye sinners,

And whither will ye flee on that day of judgement,

When ye hear the voice of the prayer of the righteous?

4 Yea, ye shall fare like unto them,

Against whom this word shall be a testimony:

" Ye have been companions of sinners."

5 And in those days the prayer of the righteous shall reach unto the Lord,

And for you the days of your judgement shall come.

6 And all the words of your unrighteousness shall be read out before the Great Holy One,

And your faces shall be covered with shame,

And He will reject every work which is grounded on unrighteousness.

7 Woe to you, ye sinners, who live on the mid ocean and on the dry land,

Whose remembrance is evil against you.

8 Woe to you who acquire silver and gold in unrighteousness and say:

" We have become rich with riches and have possessions.

And have acquired everything we have desired.

9 And now let us do what we purposed:

For we have gathered silver,

9c And many are the husbandmen in our houses."

9d And our granaries are (brim) full as with water,

10 Yea and like water your lies shall flow away.

For your riches shall not abide

But speedily ascend from you.

For ye have acquired it all in unrighteousness,

And ye shall be given over to a great curse.

CHAPTER 98

1 And now I swear unto you, to the wise and to the foolish,

For ye shall have manifold experiences on the earth.

2 For ye men shall put on more adornments than a woman,

And coloured garments more than a virgin:

In royalty and in grandeur and in power,

And in silver and in gold and in purple,

And in splendour and in food they shall be poured out as water.

3 Therefore they shall be wanting in doctrine and wisdom,

And they shall perish thereby together with their possessions.

And with all their glory and their splendour,

And in shame and in slaughter and in great destitution,

Their spirits shall be cast into the furnace of fire.

4 I have sworn unto you, ye sinners, as a mountain has not become a slave,

And a hill does not become the handmaid of a woman,

Even so sin has not been sent upon the earth,

But man of himself has created it,

And under a great curse shall they fall who commit it.

5 And barrenness has not been given to the woman,

But on account of the deeds of her own hands she dies without children.

6 I have sworn unto you, ye sinners, by the Holy Great One,

That all your evil deeds are revealed in the heavens,

And that none of your deeds of oppression are covered and hidden.

7 And do not think in your spirit nor say in your heart that ye do not know and that
ye do not see 8 that every sin is every day recorded in heaven in the presence of the
Highest. From henceforth ye know that all your oppression wherewith ye oppress is
written down every day till the day of your judgement. 9 Woe to you, ye fools, for
through your folly shall ye perish: and ye transgress against the wise, 10 and so good
hap shall not be your portion. And now, know ye that ye are prepared for the day of
destruction: wherefore do not hope to live, ye sinners, but ye shall depart and die; for
ye know no ransom; for ye are prepared for the day of the great judgement, for the day
of tribulation and great shame for your spirits. 11 Woe to you, ye obstinate of heart,
who work wickedness and eat blood: Whence have ye good things to eat and to drink
and to be filled? From all the good things which the Lord the Most High has placed
in abundance on the earth; therefore, ye shall have no peace. 12 Woe to you who love
the deeds of unrighteousness: wherefore do ye hope for good hap unto yourselves?
know that ye shall be delivered into the hands of the righteous, and they shall cut 13
off your necks and slay you and have no mercy upon you. Woe to you who rejoice in
the tribulation of the righteous; for no grave shall be dug for you. Woe to you who set
at nought the words of 15 the righteous; for ye shall have no hope of life. Woe to you
who write down lying and godless words; for they write down their lies that men may
hear them and act godlessly towards (their) 16 neighbours. Therefore, they shall have
no peace but die a sudden death.

CHAPTER 99

1 Woe to you who work godlessness,

And glory in lying and extol them:

Ye shall perish, and no happy life shall be yours.

2 Woe to them who pervert the words of uprightness,

And transgress the eternal law,

And transform themselves into what they were not [into sinners]:

They shall be trodden under foot upon the earth.

3 In those days make ready, ye righteous, to raise your prayers as a memorial,

And place them as a testimony before the angels,

That they may place the sin of the sinners for a memorial before the Highest.

4 In those days the nations shall be stirred up,

And the families of the nations shall arise on the day of destruction.

5 And in those days the destitute shall go forth and carry off their children,

And they shall abandon them, so that their children shall perish through them:

Yea, they shall abandon their children (that are still) suckling's, and not return to them,

And shall have no pity on their beloved ones.

6, 7 And again I swear to you, ye sinners, that sin is prepared for a day of unceasing bloodshed. And they who worship stones, and grave images of gold and silver and wood (and stone) and clay, and those who worship impure spirits and demons, and all kinds of idols not according to knowledge, shall get no manner of help from them.

8 And they shall become godless by reason of the folly of their hearts,

And their eyes shall be blinded through the fear of their hearts.

And through visions in their dreams.

9 Through these they shall become godless and fearful.

For they shall have wrought all their work in a lie,

And shall have worshiped a stone:

Therefore, in an instant shall they perish.

10 But in those days blessed are all they who accept the words of wisdom, and

understand them,

And observe the paths of the Highest, and walk in the path of His righteousness,

And become not godless with the godless.

For they shall be saved.

11 Woe to you who spread evil to your neighbours.

For you shall be slain in Sheol.

12 Woe to you who make deceitful and false measures,

And (to them) who cause bitterness on the earth.

For they shall thereby be utterly consumed.

13 Woe to you who build your houses through the grievous toil of others,

And all their building materials are the bricks and stones of sin.

I tell you ye shall have no peace.

14 Woe to them who reject the measure and eternal heritage of their fathers.

And whose souls follow after idols.

For they shall have no rest.

15 Woe to them who work unrighteousness and help oppression,

And slay their neighbours until the day of the great judgement.

16 For He shall cast down your glory,

And bring affliction on your hearts,

And shall arouse His fierce indignation.

And destroy you all with the sword.

And all the holy and righteous shall remember your sins.

CHAPTER 100

1 And in those days in one place the fathers together with their sons shall be smitten.

And brothers one with another shall fall in death.

Till the streams flow with their blood.

2 For a man shall not withhold his hand from slaying his sons and his sons' sons,

And the sinner shall not withhold his hand from his honoured brother:

From dawn till sunset, they shall slay one another.

3 And the horse shall walk up to the breast in the blood of sinners,

And the chariot shall be submerged to its height.

4 In those days the angels shall descend into the secret places.

And gather together into one place all those who brought down sin.

And the Highest will arise on that day of judgement.

To execute great judgement amongst sinners.

5 And over all the righteous and holy He will appoint guardians from amongst the holy angels.

To guard them as the apple of an eye,

Until He makes an end of all wickedness and all sin,

And though the righteous sleep a long sleep, they have nought to fear.

6 And (then) the children of the earth shall see the wise in security,

And shall understand all the words of this book,

And recognize that their riches shall not be able to save them.

In the overthrow of their sins.

7 Woe to you, Sinners, on the day of strong anguish,

Ye who afflict the righteous and burn them with fire:

Ye shall be requited according to your works.

8 Woe to you, ye obstinate of heart,

Who watch in order to devise wickedness:

Therefore, shall fear come upon you.

And there shall be none to help you.

9 Woe to you, ye sinners, on account of the words of your mouth,

And on account of the deeds of your hands which your godlessness as wrought,

In blazing flames burning worse than fire shall ye burn.

10 And now, know ye that from the angels He will inquire as to your deeds in heaven, from the sun and from the moon and from the stars in reference to your sins because upon the earth ye execute 11 judgements on the righteous. And He will summon to testify against you every cloud and mist and dew and rain; for they shall all be withheld because of you from descending upon you, and they 12 shall be mindful of your sins. And now give presents to the rain that it be not withheld from descending upon you, nor yet the dew, when it has received gold and silver from you that it may descend. When the hoar-frost and snow with their chilliness, and all the snowstorms with all their plagues fall upon you, in those days ye shall not be able to stand before them.

CHAPTER 101

Observe the heaven, ye children of heaven, and every work of the Highest, and fear ye Him and work no evil in His presence. If He closes the windows of heaven, and withholds the rain and the dew from descending on the earth on your account, what will ye do then? And if He sends His anger upon you because of your deeds, ye cannot petition Him; for ye spoke proud and insolent words against His righteousness: therefore, ye shall have no peace. And see ye not the sailors of the ships, how their ships are tossed to and for by the waves, and are shaken by the winds, and are in sore trouble? And therefore, do they fear because all their goodly possessions go upon the sea with them, and they have evil forebodings of heart that the sea will swallow them, and they will perish therein. Are not the entire sea and all its waters, and all its movements, the work of the Highest, and has He not set limits to its doings, and confined it throughout by the sand? And at His reproof it is afraid and dries up, and all its fish die and all that is in it; But ye sinners that are on the earth fear Him not. Has He not made the heaven and the earth, and all that is therein? Who has given understanding and wisdom to everything that moves on the earth and in the sea. Do not the sailors of the ships fear the sesea? et sinners fear not the Highest.

CHAPTER 102

In those days when He hath brought a grievous fire upon you,

Whither will ye flee, and where will ye find deliverance?

And when He launches forth His Word against you Will you not be affrighted and fear?

And all the luminaries shall be affrighted with great fear,

And all the earth shall be affrighted and tremble and be alarmed.

And all the angels shall execute their commands.

And shall seek to hide themselves from the presence of the Great Glory,

And the children of earth shall tremble and quake.

And ye sinners shall be cursed for ever,

And ye shall have no peace.

Fear ye not, ye souls of the righteous,

And be hopeful ye that have died in righteousness.

And grieve not if your soul into Sheol has descended in grief,

And that in your life your body fared not according to your goodness,

But wait for the day of the judgement of sinners.

And for the day of cursing and chastisement.

And yet when ye die the sinners speak over you:

" As we die, so die the righteous,

And what benefit do they reap for their deeds?

Behold, even as we, so do they die in grief and darkness,

And what have they more than we?

From henceforth we are equal.

And what will they receive and what will they see for ever?

Behold, they too have died,

And henceforth for ever shall they see no light."

I tell you, ye sinners, ye are content to eat and drink, and rob and sin, and strip men naked, and acquire wealth and see good days. Have you seen the righteous how their end falls out, that no manner of violence is found in them till their death? " Nevertheless, they perished and became as though they had not been, and their spirits descended into Sheol in tribulation."

CHAPTER 103

1 Now, therefore, I swear to you, the righteous, by the glory of the Great and Honoured and Mighty One in dominion, and by His greatness I swear to you.

I know a mystery.

And have read the heavenly tablets,

And have seen the holy books,

And have found written therein and inscribed regarding them:

3 That all goodness and joy and glory are prepared for them,

And written down for the spirits of those who have died in righteousness,

And that manifold good shall be given to you in recompense for your labours,

And that your lot is abundantly beyond the lot of the living.

4 And the spirits of you who have died in righteousness shall live and rejoice,

And their spirits shall not perish, nor their memorial from before the face of the Great One

Unto all the generations of the world: wherefore no longer fear their contumely.

5 Woe to you, ye sinners, when ye have died,

If ye die in the wealth of your sins,

And those who are like you say regarding you:

' Blessed are the sinners: they have seen all their days.

6 And how they have died in prosperity and in wealth,

And have not seen tribulation or murder in their life;

And they have died in honour,

And judgement has not been executed on them during their life."

7 Know ye, that their souls will be made to descend into Sheol

And they shall be wretched in their great tribulation.

8 And into darkness and chains and a burning flame where there is grievous judgement shall your spirits enter;

And the great judgement shall be for all the generations of the world.

Woe to you, for ye shall have no peace.

9 Say not in regard to the righteous and good who are in life:

" In our troubled days we have toiled laboriously and experienced every trouble,

And met with much evil and been consumed,

And have become few and our spirit small.

10 And we have been destroyed and have not found any to help us even with a word:

We have been tortured [and destroyed], and not hoped to see life from day to day.

11 We hoped to be the head and have become the tail:

We have toiled laboriously and had no satisfaction in our toil;

And we have become the food of the sinners and the unrighteous,

And they have laid their yoke heavily upon us.

12 They have had dominion over us that hated us and smote us;

And to those that hated us we have bowed our necks

But they pitied us not.

13 We desired to get away from them that we might escape and be at rest,

But found no place whereunto we should flee and be safe from them.

14 And are complained to the rulers in our tribulation,

And cried out against those who devoured us,

But they did not attend to our cries

And would not hearken to our voice.

15 And they helped those who robbed us and devoured us and those who made us few; and they concealed their oppression, and they did not remove from us the yoke of those that devoured us and dispersed us and murdered us, and they concealed their murder, and remembered not that they had lifted up their hands against us.

CHAPTER 104

1 I swear unto you, that in heaven the angels remember you for good before the glory of the Great 2 One: and your names are written before the glory of the Great One. Be hopeful; for a foretime ye were put to shame through ill and affliction; but now ye shall shine as the lights of heaven, you shall shine and ye shall be seen, and the portals of heaven shall be opened to you. And in your cry, cry for judgement, and it shall appear

to you; for all your tribulation shall be visited on the 4 rulers, and on all who helped those who plundered you. Be hopeful and cast not away your hopes for ye shall have great joy as the angels of heaven. What shall ye be obliged to do? Ye shall not have to hide on the day of the great judgement and ye shall not be found as sinners, and the eternal judgement shall be far from you for all the generations of the world. And now fear not, ye righteous, when ye see the sinners growing strong and prospering in their ways be not companions with them but keep afar from their violence; for ye shall become companions of the hosts of heaven. And, although ye sinners say: " All our sins shall not be searched out and be written down," nevertheless they shall write down all your sins every day. And now I show unto you that light and darkness, day and night, see all your sins. Be not godless in your hearts and lie not and alter not the words of uprightness, nor charge with lying the words of the Holy Great One, nor take account of your idols: for all your lying and all your godlessness issue not in righteousness but in great sin. And now I know this mystery, that sinners will alter and pervert the words of righteousness in many ways, and will speak wicked words, and lie, and practice great deceits, and write books concerning their words. But when they write down truthfully all my words in their languages, and do not change or minish ought from my words but write them all down truthfully -all that I first testified concerning them. Then, I know another mystery, that books will be given to the righteous and the wise to become a cause of joy and uprightness and much wisdom. And to them shall the books be given, and they shall believe in them and rejoice over them, and then shall all the righteous who have learnt therefrom all the paths of uprightness be recompensed.'

CHAPTER 105

1 In those days the Lord bade (them) to summon and testify to the children of earth concerning their wisdom: Show (it) unto them; for ye are their guides, and a recompense over the whole earth. 2 For I and My son will be united with them for ever in the paths of uprightness in their lives; and ye shall have peace: rejoice, ye children of uprightness. Amen.

Fragment of the Book of Noah

CHAPTER 106

And after some days my son Methuselah took a wife for his son Lamech, and she became pregnant by him and bore a son. And his body was white as snow and red as the blooming of a rose, and the hair of his head and his long locks were white as wool, and his eyes beautiful. And when he opened his eyes, he lighted up the whole house like the sun, and the whole house was very bright. And thereupon he arose in the hands of the midwife, opened his mouth, and conversed with the Lord of righteousness. And his father Lamech was afraid of him and fled and came to his father Methuselah. And he said unto him: ' I have begotten a strange son, diverse from and unlike man, and resembling the sons of the God of heaven; and his nature is different, and he is not like us, and his eyes are as the rays of the sun, and his countenance is glorious. And it seems to me that he is not sprung from me but from the angels, and I fear that in his days a wonder may be wrought on the earth. And now, my father, I am here to petition thee and implore thee that thou mayest go to Enoch, our father, and learn from him the truth, for his dwelling-place is amongst the angels.' And when Methuselah heard the words of his son, he came to me to the ends of the earth; for he had heard that was there, and he cried aloud, and I heard his voice, and I came to him. And said unto him: ' Behold, here am I, my son, wherefore hast thou come to me? ' And he answered and said: ' Because of a great cause of anxiety have I come to thee, and because of a disturbing vision 10 have I approached. And now, my father, hear me: unto Lamech my son there hath been born a son, the like of whom there is none, and his nature is not like man's nature, and the colour of his body is whiter than snow and redder than the bloom of a rose, and the hair of his head is whiter than white wool, and his eyes are like the rays of the sun, and he opened his eyes and thereupon lighted up the whole house. And he arose in the hands of the midwife and opened his mouth and blessed the Lord of heaven. And his father Lamech became afraid and fled to me and did not believe that he was sprung from him, but that he was in the likeness of the angels of heaven; and behold I have come to thee that thou mayest make known to me the truth.' And I, Enoch, answered and said unto him: 'The Lord will do a new thing on the earth, and this I have already seen in a vision, and make known to thee that in the generation of my father Jared some of the angels of heaven transgressed the word of the Lord. And behold they commit sin and transgress the law and have united themselves with women and commit sin with them, and have married some of them, and have begot children by them. And they shall produce on the earth giants not according to the spirit, but according to the flesh, and there shall be a great punishment on the earth, and the earth shall be cleansed from all impurity. Yea, there shall come a great destruction over the whole earth, and there shall be a deluge and a great destruction for one year. And this son who has been born unto you shall be left on the earth, and his three children shall be saved with him: when all mankind that are on the earth shall die [he and his sons shall be saved]. And now make known to thy son Lamech that he who has been born is in truth his son, and call his name Noah; for he shall be left to you, and he and his sons shall be saved from the destruction, which shall come upon the earth on account of all the sin and all the unrighteousness, which shall be consummated on the earth in his days. And after that there shall be still more unrighteousness than that which was first consummated on the earth; for I know the mysteries of the holy ones; for He, the Lord, has showed me and informed me, and I have read (them) in the heavenly tablets.

CHAPTER 107

And I saw written on them that generation upon generation shall transgress, till a generation of righteousness arises, and transgression is destroyed, and sin passes away from the earth, and all manner of good comes upon it. And now, my son, go and make known to thy son Lamech that this son, which has been born, is in truth his son, and that (this) is no lie.' And when Methuselah had heard the words of his father Enoch-for he had shown to him everything in secret-he returned and showed (them) to him and called the name of that son Noah; for he will comfort the earth after all the destruction.

CHAPTER 108

Another book which Enoch wrote for his son Methuselah and for those who will come after him and keep the law in the last days. Ye who have done good shall wait for those days till an end is made of those who work evil, and an end of the might of the transgressors. And wait ye indeed till sin has passed away, for their names shall be blotted out of the book of life and out of the holy books, and their seed shall be destroyed for ever, and their spirits shall be slain, and they shall cry and make lamentation in a place that is a chaotic wilderness, and in the fire shall they burn; for there is no earth there. And I saw there something like an invisible cloud; for by reason of its depth I could not look over, and I saw a flame of fire blazing brightly, and things like shining mountains circling and sweeping to and for. And I asked one of the holy angels who was with me and said unto him: ' What is this shining thing? for it is not a heaven but only the flame of a blazing fire, and the voice of weeping and crying and lamentation and strong pain.' And he said unto me: ' This place which thou seest-here are cast the spirits of sinners and blasphemers, and of those who work wickedness, and of those who pervert everything that the Lord hath spoken through the mouth of the prophets-(even) the things that shall be. For some of them are written and inscribed above in the heaven, in order that the angels may read them and know that which shall befall the sinners, and the spirits of the humble, and of those who have afflicted their bodies, and been recompensed by God; and of those who have been put to shame by wicked men: Who love God and loved neither gold nor silver nor any of the good things which are in the world, but gave over their bodies to torture. Who, since they came into being, longed not after earthly food, but regarded everything as a passing breath, and lived accordingly, and the Lord tried them much, and their spirits were 10 found pure so that they should bless His name. And all the blessings destined for them I have recounted in the books. And he hath assigned them their recompense, because they have been found to be such as loved heaven more than their life in the world, and though they were trodden under foot of wicked men, and experienced abuse and reviling from them and were put to shame, yet they blessed Me. And now I will summon the spirits of the good who belong to the generation of light, and I will transform those who were born in darkness, who in the flesh were not recompensed with such honour as their faithfulness deserved. And I will bring forth in shining light those who have loved My holy name, and I will seat each on the throne of his honour. And they shall be resplendent for times without number; for righteousness is the judgement of God; for to the faithful He will give faithfulness in the habitation of upright paths. And they shall see those who were, born in darkness led into darkness, while the righteous shall be resplendent. And the sinners shall cry aloud and see them resplendent, and they indeed will go where days and seasons are prescribed for them.'

BOOK OF 2 ENOCH

THE SECRETS OF ENOCH

CHAPTER 1

1 There was a wise man, a great artificer, and the Lord conceived love for him and received him, that he should behold the uppermost dwellings and be an eye-witness of the wise and great and inconceivable and immutable realm of God Almighty, of the very wonderful and glorious and bright and many-eyed station of the Lord's servants, and of the inaccessible throne of the Lord, and of the degrees and manifestations of the incorporeal hosts, and of the ineffable ministration of the multitude of the elements, and of the various apparition and inexpressible singing of the host of Cherubim, and of the boundless light.

2 At that time, he said, when my one hundred and sixty-fifth year was completed, I begat my son Mathusal (Methuselah).

3 After this too I lived two hundred years and completed of all the years of my life three hundred and sixty-five years.

4 On the first day of the month I was in my house alone and was resting on my bed and slept.

5 And when I was asleep, great distress came up into my heart, and I was weeping with my eyes in sleep, and I could not understand what this distress was, or what would happen to me.

6 And there appeared to me two men, exceeding big, so that I never saw such on earth; their faces were shining like the sun, their eyes too (were) like a burning light, and from their lips was fire coming forth with clothing and singing of various kinds in appearance purple, their wings (were)brighter than gold, their hands whiter than snow.

7 They were standing at the head of my bed and began to call me by my name.

8 And I arose from my sleep and saw clearly those two men standing in front of me.

9 And I saluted them and was seized with fear and the appearance of my face was changed from terror, and those men said to me:

10 Have courage, Enoch, do not fear; the eternal God sent us to you, and lo! You shalt to-day ascend with us into heaven, and you shall tell your sons and all your household all that they shall do without you on earth in your house, and let no one seek you till the Lord return you to them.

11 And I made haste to obey them and went out from my house, and made to the doors, as it was ordered me, and summoned my sons Mathusal (Methuselah) and Regim and Gaidad and made known to them all the marvels those (men) had told me.

CHAPTER 2

1 Listen to me, my children, I know not whither I go, or what will befall me; now therefore, my children, I tell you: turn not from God before the face of the vain, who made not Heaven and earth, for these shall perish and those who worship them, and may the Lord make confident your hearts in the fear of him. And now, my children, let no one think to seek me, until the Lord return me to you.

CHAPTER 3

1 It came to pass, when Enoch had told his sons, that the angels took him on to their wings and bore him up on to the first heaven and placed him on the clouds. And there I looked, and again I looked higher, and saw the ether, and they placed me on the first heaven and showed me a very great Sea, greater than the earthly sea.

CHAPTER 4

1 They brought before my face the elders and rulers of the stellar orders, and showed me two hundred angels, who rule the stars and (their) services to the heavens, and fly with their wings and come round all those who sail.

CHAPTER 5

1 And here I looked down and saw the treasure-houses of the snow, and the angels who keep their terrible store-houses, and the clouds whence they come out and into which they go.

CHAPTER 6

1 They showed me the treasure-house of the dew, like oil of the olive, and the appearance of its form, as of all the flowers of the earth; further many angels guarding the treasure-houses of these (things), and how they are made to shut and open.

CHAPTER 7

1 And those men took me and led me up on to the second heaven, and showed me darkness, greater than earthly darkness, and there I saw prisoners hanging, watched, awaiting the great and boundless judgment, and these angels (spirits) were dark-looking, more than earthly darkness, and incessantly making weeping through all hours.

2 And I said to the men who were with me: Wherefore are these incessantly tortured? They answered me: These are God's apostates, who obeyed not God's commands, but took counsel with their own will, and turned away with their prince, who also (is) fastened on the fifth heaven.

3 And I felt great pity for them, and they saluted me, and said to me: Man of God, pray for us to the Lord; and I answered to them: Who am I, a mortal man, that I should pray for angels (spirits)? Who knows whither I go, or what will befall me? Or who will pray for me?

CHAPTER 8

1 And those men took me thence, and led me up on to the third heaven, and placed me there; and I looked downwards, and saw the produce of these places, such as has never been known for goodness.

2 And I saw all the sweet-flowering trees and beheld their fruits, which were sweet-smelling, and all the foods borne (by them) bubbling with fragrant exhalation.

3 And in the midst of the trees that of life, in that place whereon the Lord rests, when he goes up into paradise; and this tree is of ineffable goodness and fragrance, and adorned more than every existing thing; and on all sides (it is) in form gold-looking and vermilion and fire-like and covers all, and it has produce from all fruits.

4 Its root is in the garden at the earth's end.

5 And paradise is between corruptibility and incorruptibility.

6 And two springs come out which send forth honey and milk, and their springs send forth oil and wine, and they separate into four parts, and go round with quiet course, and go down into the PARADISE OF EDEN, between corruptibility and incorruptibility.

7 And thence they go forth along the earth, and have a revolution to their circle even as other elements.

8 And here there is no unfruitful tree, and every place is blessed.

9 And (there are) three hundred angels very bright, who keep the garden, and with incessant sweet singing and never-silent voices serve the Lord throughout all days and

hours.

10 And I said: How very sweet is this place, and those men said to me:

CHAPTER 9

1 This place, O Enoch, is prepared for the righteous, who endure all manner of offence from those that exasperate their souls, who avert their eyes from iniquity, and make righteous judgment, and give bread to the hungering, and cover the naked with clothing, and raise up the fallen, and help injured orphans, and who walk without fault before the face of the Lord, and serve him alone, and for them is prepared this place for eternal inheritance.

CHAPTER 10

1 And those two men led me up on to the Northern side, and showed me there a very terrible place, and (there were) all manner of tortures in that place: cruel darkness and unillumined gloom, and there is no light there, but murky fire constantly flaming aloft, and (there is) a fiery river coming forth, and that whole place is everywhere fire, and everywhere (there is) frost and ice, thirst and shivering, while the bonds are very cruel, and the angels (spirits) fearful and merciless, bearing angry weapons, merciless torture, and I said:

2 Woe, woe, how very terrible is this place.

3 And those men said to me: This place, O Enoch, is prepared for those who dishonour God, who on earth practice sin against nature, which is child-corruption after the sodomitic fashion, magic-making, enchantments and devilish witchcrafts, and who boast of their wicked deeds, stealing, lies, calumnies, envy, rancour, fornication, murder, and who, accursed, steal the souls of men, who, seeing the poor take away their goods and themselves wax rich, injuring them for other men's goods; who being able to satisfy the empty, made the hungering to die; being able to clothe, stripped the naked; and who knew not their creator, and bowed to the soulless (and lifeless) gods, who cannot see nor hear, vain gods, (who also) built hewn images and bow down to unclean handiwork, for all these is prepared this place among these, for eternal inheritance.

CHAPTER 11

1 Those men took me, and led me up on to the fourth heaven, and showed me all the successive goings, and all the rays of the light of sun and moon.

2 And I measure their goings, and compared their light, and saw that the sun's light is greater than the moon's.

3 Its circle and the wheels on which it goes always, like the wind going past with very marvellous speed, and day and night it has no rest.

4 Its passage and return (are accompanied by) four great stars, (and) each star has under it a thousand stars, to the right of the sun's wheel, (and by) four to the left, each having under it a thousand stars, altogether eight thousand, issuing with the sun continually.

5 And by day fifteen myriads of angels attend it, and by night A thousand.

6 And six-winged ones issue with the angels before the sun's wheel into the fiery flames, and a hundred angels kindle the sun and set it alight.

CHAPTER 12

1 And I looked and saw other flying elements of the sun, whose names (are) Phoenixes and Chalkydri, marvellous and wonderful, with feet and tails in the form of a lion, and a crocodile's head, their appearance (is) empurpled, like the rainbow; their size (is) nine hundred measures, their wings (are like) those of angels, each (has) twelve, and they attend and accompany the sun, bearing heat and dew, as it is ordered them from God.

2 Thus (the sun) revolves and goes, and rises under the heaven, and its course goes under the earth with the light of its rays incessantly.

CHAPTER 13

1 Those men bore me away to the east, and placed me at the sun's gates, where the sun goes forth according to the regulation of the seasons and the circuit of the months of the whole year, and the number of the hours day and night.

2 And I saw six gates open, each gate having sixty-one stadia and A quarter of one stadium, and I measured (them) truly, and understood their size (to be) so much, through which the sun goes forth, and goes to the west, and is made even, and rises throughout all the months, and turns back again from the six gates according to the succession of the seasons; thus (the period) of the whole year is finished after the returns of the four seasons.

CHAPTER 14

1 And again those men led me away to the western parts, and showed me six great gates open corresponding to the eastern gates, opposite to where the sun sets, according to the number of the days three hundred and sixty-five and A quarter.

2 Thus again it goes down to the western gates, (and) draws away its light, the greatness of its brightness, under the earth; for since the crown of its shining is in heaven with the Lord, and guarded by four hundred angels, while the sun goes round on wheel under the earth, and stands seven great hours in night, and spends half (its course) under the earth, when it comes to the eastern approach in the eighth hour of the night, it brings its lights, and the crown of shining, and the sun flames forth more than fire.

CHAPTER 15

1 Then the elements of the sun, called Phoenixes and Chalkydri break into song, therefore every bird flutters with its wings, rejoicing at the giver of light, and they broke into song at the command of the Lord.

2 The giver of light comes to give brightness to the whole world, and the morning guard takes shape, which is the rays of the sun, and the sun of the earth goes out, and receives its brightness to light up the whole face of the earth, and they showed me this calculation of the sun's going.

3 And the gates which it enters, these are the great gates of the calculation of the hours of the year; for this reason the sun is a great creation, whose circuit (lasts) twenty-eight years, and begins again from the beginning.

CHAPTER 16

1 Those men showed me the other course, that of the moon, twelve great gates, crowned from west to east, by which the moon goes in and out of the customary times.

2 It goes in at the first gate to the western places of the sun, by the first gates with (thirty)-one (days) exactly, by the second gates with thirty-one days exactly, by the third with thirty days exactly, by the fourth with thirty days exactly, by the fifth with thirty-one days exactly, by the sixth with thirty-one days exactly, by the seventh with thirty days exactly, by the eighth with thirty-one days perfectly, by the ninth with thirty-one days exactly, by the tenth with thirty days perfectly, by the eleventh with thirty-one days exactly, by the twelfth with twenty-eight days exactly.

3 And it goes through the western gates in the order and number of the eastern and accomplishes the three hundred and sixty-five and a quarter day of the solar year, while

the lunar year has three hundred fifty-four, and there are wanting (to it) twelve days of the solar circle, which are the lunar epacts of the whole year.

4 Thus, too, the great circle contains five hundred and thirty-two years.

5 The quarter (of a day) is omitted for three years, the fourth fulfils it exactly.

6 Therefore they are taken outside of heaven for three years and are not added to the number of days, because they change the time of the years to two new month's towards completion, to two others towards diminution.

7 And when the western gates are finished, it returns and goes to the eastern to the lights and goes thus day and night about the heavenly circles, lower than all circles, swifter than the heavenly winds, and spirits and elements and angels flying; each angel has six wings.

8 It has a sevenfold course in nineteen years.

CHAPTER 17

1 In the midst of the heavens I saw armed soldiers, serving the Lord, with tympana and organs, with incessant voice, with sweet voice, with sweet and incessant (voice) and various singing, which it is impossible to describe, and (which) astonishes every mind, so wonderful and marvellous is the singing of those angels, and I was delighted listening to it.

CHAPTER 18

1 The men took me on to the fifth heaven and placed me, and there I saw many and countless soldiers, called Grigori, of human appearance, and their size (was) greater than that of great giants and their faces withered, and the silence of their mouth's perpetual, and there was no service on the fifth heaven, and I said to the men who were with me:

2 Wherefore are these very withered and their faces melancholy, and their mouths silent, and (wherefore) is there no service on this heaven?

3 And they said to me: These are the Grigori, who with their prince Satanail (Satan) rejected the Lord of light, and after them are those who are held in great darkness on the second heaven, and three of them went down on to earth from the Lord's throne, to the place Ermon, and broke through their vows on the shoulder of the hill Ermon and saw the daughters of men how good they are, and took to themselves wives, and befouled the earth with their deeds, who in all times of their age made lawlessness and mixing, and giants are born and marvellous big men and great enmity.

4 And therefore God judged them with great judgment, and they weep for their brethren, and they will be punished on the Lord's great day.

5 And I said to the Grigori: I saw your brethren and their works, and their great torments, and I prayed for them, but the Lord has condemned them (to be) under earth till (the existing) heaven and earth shall end for ever.

6 And I said: Wherefore do you wait, brethren, and do not serve before the Lord's face, and have not put your services before the Lord's face, lest you anger your Lord utterly?

7 And they listened to my admonition, and spoke to the four ranks in heaven, and lo! As I stood with those two men four trumpets trumpeted together with great voice, and the Grigori broke into song with one voice, and their voice went up before the Lord pitifully and affectingly.

CHAPTER 19

1 And thence those men took me and bore me up on to the sixth heaven, and there I saw seven bands of angels, very bright and very glorious, and their faces shining more than the sun's shining, glistening, and there is no difference in their faces, or behaviour, or manner of dress; and these make the orders, and learn the goings of the stars, and the alteration of the moon, or revolution of the sun, and the good government of the world.

2 And when they see evildoing, they make commandments and instruction, and sweet and loud singing, and all (songs) of praise.

3 These are the archangels who are above angels, measure all life in heaven and on earth, and the angels who are (appointed) over seasons and years, the angels who are over rivers and sea, and who are over the fruits of the earth, and the angels who are over every grass, giving food to all, to every living thing, and the angels who write all the souls of men, and all their deeds, and their lives before the Lord's face; in their midst are six Phoenixes and six Cherubim and six six-winged ones continually with one voice singing one voice, and it is not possible to describe their singing, and they rejoice before the Lord at his footstool.

CHAPTER 20

1 And those two men lifted me up thence on to the seventh heaven, and I saw there a very great light, and fiery troops of great archangels, incorporeal forces, and dominions, orders and governments, Cherubim and seraphim, thrones and many-eyed ones, nine regiments, the Ioanit stations of light, and I became afraid, and began to tremble with great terror, and those men took me, and led me after them, and said to me:

2 Have courage, Enoch, do not fear, and showed me the Lord from afar, sitting on His very high throne. For what is there on the tenth heaven, since the Lord dwells there?

3 On the tenth heaven is God, in the Hebrew tongue he is called Aravat.

4 And all the heavenly troops would come and stand on the ten steps according to their rank, and would bow down to the Lord, and would again go to their places in joy and felicity, singing songs in the boundless light with small and tender voices, gloriously serving him.

CHAPTER 21

1 And the Cherubim and seraphim standing about the throne, the six-winged and many-eyed ones do not depart, standing before the Lord's face doing his will, and cover his whole throne, singing with gentle voice before the Lord's face: Holy, holy, holy, Lord Ruler of Sabaoth, heavens and earth are full of Your glory.

2 When I saw all these things, those men said to me: Enoch, thus far is it commanded us to journey with you, and those men went away from me and thereupon I saw them not.

3 And I remained alone at the end of the seventh heaven and became afraid, and fell on my face and said to myself: Woe is me, what has befallen me?

4 And the Lord sent one of his glorious ones, the archangel Gabriel, and (he) said to me: Have courage, Enoch, do not fear, arise before the Lord's face into eternity, arise, come with me.

5 And I answered him, and said in myself: My Lord, my soul is departed from me, from terror and trembling, and I called to the men who led me up to this place, on them I relied, and (it is) with them I go before the Lord's face.

6 And Gabriel caught me up, as a leaf caught up by the wind, and placed me before the Lord's face.

7 And I saw the eighth heaven, which is called in the Hebrew tongue Muzaloth, changer of the seasons, of drought, and of wet, and of the twelve constellations of the circle of the firmament, which are above the seventh heaven.

8 And I saw the ninth heaven, which is called in Hebrew Kuchavim, where are the heavenly homes of the twelve constellations of the circle of the firmament.

CHAPTER 22

1 On the tenth heaven, (which is called) Aravoth, I saw the appearance of the Lord's face, like iron made to glow in fire, and brought out, emitting sparks, and it burns.

2 Thus (in a moment of eternity) I saw the Lord's face, but the Lord's face is ineffable, marvellous and very awful, and very, very terrible.

3 And who am I to tell of the Lord's unspeakable being, and of his very wonderful face? And I cannot tell the quantity of his many instructions, and various voices, the Lord's throne (is) very great and not made with hands, nor the quantity of those standing round him, troops of Cherubim and seraphim, nor their incessant singing, nor his immutable beauty, and who shall tell of the ineffable greatness of his glory.

4 And I fell prone and bowed down to the Lord, and the Lord with his lips said to me:

5 Have courage, Enoch, do not fear, arise and stand before my face into eternity.

6 And the archistratege Michael lifted me up, and led me to before the Lord's face.

7 And the Lord said to his servants tempting them: Let Enoch stand before my face into eternity, and the glorious ones bowed down to the Lord, and said: Let Enoch go according to Your word.

8 And the Lord said to Michael: Go and take Enoch from out (of) his earthly garments, and anoint him with my sweet ointment, and put him into the garments of My glory.

9 And Michael did thus, as the Lord told him. He anointed me, and dressed me, and the appearance of that ointment is more than the great light, and his ointment is like sweet dew, and its smell mild, shining like the sun's ray, and I looked at myself, and (I) was like (transfigured) one of his glorious ones.

10 And the Lord summoned one of his archangels by name Pravuil, whose knowledge was quicker in wisdom than the other archangels, who wrote all the deeds of the Lord; and the Lord said to Pravuil: Bring out the books from my store-houses, and a reed of quick-writing, and give (it) to Enoch, and deliver to him the choice and comforting books out of your hand.

CHAPTER 23

1 And he was telling me all the works of heaven, earth and sea, and all the elements, their passages and goings, and the thunderings of the thunders, the sun and moon, the goings and changes of the stars, the seasons, years, days, and hours, the risings of the wind, the numbers of the angels, and the formation of their songs, and all human things, the tongue of every human song and life, the commandments, instructions, and sweet-voiced singings, and all things that it is fitting to learn.

2 And Pravuil told me: All the things that I have told you, we have written. Sit and write all the souls of mankind, however many of them are born, and the places prepared for them to eternity; for all souls are prepared to eternity, before the formation of the world.

3 And all double thirty days and thirty nights, and I wrote out all things exactly, and wrote three hundred and sixty-six books.

CHAPTER 24

1 And the Lord summoned me, and said to me: Enoch, sit down on my left with Gabriel.

2 And I bowed down to the Lord, and the Lord spoke to me: Enoch, beloved, all (that) you see, all things that are standing finished I tell you even before the very beginning, all that I created from non-being, and visible (physical) things from invisible (spiritual).

3 Hear, Enoch, and take in these my words, for not to My angels have I told my secret, and I have not told them their rise, nor my endless realm, nor have they understood my creating, which I tell you to-day.

4 For before all things were visible (physical), I alone used to go about in the invisible (spiritual) things, like the sun from east to west, and from west to east.

5 But even the sun has peace in itself, while I found no peace, because I was creating all things, and I conceived the thought of placing foundations, and of creating visible (physical) creation.

CHAPTER 25

1 I commanded in the very lowest (parts), that visible (physical) things should come down from invisible (spiritual), and Adoil came down very great, and I beheld him, and lo! He had a belly of great light.

2 And I said to him: Become undone, Adoil, and let the visible (physical) (come) out of you.

3 And he came undone, and a great light came out. And I (was) in the midst of the great light, and as there is born light from light, there came forth a great age, and showed all creation, which I had thought to create.

4 And I saw that (it was) good.

5 And I placed for myself a throne, and took my seat on it, and said to the light: Go

thence up higher and fix yourself high above the throne and be A foundation to the highest things.

6 And above the light there is nothing else, and then I bent up and looked up from my throne.

CHAPTER 26

1 And I summoned the very lowest a second time, and said: Let Archas come forth hard, and he came forth hard from the invisible (spiritual).

2 And Archas came forth, hard, heavy, and very red.

3 And I said: Be opened, Archas, and let there be born from you, and he came undone, an age came forth, very great and very dark, bearing the creation of all lower things, and I saw that (it was) good and said to him:

4 Go thence down below, and make yourself firm, and be a foundation for the lower things, and it happened and he went down and fixed himself, and became the foundation for the lower things, and below the darkness there is nothing else.

CHAPTER 27

1 And I commanded that there should be taken from light and darkness, and I said: Be thick, and it became thus, and I spread it out with the light, and it became water, and I spread it out over the darkness, below the light, and then I made firm the waters, that is to say the bottomless, and I made foundation of light around the water, and created seven circles from inside, and imaged (the water) like crystal wet and dry, that is to say like glass, (and) the circumcession of the waters and the other elements, and I showed each one of them its road, and the seven stars each one of them in its heaven, that they go thus, and I saw that it was good.

2 And I separated between light and between darkness, that is to say in the midst of the water hither and thither, and I said to the light, that it should be the day, and to the darkness, that it should be the night, and there was evening and there was morning the first day.

CHAPTER 28

1 And then I made firm the heavenly circle, and (made) that the lower water, which is under heaven collect itself together, into one whole, and that the chaos become dry, and it became so.

2 Out of the waves I created rock hard and big, and from the rock I piled up the dry, and the dry I called earth, and the midst of the earth I called abyss, that is to say the bottomless, I collected the sea in one place and bound it together with a yoke.

3 And I said to the sea: Behold I give you (your) eternal limits, and you shalt not break loose from your component parts.

4 Thus I made fast the firmament. This day I called me the first-created [Sunday].

CHAPTER 29

1 And for all the heavenly troops I imaged the image and essence of fire, and my eye looked at the very hard, firm rock, and from the gleam of my eye the lightning received its wonderful nature, (which) is both fire in water and water in fire, and one does not put out the other, nor does the one dry up the other, therefore the lightning is brighter than the sun, softer than water and firmer than hard rock.

2 And from the rock I cut off a great fire, and from the fire I created the orders of the incorporeal ten troops of angels, and their weapons are fiery and their raiment a burning flame, and I commanded that each one should stand in his order.

3 And one from out the order of angels, having turned away with the order that was under him, conceived an impossible thought, to place his throne higher than the clouds above the earth, that he might become equal in rank to my power.

4 And I threw him out from the height with his angels, and he was flying in the air continuously above the bottomless.

CHAPTER 30

1 On the third day I commanded the earth to make grow great and fruitful trees, and hills, and seed to sow, and I planted Paradise, and enclosed it, and placed as armed (guardians) flaming angels, and thus I created renewal.

2 Then came evening and came morning the fourth day.

3 [Wednesday]. On the fourth day I commanded that there should be great lights on the heavenly circles.

4 On the first uppermost circle I placed the stars, Kruno, and on the second Aphrodit, on the third Aris, on the fifth Zoues, on the sixth Ermis, on the seventh lesser the moon, and adorned it with the lesser stars.

5 And on the lower I placed the sun for the illumination of day, and the moon and stars for the illumination of night.

6 The sun that it should go according to each constellation, twelve, and I appointed the succession of the months and their names and lives, their thundering, and their hour-markings, how they should succeed.

7 Then evening came and morning came the fifth day.

8 [Thursday]. On the fifth day I commanded the sea, that it should bring forth fishes, and feathered birds of many varieties, and all animals creeping over the earth, going forth over the earth on four legs, and soaring in the air, male sex and female, and every soul breathing the spirit of life.

9 And there came evening, and there came morning the sixth day.

10 [Friday]. On the sixth day I commanded my wisdom to create man from seven consistencies: one, his flesh from the earth; two, his blood from the dew; three, his eyes from the sun; four, his bones from stone; five, his intelligence from the swiftness of the angels and from cloud; six, his veins and his hair from the grass of the earth; seven, his soul from my breath and from the wind.

11 And I gave him seven natures: to the flesh hearing, the eyes for sight, to the soul smell, the veins for touch, the blood for taste, the bones for endurance, to the intelligence sweetness [enjoyment].

12 I conceived a cunning saying to say, I created man from invisible (spiritual) and from visible (physical) nature, of both are his death and life and image, he knows speech like some created thing, small in greatness and again great in smallness, and I placed him on earth, a second angel, honourable, great and glorious, and I appointed him as ruler to rule on earth and to have my wisdom, and there was none like him of earth of all my existing creatures.

13 And I appointed him a name, from the four component parts, from east, from west, from south, from north, and I appointed for him four special stars, and I called his name Adam, and showed him the two ways, the light and the darkness, and I told him:

14 This is good, and that bad, that I should learn whether he has love towards me, or hatred, that it be clear which in his race love me.

15 For I have seen his nature, but he has not seen his own nature, therefore (through) not seeing he will sin worse, and I said After sin (what is there) but death?

16 And I put sleep into him and he fell asleep. And I took from him A rib, and created him a wife, that death should come to him by his wife, and I took his last word and called her name mother, that is to say, Eva (Eve).

CHAPTER 31

1 Adam has life on earth, and I created a garden in Eden in the east, that he should observe the testament and keep the command.

2 I made the heavens open to him, that he should see the angels singing the song of victory, and the bloomless light.

3 And he was continuously in paradise, and the devil understood that I wanted to create another world, because Adam was lord on earth, to rule and control it.

4 The devil is the evil spirit of the lower places, as a fugitive he made Sotona from the heavens as his name was Satanail (Satan), thus he became different from the angels, (but his nature) did not change (his) intelligence as far as (his) understanding of righteous and sinful (things).

5 And he understood his condemnation and the sin which he had sinned before, therefore he conceived thought against Adam, in such form he entered and seduced Eva (Eve) but did not touch Adam.

6 But I cursed ignorance, but what I had blessed previously, those I did not curse, I cursed not man, nor the earth, nor other creatures, but man's evil fruit, and his works.

CHAPTER 32

1 I said to him: Earth you are, and into the earth whence I took you shalt go, and I will not ruin you, but send you whence I took you.

2 Then I can again receive you at My second presence.

3 And I blessed all my creatures visible (physical) and invisible (spiritual). And Adam was five and half hours in paradise.

4 And I blessed the seventh day, which is the Sabbath, on which he rested from all his works.

CHAPTER 33

1 And I appointed the eighth day also, that the eighth day should be the first-created after my work, and that (the first seven) revolve in the form of the seventh thousand, and that at the beginning of the eighth thousand there should be a time of not-counting, endless, with neither years nor months nor weeks nor days nor hours.

2 And now, Enoch, all that I have told you, all that you have understood, all that

you have seen of heavenly things, all that you have seen on earth, and all that I have written in books by my great wisdom, all these things I have devised and created from the uppermost foundation to the lower and to the end, and there is no counsellor nor inheritor to my creations.

3 I am self-eternal, not made with hands, and without change.

4 My thought is my counsellor, my wisdom and my word are made, and my eyes observe all things how they stand here and tremble with terror.

5 If I turn away my face, then all things will be destroyed.

6 And apply your mind, Enoch, and know him who is speaking to you, and take thence the books which you yourself have written.

7 And I give you Samuil and Raguil, who led you up, and the books, and go down to earth, and tell your sons all that I have told you, and all that you have seen, from the lower heaven up to my throne, and all the troops.

8 For I created all forces, and there is none that resists me or that does not subject himself to me. For all subject themselves to my monarchy, and labour for my sole rule.

9 Give them the books of the handwriting, and they will read (them) and will know me for the creator of all things and will understand how there is no other God but me.

10 And let them distribute the books of your handwriting–children to children, generation to generation, nations to nations.

11 And I will give you, Enoch, my intercessor, the archistratege Michael, for the handwritings of your fathers Adam, Seth, Enos, Cainan, Mahaleleel, and Jared your father.

CHAPTER 34

1 They have rejected my commandments and my yoke, worthless seed has come up, not fearing God, and they would not bow down to me, but have begun to bow down to vain gods, and denied my unity, and have laden the whole earth with untruths, offences, abominable lecheries, namely one with another, and all manner of other unclean wickedness, which are disgusting to relate.

2 And therefore I will bring down a deluge upon the earth and will destroy all men, and the whole earth will crumble together into great darkness.

CHAPTER 35

1 Behold from their seed shall arise another generation, much afterwards, but of them many will be very insatiate.

2 He who raises that generation, (shall) reveal to them the books of your handwriting, of your fathers, (to them) to whom he must point out the guardianship of the world, to the faithful men and workers of my pleasure, who do not acknowledge my name in vain.

3 And they shall tell another generation, and those (others) having read shall be glorified thereafter, more than the first.

CHAPTER 36

1 Now, Enoch, I give you the term of thirty days to spend in your house, and tell your sons and all your household, that all may hear from my face what is told them by you, that they may read and understand, how there is no other God but me.

2 And that they may always keep my commandments and begin to read and take in the books of your handwriting.

3 And after thirty days I shall send my angel for you, and he will take you from earth and from your sons to me.

CHAPTER 37

1 And the Lord called upon one of the older angels, terrible and menacing, and placed him by me, in appearance white as snow, and his hands like ice, having the appearance of great frost, and he froze my face, because I could not endure the terror of the Lord, just as it is not possible to endure A stove's fire and the sun's heat, and the frost of the air.

2 And the Lord said to me: Enoch, if your face be not frozen here, no man will be able to behold your face.

CHAPTER 38

1 And the Lord said to those men who first led me up: Let Enoch go down on to earth with you, and await him till the determined day.

2 And they placed me by night on my bed.

3 And Mathusal (Methuselah) expecting my coming, keeping watch by day and by night at my bed, was filled with awe when he heard my coming, and I told him, Let all my household come together, that I tell them everything.

CHAPTER 39

1 Oh my children, my beloved ones, hear the admonition of your father, as much as is according to the Lord's will.

2 I have been let come to you to-day, and announce to you, not from my lips, but from the Lord's lips, all that is and was and all that is now, and all that will be till judgment-day.

3 For the Lord has let me come to you, you hear therefore the words of my lips, of a man made big for you, but I am one who has seen the Lord's face, like iron made to glow from fire it sends forth sparks and burns.

4 You look now upon my eyes, (the eyes) of a man big with meaning for you, but I have seen the Lord's eyes, shining like the sun's rays and filling the eyes of man with awe.

5 You see now, my children, the right hand of a man that helps you, but I have seen the Lord's right hand filling heaven as he helped me.

6 You see the compass of my work like your own, but I have seen the Lord's limitless and perfect compass, which has no end.

7 You hear the words of my lips, as I heard the words of the Lord, like great thunder incessantly with hurling of clouds.

8 And now, my children, hear the discourses of the father of the earth, how fearful and awful it is to come before the face of the ruler of the earth, how much more terrible and awful it is to come before the face of the ruler of heaven, the controller (judge) of quick and dead, and of the heavenly troops. Who can endure that endless pain?

CHAPTER 40

1 And now, my children, I know all things, for this (is) from the Lord's lips, and this my eyes have seen, from beginning to end.

2 I know all things, and have written all things into books, the heavens and their end, and their plenitude, and all the armies and their marching.

3 I have measured and described the stars, the great countless multitude (of them).

4 What man has seen their revolutions, and their entrances? For not even the angels see their number, while I have written all their names.

5 And I measured the sun's circle, and measured its rays, counted the hours, I wrote down too all things that go over the earth, I have written the things that are nourished, and all seed sown and unsown, which the earth produces and all plants, and every grass and every flower, and their sweet smells, and their names, and the dwelling-places of the clouds, and their composition, and their wings, and how they bear rain and raindrops.

6 And I investigated all things and wrote the road of the thunder and of the lightning, and they showed me the keys and their guardians, their rise, the way they go; it is let out (gently) in measure by a chain, lest by A heavy chain and violence it hurl down the angry clouds and destroy all things on earth.

7 I wrote the treasure-houses of the snow, and the storehouses of the cold and the frosty airs, and I observed their season's key-holder, he fills the clouds with them, and does not exhaust the treasure-houses.

8 And I wrote the resting-places of the winds and observed and saw how their key-holders bear weighing-scales and measures; first, they put them in (one) weighing-scale, then in the other the weights and let them out according to measure cunningly over the whole earth, lest by heavy breathing they make the earth to rock.

9 And I measured out the whole earth, its mountains, and all hills, fields, trees, stones, rivers, all existing things I wrote down, the height from earth to the seventh heaven, and downwards to the very lowest hell, and the judgment-place, and the very great, open and weeping hell.

10 And I saw how the prisoners are in pain, expecting the limitless judgment.

11 And I wrote down all those being judged by the judge, and all their judgment (and sentences) and all their works.

CHAPTER 41

1 And I saw all forefathers from (all) time with Adam and Eva (Eve), and I sighed and broke into tears and said of the ruin of their dishonour:

2 Woe is me for my infirmity and (for that) of my forefathers, and thought in my heart and said:

3 Blessed (is) the man who has not been born or who has been born and shall not sin before the Lord's face, that he come not into this place, nor bring the yoke of this place.

CHAPTER 42

1 I saw the key-holders and guards of the gates of hell standing, like great serpents, and their faces like extinguishing lamps, and their eyes of fire, their sharp teeth, and I saw all the Lord's works, how they are right, while the works of man are some (good), and others bad, and in their works are known those who lie evilly.

CHAPTER 43

1 I, my children, measured and wrote out every work and every measure and every righteous judgment.

2 As (one) year is more honourable than another, so is (one) man more honourable than another, some for great possessions, some for wisdom of heart, some for particular intellect, some for cunning, one for silence of lip, another for cleanliness, one for strength, another for comeliness, one for youth, another for sharp wit, one for shape of body, another for sensibility, let it be heard everywhere, but there is none better than he who fears God, he shall be more glorious in time to come.

CHAPTER 44

1 The Lord with his hands having created man, in the likeness of his own face, the Lord made him small and great.

2 Whoever reviles the ruler's face, and abhors the Lord's face, has despised the Lord's face, and he who vents anger on any man without injury, the Lord's great anger will cut him down, he who spits on the face of man reproachfully, will be cut down at the Lord's great judgment.

3 Blessed is the man who does not direct his heart with malice against any man, and helps the injured and condemned, and raises the broken down, and shall do charity to the needy, because on the day of the great judgment every weight, every measure and every makeweight (will be) as in the market, that is to say (they are) hung on scales and stand in the market, (and every one) shall learn his own measure, and according to his measure shall take his reward.

CHAPTER 45

1 Whoever hastens to make offerings before the Lord's face, the Lord for his part will hasten that offering by granting of his work.

2 But whoever increases his lamp before the Lord's face and make not true judgment, the Lord will (not) increase his treasure in the realm of the highest.

3 When the Lord demands bread, or candles, or (the)flesh (of beasts), or any other sacrifice, then that is nothing; but God demands pure hearts, and with all that (only) tests the heart of man.

CHAPTER 46

1 Hear, my people, and take in the words of my lips.

2 If any one bring any gifts to an earthly ruler, and have disloyal thoughts in his heart, and the ruler know this, will he not be angry with him, and not refuse his gifts, and not give him over to judgment?

3 Or (if) one man make himself appear good to another by deceit of tongue, but (have) evil in his heart, then will not (the other) understand the treachery of his heart, and himself be condemned, since his untruth was plain to all?

4 And when the Lord shall send a great light, then there will be judgment for the just and the unjust, and there no one shall escape notice.

CHAPTER 47

1 And now, my children, lay thought on your hearts, mark well the words of your father, which are all (come) to you from the Lord's lips.

2 Take these books of your father's handwriting and read them.

3 For the books are many, and in them you will learn all the Lord's works, all that has been from the beginning of creation, and will be till the end of time.

4 And if you will observe my handwriting, you will not sin against the Lord; because there is no other except the Lord, neither in heaven, nor in earth, nor in the very lowest (places), nor in the (one) foundation.

5 The Lord has placed the foundations in the unknown, and has spread forth heavens visible (physical) and invisible (spiritual); he fixed the earth on the waters, and created countless creatures, and who has counted the water and the foundation of the unfixed,

or the dust of the earth, or the sand of the sea, or the drops of the rain, or the morning dew, or the wind's breathings? Who has filled earth and sea, and the indissoluble winter?

6 I cut the stars out of fire, and decorated heaven, and put it in their midst.

CHAPTER 48

1 That the sun go along the seven heavenly circles, which are the appointment of one hundred and eighty-two thrones, that it go down on a short day, and again one hundred and eighty-two, that it go down on a big day, and he has two thrones on which he rests, revolving hither and thither above the thrones of the months, from the seventeenth day of the month Tsivan it goes down to the month Thevan, from the seventeenth of Thevan it goes up.

2 And thus it goes close to the earth, then the earth is glad and makes grow its fruits, and when it goes away, then the earth is sad, and trees and all fruits have no florescence.

3 All this he measured, with good measurement of hours, and fixed Λ measure by his wisdom, of the visible (physical) and the invisible (spiritual).

4 From the invisible (spiritual) he made all things visible (physical), himself being invisible (spiritual).

5 Thus I make known to you, my children, and distribute the books to your children, into all your generations, and amongst the nations who shall have the sense to fear God, let them receive them, and may they come to love them more than any food or earthly sweets, and read them and apply themselves to them.

6 And those who understand not the Lord, who fear not God, who accept not, but reject, who do not receive the (books), a terrible judgment awaits these.

7 Blessed is the man who shall bear their yoke and shall drag them along, for he shall be released on the day of the great judgment.

CHAPTER 49

1 I swear to you, my children, but I swear not by any oath, neither by heaven nor by earth, nor by any other creature which God created.

2 The Lord said: There is no oath in me, nor injustice, but truth.

3 If there is no truth in men, let them swear by the words, Yea, yea, or else, Nay, nay.

4 And I swear to you, yea, yea, that there has been no man in his mother's womb, (but

that) already before, even to each one there is a place prepared for the repose of that soul, and a measure fixed how much it is intended that a man be tried in this world.

5 Yea, children, deceive not yourselves, for there has been previously prepared a place for every soul of man.

CHAPTER 50

1 I have put every man's work in writing and none born on earth can remain hidden nor his works remain concealed.

2 I see all things.

3 Now therefore, my children, in patience and meekness spend the number of your days, that you inherit endless life.

4 Endure for the sake of the Lord every wound, every injury, every evil word and attack.

5 If ill-requitals befall you, return (them) not either to neighbour or enemy, because the Lord will return (them) for you and be your avenger on the day of great judgment, that there be no avenging here among men.

6 Whoever of you spends gold or silver for his brother's sake, he will receive ample treasure in the world to come.

7 Injure not widows nor orphans nor strangers, lest God's wrath come upon you.

CHAPTER 51

1 Stretch out your hands to the poor according to your strength.

2 Hide not your silver in the earth.

3 Help the faithful man in affliction, and affliction will not find you in the time of your trouble.

4 And every grievous and cruel yoke that come upon you bear all for the sake of the Lord, and thus you will find your reward in the day of judgment.

5 It is good to go morning, midday, and evening into the Lord's dwelling, for the glory of your creator.

6 Because every breathing (thing) glorifies him, and every creature visible (physical) and invisible (spiritual) returns him praise.

CHAPTER 52

1 Blessed is the man who opens his lips in praise of God of Sabaoth and praises the Lord with his heart.

2 Cursed every man who opens his lips for the bringing into contempt and calumny of his neighbour, because he brings God into contempt.

3 Blessed is he who opens his lips blessing and praising God.

4 Cursed is he before the Lord all the days of his life, who opens his lips to curse and abuse.

5 Blessed is he who blesses all the Lord's works.

6 Cursed is he who brings the Lord's creation into contempt.

7 Blessed is he who looks down and raises the fallen.

8 Cursed is he who looks to and is eager for the destruction of what is not his.

9 Blessed is he who keeps the foundations of his fathers made firm from the beginning.

10 Cursed is he who perverts the decrees of his forefathers.

11 Blessed is he who imparts peace and love.

12 Cursed is he who disturbs those that love their neighbours.

13 Blessed is he who speaks with humble tongue and heart to all.

14 Cursed is he who speaks peace with his tongue, while in his heart there is no peace but a sword.

15 For all these things will be laid bare in the weighing-scales and in the books, on the day of the great judgment.

CHAPTER 53

1 And now, my children, do not say: Our father is standing before God, and is praying for our sins, for there is there no helper of any man who has sinned.

2 You see how I wrote all works of every man, before his creation, (all) that is done amongst all men for all time, and none can tell or relate my handwriting, because the Lord see all imaginings of man, how they are vain, where they lie in the treasure-houses of the heart.

3 And now, my children, mark well all the words of your father, that I tell you, lest you regret, saying: Why did our father not tell us?

CHAPTER 54

1 At that time, not understanding this let these books which I have given you be for an inheritance of your peace.

2 Hand them to all who want them, and instruct them, that they may see the Lord's very great and marvellous works.

CHAPTER 55

1 My children, behold, the day of my term and time have approached.

2 For the angels who shall go with me are standing before me and urge me to my departure from you; they are standing here on earth, awaiting what has been told them.

3 For to-morrow I shall go up on to heaven, to the uppermost Jerusalem to my eternal inheritance.

4 Therefore I bid you do before the Lord's face all (his) good pleasure.

CHAPTER 56

1 Mathosalam having answered his father Enoch, said: What is agreeable to your eyes, father, that I may make before your face, that you may bless our dwellings, and your sons, and that your people may be made glorious through you, and then (that) you may depart thus, as the Lord said?

2 Enoch answered to his son Mathosalam (and) said: Hear, child, from the time when the Lord anointed me with the ointment of his glory, (there has been no) food in me, and my soul remembers not earthly enjoyment, neither do I want anything earthly.

CHAPTER 57

1 My child Methosalam, summon all your brethren and all your household and the elders of the people, that I may talk to them and depart, as is planned for me.

2 And Methosalam made haste, and summoned his brethren, Regim, Riman, Uchan, Chermion, Gaidad, and all the elders of the people before the face of his father Enoch; and he blessed them, (and) said to them:

CHAPTER 58

1 Listen to me, my children, to-day.

2 In those days when the Lord came down on to earth for Adam's sake, and visited all his creatures, which he created himself, after all these he created Adam, and the Lord called all the beasts of the earth, all the reptiles, and all the birds that soar in the air, and brought them all before the face of our father Adam.

3 And Adam gave the names to all things living on earth.

4 And the Lord appointed him ruler over all, and subjected to him all things under his hands, and made them dumb and made them dull that they be commanded of man, and be in subjection and obedience to him.

5 Thus also the Lord created every man lord over all his possessions.

6 The Lord will not judge a single soul of beast for man's sake, but adjudges the souls of men to their beasts in this world; for men have a special place.

7 And as every soul of man is according to number, similarly beasts will not perish, nor all souls of beasts which the Lord created, till the great judgment, and they will accuse man, if he feed them ill.

CHAPTER 59

1 Whoever defiles the soul of beasts, defiles his own soul.

2 For man brings clean animals to make sacrifice for sin, that he may have cure of his soul.

3 And if they bring for sacrifice clean animals, and birds, man has cure, he cures his soul.

4 All is given you for food, bind it by the four feet, that is to make good the cure, he cures his soul.

5 But whoever kills beast without wounds, kills his own souls and defiles his own flesh.

6 And he who does any beast any injury whatsoever, in secret, it is evil practice, and he defiles his own soul.

CHAPTER 60

1 He who works the killing of a man's soul, kills his own soul, and kills his own body, and there is no cure for him for all time.

2 He who puts a man in any snare, shall stick in it himself, and there is no cure for him for all time.

3 He who puts a man in any vessel, his retribution will not be wanting at the great judgment for all time.

4 He who works crookedly or speaks evil against any soul, will not make justice for himself for all time.

CHAPTER 61

1 And now, my children, keep your hearts from every injustice, which the Lord hates. Just as a man asks something for his own soul from God, so let him do to every living soul, because I know all things, how in the great time to come there is much inheritance prepared for men, good for the good, and bad for the bad, without number many.

2 Blessed are those who enter the good houses, for in the bad houses there is no peace nor return from them.

3 Hear, my children, small and great! When man puts a good thought in his heart, brings gifts from his labours before the Lord's face and his hands made them not, then the Lord will turn away his face from the labour of his hand, and (that) man cannot find the labour of his hands.

4 And if his hands made it, but his heart murmur, and his heart cease not making murmur incessantly, he has not any advantage.

CHAPTER 62

1 Blessed is the man who in his patience brings his gifts with faith before the Lord's face, because he will find forgiveness of sins.

2 But if he take back his words before the time, there is no repentance for him; and if the time pass and he do not of his own will what is promised, there is no repentance after death.

3 Because every work which man does before the time, is all deceit before men, and sin before God.

CHAPTER 63

1 When man clothes the naked and fills the hungry, he will find reward from God.

2 But if his heart murmur, he commits a double evil; ruin of himself and of that which he gives; and for him there will be no finding of reward on account of that.

3 And if his own heart is filled with his food and his own flesh, clothed with his own clothing, he commits contempt, and will forfeit all his endurance of poverty, and will not find reward of his good deeds.

4 Every proud and magniloquent man is hateful to the Lord, and every false speech, clothed in untruth; it will be cut with the blade of the sword of death, and thrown into the fire, and shall burn for all time.

CHAPTER 64

1 When Enoch had spoken these words to his sons, all people far and near heard how the Lord was calling Enoch. They took counsel together:

2 Let us go and kiss Enoch, and two thousand men came together and came to the place Achuzan where Enoch was, and his sons.

3 And the elders of the people, the whole assembly, came and bowed down and began to kiss Enoch and said to him:

4 Our father Enoch, (may) you (be) blessed of the Lord, the eternal ruler, and now bless your sons and all the people, that we may be glorified to-day before your face.

5 For you shalt be glorified before the Lord's face for all time, since the Lord chose you, rather than all men on earth, and designated you writer of all his creation, visible (physical) and invisible (spiritual), and redeemed of the sins of man, and helper of your household.

CHAPTER 65

1 And Enoch answered all his people saying: Hear, my children, before that all creatures were created, the Lord created the visible (physical) and invisible (spiritual) things.

2 And as much time as there was and went past, understand that after all that he created man in the likeness of his own form, and put into him eyes to see, and ears to hear, and heart to reflect, and intellect wherewith to deliberate.

3 And the Lord saw all man's works, and created all his creatures, and divided time,

from time he fixed the years, and from the years he appointed the months, and from the months he appointed the days, and of days he appointed seven.

4 And in those he appointed the hours, measured them out exactly, that man might reflect on time and count years, months, and hours, (their) alternation, beginning, and end, and that he might count his own life, from the beginning until death, and reflect on his sin and write his work bad and good; because no work is hidden before the Lord, that every man might know his works and never transgress all his commandments, and keep my handwriting from generation to generation.

5 When all creation visible (physical) and invisible (spiritual), as the Lord created it, shall end, then every man goes to the great judgment, and then all time shall perish, and the years, and thenceforward there will be neither months nor days nor hours, they will be adhered together and will not be counted.

6 There will be one aeon, and all the righteous who shall escape the Lord's great judgment, shall be collected in the great aeon, for the righteous the great aeon will begin, and they will live eternally, and then too there will be amongst them neither labour, nor sickness, nor humiliation, nor anxiety, nor need, nor brutality, nor night, nor darkness, but great light.

7 And they shall have a great indestructible wall, and a paradise bright and incorruptible (eternal), for all corruptible (mortal) things shall pass away, and there will be eternal life.

CHAPTER 66

1 And now, my children, keep your souls from all injustice, such as the Lord hates.

2 Walk before his face with terror and trembling and serve him alone.

3 Bow down to the true God, not to dumb idols, but bow down to his similitude, and bring all just offerings before the Lord's face. The Lord hates what is unjust.

4 For the Lord sees all things; when man takes thought in his heart, then he counsels the intellects, and every thought is always before the Lord, who made firm the earth and put all creatures on it.

5 If you look to heaven, the Lord is there; if you take thought of the sea's deep and all the under-earth, the Lord is there.

6 For the Lord created all things. Bow not down to things made by man, leaving the Lord of all creation, because no work can remain hidden before the Lord's face.

7 Walk, my children, in long-suffering, in meekness, honesty, in provocation, in grief, in faith and in truth, in (reliance on) promises, in illness, in abuse, in wounds, in temptation, in nakedness, in privation, loving one another, till you go out from this age

of ills, that you become inheritors of endless time.

8 Blessed are the just who shall escape the great judgment, for they shall shine forth more than the sun sevenfold, for in this world the seventh part is taken off from all, light, darkness, food, enjoyment, sorrow, paradise, torture, fire, frost, and other things; he put all down in writing, that you might read and understand.

CHAPTER 67

1 When Enoch had talked to the people, the Lord sent out darkness on to the earth, and there was darkness, and it covered those men standing with Enoch, and they took Enoch up on to the highest heaven, where the Lord (is); and he received him and placed him before his face, and the darkness went off from the earth, and light came again.

2 And the people saw and understood not how Enoch had been taken, and glorified God, and found a roll in which was traced The Invisible (spiritual) God; and all went to their dwelling places.

CHAPTER 68

1 Enoch was born on the sixth day of the month Tsivan, and lived three hundred and sixty-five years.

2 He was taken up to heaven on the first day of the month Tsivan and remained in heaven sixty days.

3 He wrote all these signs of all creation, which the Lord created, and wrote three hundred and sixty-six books, and handed them over to his sons and remained on earth thirty days, and was again taken up to heaven on the sixth day of the month Tsivan, on the very day and hour when he was born.

4 As every man's nature in this life is dark, so are also his conception, birth, and departure from this life.

5 At what hour he was conceived, at that hour he was born, and at that hour too he died.

6 Methosalam and his brethren, all the sons of Enoch, made haste, and erected an altar at that place called Achuzan, whence and where Enoch had been taken up to heaven.

7 And they took sacrificial oxen and summoned all people and sacrificed the sacrifice before the Lord's face.

8 All people, the elders of the people and the whole assembly came to the feast and brought gifts to the sons of Enoch.

9 And they made a great feast, rejoicing and making merry three days, praising God, who had given them such a sign through Enoch, who had found favour with him, and that they should hand it on to their sons from generation to generation, from age to age.

10 Amen.

BOOK OF 3 ENOCH

THE HEBREW BOOK OF ENOCH

CHAPTER I

INTRODUCTION: Rabbi Ishmael ascends to heaven to witness the vision of the Merkaba (chariot). He is given to Metatron

AND ENOCH WALKED WITH GOD: AND HE WAS NOT; FOR GOD TOOK HIM.

(1) I ascended on high to witness the vision of the Merkaba (the divine chariot) and I had entered the six Halls, which were situated within one another.

The halls were in concentric circles, one within the other.

(2) As soon as I reached the door of the Seventh Hall I stood still in prayer before the Holy One, blessed be He. I lifted up my eyes on high towards the Divine Majesty and I said:

(3) "Lord of the Universe, I pray you, that the worthiness of Aaron the son of Amram, who loves and pursues peace, and who received the crown of priesthood from Your Glory on Mount Sinai, be upon me in this hour, so that Khafsiel, (Qafsiel) the prince, and the angels with him may not overcome (overpower) me nor cast me down from the heavens."

[Qafsiel or Qaphsiel is an angel of a high order set to guard the seventh hall of heaven.]

(4) At that moment the Holy One, blessed be He, sent Metatron, his Servant, also called Ebed, to me. He is the angel, the Prince of the Presence. With great joy he spread his wings as he came to meet me in order to save me from their hand.

(5) And by his hand he took me so that they could see us, and he said to me: "Enter in peace before the high and exalted King and see the picture of Merkaba (chariot)."

(6) Then I entered the seventh Hall, and he led me to the camps of Shekina (understanding) and stood me in front of the Holy One, blessed be He, to see the Merkaba (chariot).

(7) As soon as the princes of the Merkaba (chariot) and the flaming Seraphim knew I was there, they fixed their gaze on me. Trembling and shuddering seized me at once and I fell down and was numbed by the brightness of the vision of their faces; until the Holy One, blessed be He, chastised them, saying:

(8)" My servants, my Seraphim, my Cherubim and my Ophannim! Cover your eyes before Ishmael, my son, my friend, my beloved one and (my) glory, so that he ceases trembling and shaking!

(9) Then Metatron, the Prince of the Presence, came and placed my spirit in me again and he stood me up on my feet.

(10) After that (moment) for an hour I did not have enough strength to sing a song before the Throne of Glory of the Glorious King, the mightiest of all kings, the most excellent of all princes.

(11) After an hour had passed the Holy One, blessed be He, opened the gates of Shekina (understanding) to me. These are the gates of Peace, and of Wisdom, and of Strength, and of Power, and of Speech (Dibbur), and of Song, and of Kedushah (Sacred Salutation of Holy, Holy, Holy), and the gates of Chanting.

(12) And he opened and shined His light in my eyes and my heart by words of psalm, song, praise, exaltation, thanksgiving, extolment, glorification, hymn and eulogy (to speak well of).

And as I opened my mouth, singing a song before the Holy One, blessed be He the Holy Chayoth beneath and above the Throne of Glory answered and said (chanted the prayer): "HOLY!" and "BLESSED BE THE GLORY OF YHWH FROM HIS PLACE!"

[The Chayot (or Chayyot) are a class of Merkabah, or Jewish Mystical Angels, reported in Ezekeil's vision of the Merkabah and its surrounding angels as recorded in the first chapter of the Book of Ezekiel describing his vision by the river Chebar.

Kedushnh (Sacred Salutation of Holy, Holy, Holy) is a call to greet and glorify God. KODOISH, KODOISH, KODOISH ADONAI TSEBA YOTH: Holy, Holy, Holy, is the Lord God of Hosts.

This is the Sacred Salutation, the Kedushah (Sacred Salutation of Holy, Holy, Holy), which is used by all the heavenly hosts to worship The Father before His Throne.]

CHAPTER 2

The highest classes of angels make inquiries about Rabbi Ishmael, which are answered by Metatron.

Rabbi Ishmael said:

(1) Within the hour the eagles of The Chariot (Merkaba), the flaming Ophannim and the Seraphim of consuming fire asked Metatron:

(2) "Youth! Why do you permit one born of woman to enter and see the chariot (Merkaba)? From which nation and from which tribe is this one? What is his nature?"

(3) Metatron answered and said to them: "From the nation of Israel whom the Holy One, blessed be He, chose for his people from among seventy tongues (nations of the world). He is from the tribe of Levi, whom He set aside as a contribution to his name.

He is from the seed of Aaron whom the Holy One, blessed be He, chose for his servant and He put upon him the crown of priesthood on Sinai."

(4) Then they spoke and said: "Happy is the people (nation) that is in that position!" (Ps. 144:15).

CHAPTER 3

Metatron has 70 names, but God calls him 'Youth'.

Rabbi Ishmael said:

(1) In that hour I asked Metatron, the angel, the Prince of the Presence: "What is your name?"

(2) He answered me: "I have seventy names, corresponding to the seventy nations of the world and all of them are based upon the name Metatron, angel of the Presence; but my King calls me 'Youth' (Naar)."

CHAPTER 4

Metatron is Enoch who was translated to heaven at the time of the flood.

Rabbi Ishmael said:

(1) I asked Metatron and said to him: "why does your Creator call you by seventy names? You are greater than all the princes, higher than all the angels, beloved more than all the servants, honoured above all the mighty ones in kingship, greatness and glory, so why do they in the high heavens call you 'Youth'?

(2) He answered and said to me: " Because I am Enoch, the son of Jared.

(3) When the generation of the flood sinned and were twisted and contorted in their deeds, saying unto God: "Depart from us! We do not want the knowledge of your ways," (See Job 21:14), then the Holy One, blessed be He, removed me from their midst so that I could be a witness against them in the high heavens to all the inhabitants of the world, so that they cannot say: 'The Merciful One is cruel'.

(4) "What sin did all those throngs of their wives, their sons and their daughters, their horses, their mules and their cattle and their property, and all the birds of the world commit so that the Holy One, blessed be He, destroyed the world, together with them in the waters of the flood?" They cannot say: "What in the generation of the flood sinned and what sin did they do so that the beasts and the birds should perish with them?"

(5) Then the Holy One, blessed be He, lifted me up in their lifetime in their sight to be a witness against them to the future world. And the Holy One, blessed be He, assigned me to be a prince and a ruler among the ministering angels.

(6) In that hour three of the ministering angels, UZZA, 'AZZA and AZZAEL came out and accused me in the high heavens in front of the Holy One, blessed be He: And they said, "The Progenitors, The Ancient Ones, said before You with justification: Do not create man! The Holy One, blessed be He, answered and said unto them: "I have made and I will bear, and yes, I will carry and will deliver."

(7) As soon as they saw me, they said before Him: "Lord of the Universe! What is this one that he should ascend to the highest heights? Is he not one from among the sons of those who perished in the days of the Flood? What is he doing in the Raqia? (firmament / heavens)." (What business does he have been in heaven?)

[Some sources have the names of the angels include Mal'aki or Mamlaketi. Azzael is one of the ten heads of the heavenly Sanhedrin.

Rabbinical sources have Azza and Azzael as giants. All three are said to be agents of evil who accuse man of sins. These are the fallen angels. Another theory is that Azza and Azzael are not individual angels but are orders of angels.

Raquia is a key Hebrew word in Genesis 16-8a. It is translated "firmament" in the King James Version and "expanse" in most Hebrew dictionaries and modern translations. Raqa means to spread out, beat out, or hammer as one would a malleable metal. It can also mean "plate. " The Greek Septuagint translated raqia 16 out of 17 times with the Greek word stereoma, which means a firm or solid II structure. " The Latin Vulgate (A.D.) used the Latin term "firmamentum, " which also denotes solidness and firmness. The King James translators coined the word 'firmament" because there was no single word equivalent in English. Today, 'firmament" is usually used poetically to mean sky, atmosphere, or heavens. In modern Hebrew, raqia means sky or heavens. However, originally it probably meant something solid or firm that was spread out.

Azzael is likely the same being as Azazel, the accuser angel who was the leader of the fallen ones. Etymologlj connects the word with the mythological " Uza " and "Azael", the fallen angels, to whom a reference is believed to be found in Gen. 6:2,4. In accordance with this etymologlj, the sacrifice of the goat atones for the sin of fornication of which those angels were guilty. (See 1 Enoch.) Leviticus 16:8-10 "and Aaron shall cast lots upon the two goats, one lot for the Lord and the other lot for Azazel. And Aaron shall present the goat on which the lot fell for the Lord and offer it as a sin offering; but the goat on which the lot fell for Azazel shall be presented alive before the Lord to make atonement over it, that it may be sent away into the wilderness to Azazel."]

(8) Again, the Holy One, blessed be He, answered and said to them: "What are you, that you enter and speak in my presence? I delight more in this one than in all of you put together, and therefore he will be a prince and a ruler over you in the high heavens."

(9) Then they all stood up and went out to meet me, and bowed themselves down before me and said: "Happy are you and happy is your father for your Creator favors

you."

(10) And because I am small and a youth among them in days, months and years, therefore they call me "Youth."

CHAPTER 5

The idolatry of the generation of Enosh causes God to remove the Shekina from earth. Idolatry was inspired by Azza, Uzza and Azzael

Rabbi Ishmael said: Metatron, the Prince of the Presence, said to me:

(1) From the day when the Holy One, blessed be He, evicted the first Adam from the Garden of Eden, and continuing from that day, the Shekina (glory) was dwelling upon a Cherub under the Tree of Life.

(2) And the ministering angels were gathering and going down from heaven in groups.

From the Raqia (heaven) they went in companies from the heavens in camps to perform His will in the entire world.

(3) And the first man and his children were sitting outside the gate of the Garden to see the glowing, bright appearance of the Shekina (glory).

(4) For the splendor of the Shekina (glory) enfolds the world from end to end with its splendor, times that of the orb of the sun. And everyone who made use of the splendor of the Shekina, on him no flies and no gnats lit, and he was not ill and he suffered no pain. No demons could overpower him, neither were they able to injure him.

(5) When the Holy One, blessed be He, went out and went in from the Garden to Eden, from Eden to the Garden, from the Garden to Raqia (heaven) and from Raqia (heaven) to the Garden of Eden then everything and everyone saw His magnificent Shekina and they were not injured;

(6) until the time of the generation of Enosh who was the head of all idol worshippers of the world.

[The Shekina was an energy or substance that was protecting those who used it from illness, demons, and even bugs.]

(7) And what did the generation of Enosh do? They went from one end of the world to the other, and each person brought silver, gold, precious stones and pearls in heaps the size of mountains and hills to make idols out of them throughout the entire world. And they erected the idols in every corner of the world: the size of each idol was 1000 parasangs.

[The generations of Enoch are as follows: Adam, Seth, Enosh, Kenan, Mahalalel, Jared, Enoch.

The highest (worst) sins, according to Rabbis, are idolatry, adultery, bloodshed, and sorcery) and calling God's name in vain.

A parasang is a length or measurement of distance used in 'what is now Iran. It varied according to the region. The north-eastern parasang was about 15,000 paces, the north-western parasang was 18,000 paces, and the one of the south-west was merely 6,000 paces.

The measurement called the "true parasang" was about 9,000 paces.]

(8) And they brought down the sun, the moon, planets and constellations, and placed them in front of the idols on the right side and on the left side of the idols, to attend to them just like they attend the Holy One, blessed be He, for it is written (I Kings 22:19): " And all the hosts of heaven were standing by him on his right hand and on his left."

(9) What power was in them to enable to bring them down? They would not have been able to bring them down, if it had not been for the fact that UZZA, and AZZIEL (other sources have Azzael) taught them sorceries by which they brought them down and enslaved them.

[It is obvious that the actual sun and stars were not brought down, but the angelic powers controlling them were summoned. Also, keep in mind that some cultures thought stars to be evil angels 'who flew across the sky. These agents were summoned and used.]

(10) In that time the ministering angels accused them before the Holy One, blessed be He, saying: "Master of the World! Why do you bother with the children of men? As it is written (Ps. 8:4) 'What is man (Adam) that you are mindful of him?' But it was not about Adam that this was written but about Enosh, for he is the head of the idol worshippers.

(11) Why have you left the highest of the high heavens which are filled with the majesty of your glory and are high, lifted up, and exalted on the high and exalted throne in the Raqia (heaven) of Araboth (highest heaven) and are gone and dwell with the children of men who worship idols and equate you to (place you on the same level as) the idols.

[The word "Araboth (highest heaven) " occurs in Psalm 68:4 'Extol him who rides upon the Araboth (highest heaven) I in which it is usually translated simply as the highest heaven. In the case of Enoch, this would be the throne of God. In the Zoharic commentary on Exodus it is referred to thus: 'Be glad in the presence of him who rides upon that concealed heaven which is supported by the Chayoth.

The Zohar also interprets the word to mean 'mixture' because, it says, this heaven is a mixture of fire and 'water. This is a mystical statement of a place containing opposites, and thus everything.]

(12) Now you are on earth just like the idols, What have you to do with the inhabitants of the earth who worship idols?

(13) Then the Holy One, blessed be He, lifted up His Shekina from the earth, from their midst

(14) In that moment the ministering angels came. They are troops of the host and the armies of Araboth (highest heaven) in thousand camps and ten thousand host. They brought trumpets and took the horns in their hands and surrounded the Shekina with all kinds of songs. And He ascended to the high heavens, for it is written (Ps. 47:5) "God is gone up with a shout, the Lord with the sound of a trumpet."

[Here the presence and dwelling of God is the Shekina. When the Shekina was taken, God himself left them and took his glory because of idolatry.]

CHAPTER 6

Enoch is lifted to heaven together with the Shekina.

Rabbi Ishmael said: Metatron, the Angel, the Prince of the Presence, said to me:

(1) When the Holy One, blessed be He, wanted to lift me up on high, He first sent Anaphiel YHWH, the Prince, and he took me from their company out of their sight and carried me away in great glory on a chariot of fire pulled by horses of fire, and servants of glory. And he lifted me up to the high heavens together with the Shekina.

(2) As soon as I reached the high heavens, the Holy Chayoth, the Ophannim, the Seraphim, the Cherubim, the Wheels of the Merkaba (chariot) (the Galgallim), and the ministers of the consuming fire, all smelled my scent from a distance of 365,000 myriads of parasangs, and said: "What smells like one born woman and what tastes like a white drop? Who is this that ascends on high. He is merely a gnat among those who can divide flames of fire?"

Chayot are considered angels of fire, who hold up the throne of God and the earth itself.

The angel smells the scent of human, which he finds revolting. He can taste it is the air. The white drop refers to semen. This is an extremely hateful and distasteful statement for the angel to make.

The Holy One, blessed be He, answered and spoke to them:

"My servants, my host, my Cherubim, my Ophannim, my Seraphim! Do not be displeased on account of this! Since all the children of men have denied me and my great Kingdom and have all gone worshipping idols, I have removed my Shekina from among them and have lifted it up on high. But this one whom I have taken from among them is an Elect One among (the inhabitants of) the world and he is equal to all of them (put together) in his faith, righteousness and perfection of deed and I have taken him as a tribute from my world under all the heavens.

[The statement of "taking a tribute" can be better understood if one looks at Enoch as the best mankind has to offer and God took him as a an act of admiration indicating the intended worth of mankind, had they not turned away from him. The term "Elect

One" is very important. It occurs in 1 Enoch and in certain scripture regarding Christ.]

CHAPTER 7

Enoch is raised upon the wings of Shekina to the place of the Throne.

Rabbi Ishmael said: Metatron, the Angel, the Prince of the Presence, said to me:

(1) When the Holy One, blessed be He, took me away from the generation of the Flood, he lifted me on the wings of the wind of Shekina (his glory/ understanding) to the highest heaven and brought me to the great palaces of the Araboth (highest heaven) in Raqia (heaven), where the glorious Throne of Shekina, the Merkaba (chariot), the troops of anger, the armies of vehemence, the fiery Shin'anim (accusers), and the flaming Cherubim, the burning Ophanim, the flaming servants, the flashing Chashmallin, the lightning Seraphim live.

And he placed me (there) to attend daily to the Throne of Glory.

[In some Jewish mystical writings, the attributes of Elijah and those of Enoch are interchangeable. Here Enoch takes the same trip to heaven on a fiery chariot.

Here we have various classes of angels, on which we have little information. The Chashmallin are one of the ten classes, which are sometimes silent for a time in heaven. They cease speaking or singing when "The Word" emanates from the throne.

Shinanim are a class of angel seen in lists of angelic orders. Their name seems to come from a word for accuser" and thus could be the satans in heaven.]

CHAPTER 8

The gates of heaven opened to Metatron.

Rabbi Ishmael said: Metatron, the Prince of the presence, said to me:

(1) Before he appointed me to attend the Throne of Glory, the Holy One, blessed be He, opened to me three hundred thousand gates of Understanding three hundred thousand gates of Wisdom

three hundred thousand gates of Life

three hundred thousand gates of Grace and Loving-kindness three hundred thousand gates of Love

three hundred thousand gates of The Torah

three hundred thousand gates of Meekness

three hundred thousand gates of Steadfastness

three hundred thousand gates of Mercy

three hundred thousand gates of Respect for heaven

[other readings add three hundred thousand gates of Shekina, three hundred thousand gates of fear of sin, three hundred thousand gates of power. The gate of steadfastness is also rendered as maintenance and refers to the sustenance to maintain life. All of man's needs come from heaven. Subtlety is rendered as wisdom but includes diplomacy, and craftiness.]

(2) Within the hour the Holy One, blessed be He, gave me additional wisdom and to wisdom He added understanding unto understanding, cunning unto cunning, knowledge unto knowledge, mercy unto mercy, instruction unto instruction, love unto love, loving-kindness unto loving-kindness, goodness unto goodness, meekness unto meekness, power unto power, strength unto strength, might unto might, brightness unto brightness, beauty unto beauty, splendor unto splendor, and I was honoured and adorned with all these good praiseworthy things more than all the children of heaven.

[Enoch has become more blessed or equipped than "all the children of heaven. Loving-kindness equates to "Grace" of the New Testament.]

CHAPTER 9

Enoch receives blessings from the Highest and is adorned with angelic attributes.

Rabbi Ishmael said: Metatron, the Prince of the Presence, said to me:

(1) After all these things the Holy One, blessed be He, put His hand on me and blessed me with 5360 blessings.

(2) And I was raised up and grew to the size of the length and width of the world.

(3) And he caused 72 wings to grow on me, 36 on each side. And each wing covered the entire world.

(4) And He attached to me eyes: each eye was as the great luminary (moon?).

(5) And He left no kind of splendor, brilliance, radiance, beauty of all the lights of the universe that He did not affix to me.

CHAPTER 10

God places Metatron on a throne as ruler in the seventh Hall.

Rabbi Ishmael said: Metatron, the Prince of the Presence, said to me:

(1) All these things the Holy One, blessed be He, made for me. He made me a Throne, similar in form and substance to the Throne of Glory. And He spread a curtain of magnificently bright appearance over me. And it was of beauty, grace, and mercy, similar to the curtain of the Throne of the Glory; and on it were affixed all kinds of lights in the universe.

[The idea of a curtain could represent the divine secrets and processes unknown and not available to others.]

(2) And He placed the curtain at the door of the Seventh Hall and sat me down on it.

(3) And the announcement went forth into every heaven, saying: "This is Metatron, my servant. I have made him a prince and ruler over all the princes of my kingdoms and over all the children of heaven, except the eight great, honoured, and revered princes who are the ones called YHWH, by the name of their King."

[The eight beings who are called YHWH may refer to those angels who have the Tetragram Maton as part of their name. These are highly ranked angels that are outside the normal system of authority. They are the ones God uses as his counsel.]

(4) "And every angel and prince who has a word to speak to me shall now go before him and they shall speak to him instead of Me.

(5) And every command that he speaks to you in my name, you will obey, carry out, and fulfil. (Some sources add "Beware of him and do not provoke him.") For the Prince of Wisdom and the Prince of Understanding have I committed to him to instruct him in the wisdom of heavenly things and earthly things, in the wisdom of this world and of the world to come. (6) Moreover, I have set him over all the storehouses of the palaces of Araboth (highest heaven) and over all the storehouses (reserves) of life that I have in the high heavens."

CHAPTER 11

God reveals all of the great mysteries to Metatron

Rabbi Ishmael said: Metatron, the angel, the Prince of the Presence, said to me:

(1) The Holy One, blessed be He, began revealing to me all the mysteries of Torah and all the secrets of wisdom and the deep mysteries of the Perfect Law. He revealed the thoughts of all living beings and their feelings and all the secrets of the universe and all the secrets of creation. All these were revealed to me just as they are known to the

Maker of Creation.

(2) And I watched intently to see and understand the secrets and depths of the wonderful mystery. Before a man thought a thought in secret, I saw it and before a man made a thing I watched it.

(3) And there was nothing on high or in the depth of the world that was hidden from me.

[Here Metatron is given the omniscient power of God.]

CHAPTER 12

God puts a crown on him and calls him "the Lesser YHWH".

Rabbi Ishmael said: Metatron, the Prince of the Presence, said to me:

(1) Because of the love that the Holy One, blessed be He, loved me with, was more than all the children of heaven, He made me a garment of glory on which were affixed lights of all varieties, and He clothed me in it.

(2) And He made me a robe of honour on which were affixed beauty, magnificent brilliance and majesty of all sorts.

(3) And he made me a crown of royalty on which were affixed forty-nine stones of worth, which were like the light of the orb of the sun.

[Forty-nine is a mystical number of seven sevens. The number seven represents spiritual perfection.]

(4) Its splendor went out into the four corners of the Araboth (highest heaven) of Raqia (heaven), and through the seven heavens, and throughout the four comers of the world. He placed it on my head.

(5) And He called me THE LESSER YHWH in the presence of all His heavenly household; for it is written (Ex. 22: 21): "For my name is in him."

[Without delving too deeply into Jewish mysticism, it should be pointed out that the numerical value (gematria) of the name Metatron and that of Shahhdai are the same.]

CHAPTER 13

God writes with a flaming pen on Metatron's crown the letters by which heaven and earth were created.

Rabbi Ishmael said: Metatron, the angel, the Glory of all heavens and the Prince of the Presence, said to me:

(1) Holy One, blessed be He, loved and cherished me with great love and mercy, more than all the children of heaven. Thus, He wrote with his finger with a flaming pen on the crown upon my head the letter by which heaven and earth, the seas and rivers, the mountains and hills, the planets and constellations, the lightning, winds, earthquakes and thunders, the snow and hail, the wind of the storm and the tempest were created. These are the letters by which all the needs of the world and all the orders of Creation were created.

(2) And every single letter flashed out time after time like lightning, and time after time like lanterns, time after time like flames of fire, time after time rays like those of the rising of the sun and the moon and the planets.

[There are 22 letters in the Hebrew alphabet. It is thought that all things were created when God spoke the words in the Hebrew tongue.

These words are symbolized by the combinations of the 22 letters.]

CHAPTER 14

All the highest of the princes and lowest angels fear and tremble at the sight of Metatron crowned.

Rabbi Ishmael said: Metatron, the Angel, the Prince of the Presence, said to me:

(1) When the Holy One, blessed be He, put this crown on my head, all the Princes of Nations who are in the height of Araboth (highest heaven) of Raqia (heaven) and all the host of every heaven and even the prince of the Elim, the princes of the 'Er'ellim and the princes of the Tafsarim, who are greater than all the ministering angels who minister before the Throne of Glory trembled before me. They shook, feared and trembled before me when they looked at me.

[This is a very interesting list of angels and princes. According to Jewish mystical sources, such as the Zohar, there are ten classes of angels under Mikael (Michael). The Er'ellim denotes a general class of angels, while the Elim minster before God in the high heavens. The Tafsarim are the princes of the Elim.]

(2) Even Sammael, the Prince of the Accusers, who is greater than all the princes of Nations on high, feared me and shook before me.

[Sammael is the head of the satans or accusers. He is also the ruling angel over Rome, the archenemy of Israel.]

(3) And even the angel of fire, and the angel of hail, and the angel of wind, and the angel of the lightning, and the angel of wrath, and the angel of the thunder, and the angel of the snow, and the angel of the rain; and the angel of the day, and the angel of the night, and the angel of the sun, and the angel of the moon, and the angel of the planets, and the angel of the constellations whose hands rule the world, all of them feared and shook and were frightened when they looked at me.

(4) These are the names of the rulers of the world: Gabriel, the angel of fire, Baradiel, the angel who controls hail, Ruchi-el who controls the wind, Baraqi-el who controls the lighting, Zahafi-el who controls the winds of the storm, Rahami-el who controls the thunders, Rahashi-el who controls the earthquake, Shalgiel who controls the snow, Matari-el who controls the rain, Shimshi-el who controls the planets, Rahati-el who controls the constellations.

(5) And they all fell to the ground and bowed when they saw me. And they were not able to look at me because of the majestic glory of the crown on my head.

CHAPTER 15

Metatron is transformed into fire

Rabbi Ishmael said: Metatron, the angel, the Prince of the Presence, and the Glory of all heavens, said to me:

(1) As soon as the Holy One, blessed be He, took me into (His) service to attend the Throne of Glory and the Wheels (Galgallim) of the Merkaba (chariot) and the service of Shekina, suddenly my flesh was changed into flames, my muscles into flaming fire, my bones into coals of juniper wood, the light of my eye-lids into hot flames, and all of my limbs into wings of burning fire and my entire body into glowing fire.

[Galgallim (sometimes spelled Galgalim) are a high-ranking order of angels, the equivalent of Seraphim. They are metaphorically called " the wheels of the Merkabah" (the ' divine chariot' used to connect people to the divine) and are considered the equivalent of the Orphanim (Cherubim). Galgalim is Hebrew for " wheels."]

(2) And on my right flames were burning and dividing, on my left staves of wood (burning staves) were burning, around me the winds of storms and tempests were blowing and in front of me and behind me was roaring thunder accompanied by earthquakes.

CHAPTER 15 B

[This chapter does not occur in all manuscripts. It seems to be a later addition.]

Rabbi Ishmael said to me: Metatron, the Prince of the Presence and the prince ruling over all the princes, stands before Him who is greater than all the Elohim. And he enters in under the Throne of Glory. And he has a great dwelling of light on high.

And he brings into existence the fire of deafness and places it in the ears of the Holy Chayoth, so that they cannot hear the voice of the Word that sounds from the mouth of the Divine Majesty.

[This may indicate that he goes into the holy of holies where he worships and has his own sanctuany.

The idea of more than one Elohim is not new. It is addressed in Psalm 82:

1, The Psalm of Asaph. God stands in the council of the gods; he judges among the gods. 2. How long will you judge unjustly, and show preference to the wicked? Selah. 3. Judge the poor and the orphans; do righteousness to the afflicted and dispossessed. 4. Deliver the poor and oppressed; save them from the hand of the evil. 5. They do not know, and they have no understanding; they walk about in darkness. All the foundations of the earth are shaken. 6. I said, "You are gods, and children of Elyon, even) one of you." 7. But you will die like mortals and fall like one of the princes. 8. Rise up, 0 God, and judge the earth, for you have inherited all the nations.

This section seems to preserve a fragment of a book called, "The Ascension of Moses. " The chashmal is the highest point of heaven. It is like a zenith line out of which a window opens.]]]

(2) And when Moses ascended on high, he fasted fasts, until the places where the chashmal live were opened to him; and he saw that the place was as white as a Lion's heart and he saw the companies of the host round about him, which could not be counted. And they wished to burn him. But Moses prayed for mercy, first for Israel and then for himself: and He who was sitting on the Merkaba (chariot) opened the windows above the heads of the Cherubim. And a host of 0 helpers along with the Prince of the Presence, Metatron, all went out to meet Moses. They took the prayers of Israel and placed them like a crown on the head of the Holy One, blessed be He.

(3) The they said (Deut. 6:4): "Hear, O Israel; the Lord our God is one Lord." And their face were shining and they rejoiced over Shekina and they said to Metatron: "What are these? And to whom do they give all honor and glory?" And they answered: "To the Glorious Lord of Israe1." And they spoke: Hear, O Israel: the Lord, our God is one Lord. To Whom else shall be given this abundance of honor and majesty but to You YHWH, the Divine Majesty, the King, the living and eternal one."

(4) In that moment Akatriel Ya Yehod Sebaoth (a name of the most high) spoke and said to Metatron, the Prince of the Presence and said, "Let no prayer that he prays before me return to him empty (not done). Hear his prayer and fulfil his desire whether it is great or small

(5) Then Metatron, the Prince of the presence, said to Moses, "Son of Amram! Do not be afraid. God delights in you. He asks you what you desire from the Glory and Majesty. Your face shines from one end of the world to the other." But Moses answered him: "I fear that I should bring guiltiness upon myself." Metatron said to him, "Receive the letters of the oath, which makes a covenant that cannot be broken."

[Metatron is moving through time to and from the time of Moses.

The letters make up the divine names, which are eternal.]

CHAPTER 16

[This continues the additional material.]

His privilege of presiding on a Throne are taken.

Rabbi Ishmael said: Metatron, the Angel, the Prince of the Presence, the Glory of all heaven, said to me:

(1) At first I was sitting on a large Throne at the door of the Seventh Hall. There, by authority of the Holy One, blessed be He, I was judging the children of heaven and the servants on high. And I judged Greatness, Kingship, Dignity, Rulership, Honor and Praise, and the Diadem and Crown of Glory for all the princes of kingdoms. While I was presiding in the Court of the Sky (Yeshiba), the princes of nations were standing before me, on my right and on my left, by authority of the Holy One, blessed be He.

(2) But when Acher came to see the vision of the Merkaba (chariot) and locked his eyes on me, he was afraid and shook before me so much that his soul was departing from him, because of fear, horror and dread of me, when he saw me sitting upon a throne like a king with all the ministering angels standing by my side serving me and all the princes of kingdoms adorned with crowns all around me. (3) At that moment he opened his mouth and said, "Surely there are two Divine Powers in heaven" (4) Then the Divine Voice went out from heaven from the Shekina and said: "Return, you backslide children (Jer.3:22), except for Acher!"

(5) Then Anieyel came (Other sources have " Anaphiel YHWH), the prince, the honoured, glorified, beloved, wonderful, revered and fearful one, as ordered by the Holy One, blessed be He and beat me sixty times with whips of fire and made me stand to my feet.

[Anieyel, or Anaphiel YHWH is higher in status than Metatron. It is possible the Anieyel is the angel who punishes. The purpose of this chapter is to refute the heresy of the Rabbi called Acher, 'who believed that there were now two deities in heaven, God and Metatron. To show Metatron is not a deity God sends in a higher angel to take him off his throne and beat him, proving Metatron is not God, nor is he a god. The chapter goes on to call all of Israel to return to God, except for Acher, who has committed an unforgivable sin against the monotheists and against God.]

CHAPTER 17

The princes of the seven heavens, and of the sun, moon, planets and constellations.

Rabbi Ishmael said: Metatron, the angel, the Prince of the Presence, the glory of all heavens, said to me:

(1) The number of princes are seven. They are the great, beautiful, wonderful, honored, and revered ones. They are assigned over the seven heavens, and these are they: MIKAEL (Michael), GABRIEL, SHATQIEL, BAKARIEL, BADARIEL, PACHRIEL. (Some sources omit Parchriel and add Sidriel.)

(2) And every one of them is the prince of the host of one heaven. And each one of them is accompanied by, groups of ten-thousand ministering angels is the numerical value of the word Malkut (kingdom). These, angels are the ones who sing of the glory of God, singing. "Holy, Holy. Holy. "

(3) MIKAEL is the great prince assigned to ruler over the seventh heaven, the highest one, which is in the Araboth (highest heaven). Gabriel is the prince of the host assigned to rule over the sixth heaven which is in Makon. SHATAQIEL is the prince of the host assigned to rule over the fifth heaven which is in Makon. SHAHAQIEL is the prince of the host assigned to rule over the fourth heaven which is in Zebul.

BAD ARIEL is the prince of the host assigned to rule over the third heaven which is in Shehaqim. BARAKIEL is the prince of the host assigned to rule over the second heaven which is in the height of Raqia (heaven). PAZRIEL is the prince of the host assigned to rule over the first heaven which is in Wilon (or Velum, as the first heaven is called), which is in Shamayim.

(4) Under them in GALGALLIEL, the prince who is assigned as ruler over the orb (gal gal) of the sun, and with him are 96 great and revered angels who moves the sun in Raqia (heaven) a distance of, parasangs each day.

(5) Under them is OPHANNIEL, the prince who is set the globe (Orphan) of the moon. And with him are 88 (some have it as 68) angels who move the globe of the moon thousand parasangs every night at the time when the moon stands in the East at its turning point. And the moon is situated in the East at its turning point in the fifteenth day of every month.

(6) Under them is RAHATIEL, the prince who is appointed to rule over the constellations. He is accompanied by 72 great and revered angels. And why is he called RAHATIEL? Because he makes the stars run (marhit) in their orbits and courses, which is thousand parasangs every night from the East to West, and from West to East. The Holy One, blessed be He, has made a tent for all of them, for the sun, the moon, the planets and the stars, and they travel in it at night from the West to the East.

(7) Under them is KOKBIEL, the prince who is assigned to rule over all the planets. And with him are, groups of ten thousand ministering angels, great and revered ones who move the planets from city to city and from province to province in Raqia (the heaven) of heavens.

(8) And ruling over them are seventy-two princes of nations (kingdoms) on high corresponding to the 72 nations of the world. And all of them are crowned with crowns of royalty and clothed in royal clothes and wrapped in royal robes. And all of them are riding on royal horses and holding royal scepters in their hands. In front of each of them when he is traveling in Raqia (heaven), royal servants are running with great glory and majesty just as on earth the princes are traveling in chariots with horsemen and great armies and in glory and greatness with praise, song and honour.

CHAPTER 18

The order of ranks of the angels is established by the homage.

Rabbi Ishmael said: Metatron, the Angel, the Prince of the Presence, the glory of all heaven, said to me:

(1) THE ANGELS OF THE FIRST HEAVEN, when (ever) they see their prince, they dismount from their horses and bow themselves. And THE PRINCE OF THE FIRST HEA VEN, when he sees the prince of the second heaven, he dismounts, removes the glorious crown from his head and bows himself to the ground.

AND THE PRINCE OF THE SECOND HEAVEN, when he sees the prince of the third heaven, he removes the glorious crown form his head and bows himself to the ground. AND THE

PRINCE OF THE THIRD HEAVEN, when he sees the prince of the fourth heaven, he removes the glorious crown form his head and bows himself to the ground. AND THE PRINCE OF

THE FOURTH HEAVEN, when he sees the prince of the fifth heaven, he removes the glorious crown form his head and bows himself to the ground. AND THE PRINCE OF THE FIFTH HEAVEN, when he sees the prince of the sixth heaven, he removes the glorious crown from his head and bows himself to the ground. AND THE PRINCE OF THE SIXTH HEAVEN, when he sees the prince of the seventh heaven, he removes the glorious crown from his head and bows himself to the ground.

(2) AND THE PRINCE OF THE SEVENTH HEAVEN, when he sees THE SEVENTY-TWO PRINCES OF KINGDOMS, he removes the glorious crown from his head and bows himself to the ground.

[The number 70 appears as does the number 72. It is possible the difference can be explained by the 70 angels along with two leaders, such as Mikael (Michael) and Sammael. In the following section the names of the angels do not follow their junction, as in the prior portion of the book. The names are obscure, and it is difficult to understand their meanings. The expression "bows himself to the ground" and "bow themselves" likely indicates a complete kneeling position with the head touching the earth.]

(3) And the seventy-two princes of kingdoms, when they see The door keepers of

the first hall in the ARABOTH RAQIA in the highest heaven, they remove the royal crown from their head and bow themselves. And The door keepers of the first hall, when they see the doorkeepers of the second Hall, they remove the glorious crown form their head and bow themselves. The door keepers of the second hall, when they see the door keepers of the third hall, they remove the glorious crown from their head and bow themselves. The door keepers of the third hall, when they see the door keepers of the fourth Hall, they remove the crown from their head and bow themselves. The door keepers of the fourth hall, when they see the door keepers of the fifth Hall, they remove the glorious crown from their head and bow themselves. The door keepers of the fifth hall, when they see the doorkeepers of the sixth Hall, they remove the crown from their head and fall to their face. The door keepers of the sixth hall, when they see the door keepers of the seventh hall, they remove the glorious crown from their head and bow themselves.

(4) And the door keepers of the seventh Hall, when they see The Four Great Princes, the honoured ones, who are appointed over the four Camps Of SHEKINA, they remove the crowns of glory from their head and bow themselves. (5) And the four great prince, when they see TAGHAS, the prince, great and honoured with song (and) praise, at the head of all the children of heaven, they remove the glorious crown from their head and bow themselves.

(6) And Taghas, the great and honoured prince, when he sees BARATTIEL, the great prince of three fingers in the height of Araboth, the highest heaven, he removes the glorious crown from his head and bows himself to the ground. Three fingers in height - Hold your hand out at arm's length with three fingers held out horizontally in front of your eyes. This is the measurement.

(7) And Barattiel, the great prince, when he sees HAMON, the great prince, the fearful and honoured, beautiful and terrible, he who makes all the children of heaven to shake, when the time draws near that is set for the saying of the 'Thrice Holy', he removes the glorious crown form his head and bows himself to the ground. For it is written (Isa.33:3): " At noise of the confusion at the anxious preparation of the salutation of "Holy, Holy, Holy" the people are fled; at the lifting up of yourself the nations are scattered,"

(8) And Hamon, the great prince, when he sees TUTRESSIEL, the great prince he removes the glorious crown from his head and bows himself to the ground.

(9) And Tutresiel YHWH, the great prince, when he sees ATRUGIEL, the great prince, he removes the glorious crown from his head and bows himself to the ground. (10) And Aatrugiel the great prince, when he sees NA' ARIRIEL YHWH, the great prince, he removes the glorious crown from his head and bows himself to the ground.

(11) And Na'aririel YHWH, the great prince when he see SAANIGIEL, the great prince, he removes the glorious crown from his head and bows himself to the ground.

(12) And Sasnigiel YHWH, when he sees ZAZRIEL YHWH, the great prince, he removes the glorious crown from his head and bows himself to the ground.

(13) And Zazriel YHWH, the prince, when he sees GEBURATIEL YHWH, the prince,

he removes the glorious crown from his head and bows himself to the ground.

(14) And Geburatiel YHWH, the prince, when he sees ARAPHIEL YHWH, the prince, he removes the glorious crown from his head and bows himself to the ground.

(15) And Araphiel YHWH, the prince, when he sees ASHRUYLU, the prince, who presides in all the sessions of the children of heaven, he removes the glorious crown from his head and bows himself to the ground.

(16) And Ashruylu YHWH, the prince, when he sees GALLISUR YHWH, THE PRINCE, WHO REVEALS ALL THE SECRETS OF THE LAW (Torah), he removes the glorious crown from his head and bows himself to the ground.

(17) And Gallisur YHWH, the prince, when he sees ZAKZAKIEL YHWH, the prince who is appointed to write down the merits of Israel on the Throne of Glory, he removes the glorious crown form his head and bows himself to the ground.

(18) And Zakzakiel YHWH, the great prince, when he sees ANAPHIEL YHWH, the prince who keeps the keys of the heavenly Halls, he removes the glorious crown from his head and bows himself to the ground. Why is he called by the name of Anaphiel? Because the shoulders of his honor and majesty and his crown and his splendor and his brilliance overshadow all the chambers of Araboth (highest heaven) of Raqia (heaven) on high even as the Maker of the World overshadows them.

[Regarding the Maker of the world, it is written that His glory covered the heavens, and the earth was full of His praise. The honor and majesty of Anaphiel cover all the glories of Araboth (highest heaven) the highest.

Araphiel means "Neck or Strength of God. " Ashruylu means "To cause to rest / dwell. " It is one of the names of the Godhead. Gallisur means, "reveal the secrets of the Law. " He reveals the reasons and secrets of the Creator. Raziel means, "Secrets of God. " He hears the divine decrees. Anaphiel means "Branch of God. " Zakzakiel means, "Merit of God." The glorious crowns signify honour and status.]

(19) And when he sees SOTHER ASHIEL YHWH, the prince, the great, fearful and honoured one, he removes the glorious crown from his head and bows himself to the ground. Why is he called Sother Ashiel? Because he is assigned to rule over the four heads of the river of fire, which are beside the Throne of Glory; and every single prince who goes out or enters before the Shekina, goes out or enters only by his permission.

For the seals of the river of fire are entrusted to him. And furthermore, his height is 0 groups of ten-thousand parasangs. And he stirs up the fire of the river; and he goes out and enters before the Shekina to expound what is recorded concerning the inhabitants of the world. According for it is written (Dan. 7:10): lithe judgment was set, and the books were opened."

(20) And Sother Ashiel the prince, when he sees SHOQED CHOZI, the great prince, the mighty, terrible and honoured one, he removes the glorious crown from his head and falls upon his face. And why is he called Shoqed Chozi? Because he weighs all the merits of man on a scale in the presence of the Holy One, blessed be He. (21)

And when he sees ZEHANPURYU YHWH, the great prince, the mighty and terrible one, honored, glorified and feared in the entire heavenly household, he removes the glorious crown from his head and bows himself to the ground.

Why is he called Zehanpuryu? Because he commands the river of fire and pushes it back to its place.

(22) And when he sees AZBUGA YHWH, the great prince, glorified, revered, honored, adorned, wonderful, exalted, loved and feared among all the great princes who know the mystery of the Throne of Glory, he removes the glorious crown from his head and bows himself to the ground. Why is he called Azbuga? Because in the future he will clothe the righteous and pious of the world with garments of life and wrap them in the cloak of life, so that they can live an eternal life in them.

(23) And when he sees the two great princes, the strong one and the glorified one who are standing above him, he removes the glorious crown from his head and bows himself to the ground. And these are the names of the two princes: SOPHERIEL YHWH (Sopheriel YHWH the Killer), the great prince, the honoured, glorified, blameless, venerable, ancient and mighty one.

(24) Why is he called Sop he riel YHWH who kills (Sopheriel YHWH the Killer)? Because he is assigned to control the books of the dead, so that everyone, when the day of his death draws near, is written by him in the books of the dead. Why is he called Sopheriel YHWH who makes alive (Sopheriel YHWH the Lifegiver)? Because he is assigned control over the books of life, so that every one whom the Holy One, blessed be He, will bring into life, he writes him in the book of life, by authority of The Divine Majesty. Perhaps he might say: "Since the Holy One, blessed be He, is sitting on a throne, they are also sitting when writing." The Scripture teaches us (I Kings 22:19, 2 Chron. 28:18): "And all the host of heaven are standing by him." They are called "The host of heaven" in order to show us that even the Great Princes and all like them in the high heavens, fulfil the requests of the Shekina in no other way than standing. But how is it possible that they can write, when they are standing?

[This section is very important to Jewish mystics and Cabbalists in that it sets the balance within the act of judgment between mercy and justice. If one were to strip down to the barest essentials the spiritual life of a person some may conclude it is to find balance between mercy and justice. The books of life and death are records of the birth and death of individuals. This is not the same as the Book of Life referred to in the Bible, which contains the names of the righteous.]

(25) It is done thusly. One is standing on the wheels of the tempest and the other is standing on the wheels of the wind of the storm. The one is clothed in kingly garments, the other is clothed in kingly garments. The one is wrapped in a mantle of majesty and the other is wrapped in a mantle of majesty. One is crowned with a royal crown, and the other is crowned with a royal crown. The one's body is full of eyes, and the other's body is full of eyes. One looks like lightning, and the other looks like lightning. The eyes of the one is like the sun in its power, and the eyes of the other are like the sun in its power.

The one's height is the height of the seven heavens, and the other's height is the height of the seven heavens. The wings of the one is as many as the days of the year, and the wings of the other are as many as the days of the year. The wings of one reach over the width of Raqia (heaven), and the wings of the other reach over the width of Raqia (heaven). The lips of one look like the gates of the East, and the lips of the other look like the gates of the East. The tongue of the one is as high as the waves of the sea, and the tongue of the other is as high as the waves of the sea. From the mouth of the one a flame proceeds, and from the mouth of the other a flame proceeds. From the mouth of the one lightning is emitted and from the mouth of the other lightning is emitted. From the sweat of one fire is kindled, and from the sweat of the other fire is kindled. From the one's tongue a torch is burning, and from the tongue of the other a torch is burning. On the head of the one there is a sapphire stone, and upon the head of the other there is a sapphire stone. On the shoulders of the one there is a wheel of a swift cherubim, and on the shoulders of the other there is a wheel of a swift cherubim. One has in his hand a burning scroll; the other has in his hand a burning scroll. The length of the scroll is 3000 times ten-thousand parasangs; the size of the pen is 3000 times ten-thousands of parasangs; the size of every single letter that they write is 365parasangs.

[Sopheriel is the prince appointed over the book of life. The name means Scribe of God. " Azbuga is a messenger. The name denoted strength, as many angelic names do. Zehanpunju means "the face of fear." To be full of eyes is a symbol of omniscience, Eastern gates were large, tall structures. The two symbolic uses of fire are destruction and purification.]

CHAPTER 19

Rikbiel, the prince of the wheels of the Merkaba (chariot). And the Sacred Salutation of Holy, Holy, Holy

Rabbi Ishmael said: Metatron, the Angel, the Prince of the Presence, said to me:

(1) Above these three angels, who are these great princes, there is one Prince, distinguished, revered, noble, glorified, adorned, fearful, fearless, mighty, great, uplifted, glorious, crowned, wonderful, exalted, blameless, loved, like a ruler, he is high and lofty, ancient and mighty, there is none among the princes like him. His name is RIKBIEL.

YHWH, the great and revered prince who is standing by Merkaba (chariot).

(2) And why is he called RIKBIEL? Because he is assigned to rule over the wheels of the Merkaba (chariot), and they are given to his authority.

(3) And how many are the wheels? Eight; two in each direction. And there are four winds compassing them round about. And these are their names: "the Winds of the Storm", "the Tempest", "the Strong Wind", and lithe Wind of Earthquake."

(4) And under them four rivers of fire are constantly running and there is one river of fire on each side. And around them, between the rivers, four clouds are affixed. They

are “clouds of fire", "clouds of torches", “clouds of coal", "clouds of brimstone" and they are standing by their wheels.

]There is much number symbolism here. Some Eastern cultures believe there are only eight possible directions of movement. They could be looked at as north, south, east, west, up, down, in, out. Anything else must be a combination of these. Four is the number of limits and testing. Two is the number of assistances, witness, or duplicih.]

(5) And the feet of the Chayoth are resting on the wheels. And between two wheels an earthquake is roaring, and thunder is sounding.

(6) And when the time draws near for the recital of the Song, numerous wheels are moved, the numerous clouds tremble, all the chieftains (shallishim) become afraid, and all the horsemen (parashim) become angry, and all the mighty ones (gibborim) are excited, all the host (seba'im) are frightened, and all the troops (gedudim) are fearfuC all the appointed ones (memunnim) hurry away, all the princes (sarim) and armies (chayelim) are confused, all the servants (mesharetim) faint and all the angels (mal' akim) and divisions (degalim) suffer with pain.

(7) And one wheel makes a sound to be heard by the other and one Cherub speaks to another, one Chayya to another, one Seraph to another (saying) (Ps. 68:5)

"Extol to him that rides in Araboth (highest heaven), by his name Jah (Yah) and rejoice before him!"

[The name Jah (Yah) is a shortened and "speak able" version of YHWH or Jehovah.]

CHAPTER 20

CHAYYIEL, the prince of the Chayoth

Rabbi Ishmael said: Metatron, the angel, the Prince of the Presence, said to me:

(1) Above these there is one great and mighty prince. His name is CHAYYUEL YHWH, a noble and honourable prince, a prince before whom all the children of heaven tremble, a prince who is able to swallow up the entire earth in one moment at a single mouthful.

(2) And why is he called CHA YYLIEL YHWH? Because he is assigned to rule over the Holy Chayoth and he strikes the Chayoth with lashes of fire: and glorifies them, when they give praise and glory and rejoicing, and he causes them to hurry and say "Holy" "Blessed be the Glory of YHWH from His place!" (The Kedushah Sacred Salutation of Holy, Holy, Holy).

CHAPTER 21

The Chayoth Rabbi Ishmael said: Metatron, the angel, the Prince of the Presence, said to me:

(1) The Four Chayoth correspond to the four winds. Each Chayya is as big as the space of the entire world. And each one has four faces; and each face is like the face of the East (sunrise).

(2) Each one has four wings, and each wing is like the tent (ceiling) of the universe.

(3) And each one has faces in the middle of faces and wings in the middle of wings. The size of the faces is 248 faces, and the size of the wings is 365 wings.

(4) And everyone is crowned with 2000 crowns on his head. And each crown is like the rainbow in the cloud. And its splendor is like the magnificence of the circle of the sun. And the sparks that go out from everyone are like the glory of the morning star (planet Venus) in the East.

CHAPTER 22

KERUBIEL, the Prince of the Cherubim.

Description of the Cherubim

Rabbi Ishmael said: Metatron, the angel, the Prince of the Presence, said to me:

(1) Above these there is one prince, noble, wonderful, strong, and praised with all kinds of praise. His name is CHERUBIEL YHWH, a mighty prince, full of power and strength, a prince of highness, and Highness (is) with him, a righteous Prince, and Righteousness (is) with him, a holy prince, and holiness (is) with him, a prince of glorified in (by) thousand host, exalted by ten thousand armies

(2) At his anger the earth trembles, at his anger the camps (of armies) are moved, from fear of him the foundations are shaken, at his chastisement the Araboth (highest heaven) trembles.

(3) His stature is full of (burning) coals. The height is that of the seven heavens and the breadth of his stature is like the sea.

(4) The opening of his mouth is like a lamp of fire. His tongue is a consuming fire. His eyebrows are like the splendor of the lightning. His eyes are like sparks of bright light. His face is like a burning fire.

(5) And there is a crown of holiness upon his head on which the Explicit Name is graven, and lightning proceeds from it. And the bow of the Shekina is between his shoulders. And his sword is like lightning; and on his thighs there are arrows like

flames, and upon his Armor and shield there is a consuming fire, and on his neck, there are coals of burning juniper wood and (also) around him (there are coals of burning juniper).

[The bow can represent a rainbow, but it is certainly a weapon of great power. Juniper is a symbol of strength and longevity. It was said to shelter the prophet Elijah from Queen Jezebel ' s pursuit. Tales in the apocryphal books tell of how the infant Jesus and his parents were hidden from King Herod's soldiers by a juniper during their flight into Egypt.]

(7) And the splendor of Shekina is on his face; and the horns of the majesty on his wheels; and a royal diadem upon his head.

(8) And his body is full of eyes. And wings are covering the entire of his high stature (lit. the height of his stature is all wings).

(9) On his right hand a flame is burning, and on his left a fire is glowing; and coals are burning from it. And burning staves go forth from his body. And lightning is projected from his face. With him there is always thunder within thunder, and by his side there is a never-ending earthquake within an earthquake.

(10) And the two princes of the Merkaba (chariot) are together with him.

(11) Why is he called CHERUBIEL YHWH, the Prince. Because he is assigned to rule over the chariot of the Cherubim. And the mighty Cherubim are subject to his authority. And he adorns the crowns on their heads and polishes the diadem upon their heads (skulls).

(12) He increases the glory of their appearance. And he glorifies the beauty of their majesty. And he expands the greatness of their honor. He makes their songs of praise to be sung. He makes the strength of their beauty increase. He causes the brightness of their glory to shine forth. He makes their goodness, mercy, and lovingkindess to grow. He separates their radiance, so it shows even more. He makes the beauty of their mercy even more beautiful. He glorifies their upright majesty. He sings the order of their praise to establish the dwelling place of Him who dwells on the Cherubim.

(13) And the Cherumim are standing by the Holy Chayoth, and their wings are raised up to their heads (are as the height of their heads) and Shekina is (resting) upon them and the bright Glory is upon their faces and songs of praise are in their mouth and their hands are under their wings and their feet are covered by their wings and horns of glory are upon their heads and the splendor of Shekina on their face and Shekina is resting on them and sapphire stones surround them and columns of fire are on their four sides and columns of burning staves are beside them.

(14) There is one sapphire on one side and another sapphire on the other side and under the sapphires there are coals of burning juniper wood.

(15) And a Cherub is standing in each direction, but the wings of the Cherubim surround each other above their heads in glory; and they spread them to sing with them a song to him that inhabits the clouds and to praise the fearful majesty of the king

of kings with their wings.

The sound coming from their wings is heard as a song. This hearkens back to a description of Lucifer before the fall. It was said that his body had instruments made within it, which made beautiful music.]

(16) And CHERUBIEL YHWH, is the prince who is assigned to rule over them. He arrays them in proper, beautiful, and pleasant orders and he exalts them in all manner of exaltation, dignity and glory. And he hurries them in glory and might to do the will of their Creator every moment. Above their high heads continually dwells the glory of the high king "who dwells on the Cherubim."

[Names in this section are related to the station of the angels.

Chayyliel is the prince of the Chayyoth, Cherubiel or Kerubiel is the prince of the Kerubim or Cherubim, and so on.]

CHAPTER 22-B

Rabbi Ishmael said to me: Metatron, the angel, the Prince of the Presence, said to me:

(1) How are the angels standing on high?

He said: A bridge is placed from the beginning of the doorway to the end, like a bridge that is placed over a river for everyone to pass over it. And three ministering angels surround it and sing a song before YHWH, the God of Israel. And standing before it is the lords of dread and captains of fear, numbering a thousand times thousand and ten thousand times ten thousand, and they sing praises and hymns before YHWH, the God of Israel.

(3) Many bridges are there. There are bridges of fire and many bridges of hail. Also, many rivers of hail, numerous storehouses of snow, and many wheels of fire.

(4) And how many are the ministering angels are there? 12, times ten thousand: six-thousand time ten thousand above and six (thousand times ten-thousand) below. And 12, are the storehouses of snow, six above and six below. And 24 times ten-thousand wheels of fire, 12 times ten thousand above and 12 times ten thousand below. And they surround the bridges and the rivers of fire and the rivers of hail. And there are numerous ministering angels, forming entries, for all the creatures that are standing in the midst thereof, over against the paths of Raqia (heaven) Shamayim.

(5) What does YHWH, the God of Israel, the King of Glory do? The Great and Fearful God, mighty in strength, covers His face.

(6) In Araboth (highest heaven) are, times ten-thousand angels of glory standing over against the Throne of Glory and the divisions of flaming fire. And the King of Glory covers His face; for else the Araboth (highest heaven) of Raqia (heaven) would be torn

apart from its centre because of the majesty, splendor, beauty, radiance, loveliness, brilliancy, brightness and Excellency of the appearance of (the Holy One) blessed be He.

(7) There are innumerable ministering angels carrying out his will, many kings and princes in the Araboth

(highest heaven) of His delight. They are angels who are revered among the rulers in heaven, distinguished, adorned with song and they bring love to the minds of those who are frightened by the splendor of Shekina, and their eyes are dazzled by the shining beauty of their King, their faces grow black and their strength fails.

(8) There are rivers of joy, streams of gladness, rivers of happiness, streams of victory, rivers of life, streams of friendship and they flow over and go out from in front of the Throne of Glory and grow large and wend their way through the gates on the paths to Araboth (highest heaven) of Raqia (heaven) at the voice of shouting and music of the CHA YYOTH, at the voice of the rejoicing of the cymbals of his OPHANNIM and at the melody of the cymbals of His Cherubim. And they grow great and go out with noise and with the sound of the hymn: "HOLY, HOLY, HOLY, IS THE LORD OF HOST; THE WHOLE EARTH IS FULL OF HIS GLORY!"

CHAPTER 22 -C

Rabbi Ishmael said: Metatron, the Prince of the Presence said to me:

(1) What is the distance between one bridge and another?

Tens of thousands of parasangs. They rise up tens of thousands of parasangs, and the go down tens of thousands of parasangs.

(2) The distance between the rivers of dread and the rivers of fear is 22 times ten-thousand parasangs; between the rivers of hail and the rivers of darkness 36 times ten-thousand paragangs; between the chambers of lightnings and the clouds of compassion 42 times ten-thousand parasangs; between the clouds of compassion and the Merkaba (chariot) 84 times tenthousand parasangs; between the Merkaba (chariot) and the Cherubim times ten-thousand parasangs; between the Cherubim and the Ophannim 24 times ten-thousand parasangs; between the chambers of chambers and the Holy Chayoth 40,000 times ten-thousand parasangs; between one wing (of the Chayoth) and another 12 times ten-thousand parasangs; and the breadth of each one wing is of that same measure; and the distance between the Holy Chayoth and the Throne of Glory is 30, times ten-thousand parasangs.

(3) And from the foot of the Throne to the seat there are 40, times ten thousand parasangs. And the name of Him that sits on it: let the name be sanctified!

(4) And the arches of the Bow are set above the Araboth (highest heaven), and they are thousand and 10, times ten thousand of parasangs high. Their measure is after the

measure of the 'Irin and Qaddishin (the Watchers and the Holy Ones). As it is written, (Gen. 9:13) "My bow I have set in the cloud." It is not written here "I will set" but "I have set," that is to say; I have already set it in the clouds that surround the Throne of Glory. As His clouds pass by, the angels of hail turn into burning coal.

(5) And a voice of fire goes down from the Holy Chayoth. And because of the breath of that voice, they run (Ezek. 1 :14) to another place, fearing that it could command them to go; and they return for fear that it may injure them from the other side. Therefore "they run and return."

(6) And these arches of the Bow are more beautiful and radiant than the radiance of the sun during the summer solstice. And they are brighter (whiter) than a flaming fire and they are large and beautiful.

(7) Above the arches of the Bow are the wheels of the Ophannim. Their height is 0 thousand and 10, times 10, units of measure after the measure of the Seraphim and the Troops (Gedudim).

[The Irin and Qaddishin are the highest ranked of all the angels. They constitute the supreme council of heaven. These angels are the twin sentinels. The Irin decrees while the Qaddishin sentences every case in the court of heaven. In Daniel 4:14 we find references. "By decree of the sentinels is this decided, by order of the holy ones, this sentence, that all who live may know that the Highest rules over the kingdom of men: he can give it to whom he will, or set over it the lowliest of men. For the words rendered, "of the holy god, II we read in Chaldee (in which Daniel was composed) the words elain cadisin (' -l-h-y-n qd-y-sh-y-n) [vocalized this would be 'elahin qaddishinJ, which means " holy gods, " not " holy God, " (St. Jerome, Commentary on Daniel (1).]

CHAPTER 23

The winds are blowing under the wings of the Cherubim

Rabbi Ishmael said: Metatron, the Angel, the Prince of the Presence, said to me:

(1) There are numerous winds blowing under the wings of the Cherubim. There blows " the Brooding Wind", for it is written (Gen. 1: 2): "and the wind of God was brooding upon the face of the waters."

(2) There blows "the Strong Wind", as it is said (Ex.14: 21): "and the Lord caused the sea to go back by a strong east wind all that night."

(3) There blows "the East Wind" for it is written (Ex. 10: 13): "the east wind brought the locusts."

(4) There blows " the Wind of Quails for it is written (Num. 9: 31): And there went forth a wind II from the Lord and brought quails."

(5) There blows " the Wind of Jealousy" for it is written (Num. 5:14): "And the wind of jealousy came upon him."

(6) There blows the "Wind of Earthquake" and it is written (I Kings. 19: 11): "and after that the wind of the earthquake; but the Lord was not in the earthquake."

(7) There blows the "Wind of YHWH" for it is written (Ex. 37: 1): "and he carried me out by the wind of YHWH and set me down."

(8) There blows the "Evil Wind" for it is written (I Sam. 14: 23): "and the evil wind departed from him."

(9) There blows the "Wind of Wisdom" and the "Wind of Understanding" and the "Wind of Knowledge" and the "Wind of the Fear of YHWH" for it is written (Is. 11: 2): “And the wind of YHWH shall rest upon him; the wind of wisdom and understanding, the wind of counsel and might, the wind of knowledge and the fear of YHWH."

(10) There blows the "Wind of Rain", for it is written (Prov. 25: 23) "the north wind brings forth rain."

(11) There blows the "Wind of Lightning", for it is written (Jer. 10: 13): "he makes lightning for the rain and brings forth the wind out of his storehouses."

(12) There blows the "Wind, Which Breaks the Rocks", for it is written (1 Kings 19: 11): "the Lord passed by and a great and strong wind (rent the mountains and break in pieces the rocks before the Lord.)

(13) There blows the Wind of Assuagement of the Sea", for it is written (Gen. 7:1): "and God made a wind to pass over the earth, and the waters assuaged."

(14) There blows the "Wind of Wrath", for it is written (Job1: 19): 'and behold there came a great wind from the wilderness and smote the four corners of the house and it fell."

(15) There blows the "Wind of Storms", for it is written (Ps.: 8): "Winds of the storm, fulfilling his word."

(16) And Satan is standing among these winds, for "the winds of the storm" is nothing else, but "Satan" and all these winds do not blow but under the wings of Cherubim, for it is written (Ps. 18.11): "and he rode upon a cherub and £lew, yes, and he £lew with speed upon wings of the wind."

(17) And where do all these winds go? The Scripture teaches us, that they go out from under the wings of the Cherubim and descend on the globe of the sun, for it is written (EceI. 1 :6): "The wind goes toward the south and turns around to the north; it turns around over and over in its course and the wind returns again to its route." And from the orb of the sun, they return and go down on to the rivers and the seas, then up on the mountains and up on the hills, for it is written (Am. 55:13): "For 10, he that forms the mountains and creates the wind."

(18) And from the mountains and the hills they return and go down again to the seas

and the rivers; and from the seas and the rivers they return and go up to the cities and provinces: and from the cities and provinces they return and go down into the Garden, and from the Garden they return and descend to Eden, for it is written (Gen. 3: 8) "walking in the Garden in the wind (cool) of day." In the middle of the Garden, they come together and blow from one side to the other. In the Garden they are perfumed with spices from the Garden in its most remote parts, until the winds again separate from each other. Filled with the odor of the pure spices, the winds bring the aroma from the most remote parts of Eden. They carry the spices of the Garden to the righteous and godly who in time to come will inherit the Garden of Eden and the Tree of life, for it is written (Can't 45: 16): "Awake, north wind; and come you south; blow upon my garden and eat his precious fruits."

[The same word used for "wind" is also used for "spirit. " It is interesting to read the same verses using the word " spirit. " It should also be noted that when certain attributes are associated with "wind, " such as the wind of jealousy, it could be seen to be an agent of God, such as an angel or demon.]

CHAPTER 24

The different chariots of the Holy One, blessed be He

Rabbi Ishmael said: Metatron, the Angel, the Prince of the Presence, the glory of all heaven, said to me:

(1) The Holy One blessed be He, has innumerable chariots. He has the " Chariots of the Cherubim", for it is written (Ps. 18:11, 2 Sam 22: 11): "And he rode upon a cherub and did fly."

(2) He has the "Chariots of Wind", for it is written: "and he flew swiftly upon the wings of the wind."

(3) He has the "Chariots of the Swift Cloud", for it is written (ls.19:1): "Behold, the Lord rides upon a swift cloud:

(4) He has "Chariots of Clouds", for it is written (Ex. 19:9): "Lo, I come unto you in a cloud."

(5) He has the "Chariots of the Altar", for it is written, " I saw the Lord standing upon the Altar."

(6) He has the "Chariots of Ribbotaim", for it is written (Ps. 68:18): "The chariots of God are Ribbotaim; thousands of angels."

[Ribbotaim appear to be used as the chariot and are a type of Cherub.]

(7) He has the "Chariots of the Tent", for it is written (Deut. 31:15): "And the Lord appeared in the Tent in a pillar of cloud."

(8) He has the "Chariots of the Tabernacle", for it is written (Lev. 1:1): "And the Lord spoke unto him out of the tabernacle."

(9) He has the " Chariots of the Mercy-Seat", for it is written (Num. 7:89): "then he heard the Voice speaking unto him from upon the mercy-seat."

(10) He has the "Chariots of Sapphire", for it is written (Ex. 24:10): "and there was under his feet a paved street of sapphires."

(11) He has the "Chariots of Eagles", for it is written (Ex. 19:4): "I bare you on eagles' wings." It is not Eagles that are not meant here but "they that fly as swiftly as the eagles."

(12) He has the "Chariots of a Shout", for it is written: "God is gone up with a shout."

(13) He has the "Chariots of Araboth (highest heaven)," for it is written (Ps 68:5): " Praise Him that rides upon the Araboth (highest heaven)."

(14) He has the "Chariots of Thick Clouds", for it is written (Ps. 104:3): "who makes the thick clouds His chariot."

(15) He has the "Chariots of the Chayoth," for it is written (Ezek. 1 :14): "and the Chayoth ran and returned. They run by permission and return by permission, for Shekina is above their heads.

(16) He has the "Chariots of Wheels (Galgallim)", for it is written (Ezek. 10: 2): " And he said: Go in between the whirling wheels."

(17) He has the "Chariots of a Swift Cherub," for it is written, "riding on a swift cherub." And at the time when He rides on a swift cherub, as he sets one of His feet upon his back, and before he sets the other foot upon his back, he looks through eighteen thousand worlds at one glace. And he perceives and understands and sees into them all and knows what is in all of them, and then he sets down the other foot upon the cherub, for it is written (Ezek. 48:35): " Round about eighteen thousand." How do we know that He looks through every one of them every day? It is written

(Ps. 14: 2): "He looked down from heaven upon the children of men to see if there were any that understand, that seek after God."

(18) He has the "Chariots of the Ophannim", for it is written (Ezek. 10:12): "and the Ophannim were full of eyes round about."

(19) He has the "Chariots of His Holy Throne", for it is written (Ps. 67:8): "God sits upon his holy throne"

(20) He has the "Chariots of the Throne of Yah (Jah)", for it is written (Ex. 17:16): "Because a hand is lifted up upon the Throne of Jah (Yah)."

(21) He has the " Chariots of the Throne of Judgment," for it is written (Is. 5: 16): "but the Lord of hosts shall be exalted in judgment."

(22) He has the "Chariots of the Throne of Glory", for it is written (Jer. 17:12): "The

the crown is the distance of years' journey. There is no kind of splendor, no kind of brilliance, no kind of radiance, no kind of light in the universe that is not affixed to the crown.

[As in the prior chapter, the number seven is the result of the addition of the digits in the measurement.]

(8) The name of that prince is SERAPHIEL YHWH. And the crown on his head, its name is lithe Prince of Peace." And why is he called by the name of SERAPHIEL YHWH? Because he is assigned to rule over the Seraphim. And the flaming Seraphim are under his authority. And he presides over them by day and night and teaches them to sing, praise, and proclaim the beauty, power and majesty of their King. They proclaim the beauty of their King through all types of Praise and Sanctification.

(Kedushah - Sacred Salutation of Holy, Holy, Holy).

(9) How many Seraphim are there? Four, equating to the four winds of the world. And how many wings have each one of them? Six, relating to the six days of Creation. And how many faces do they have? Each one of them have four faces.

(10) The height measurement of the Seraphim is the height of the seven heavens. The size of each wing is like the span of all Raqia (heaven). The size of each face is like the face of the East.

(11) And each one of them gives out light, adding to the splendor of the Throne of Glory, so that not even the Holy Chayoth, the honored Ophannim, nor the majestic Cherubim are able to look on it. Anyone who gazes at it would be blinded because of its great splendor.

(12) Why are they called Seraphim? Because they burn (saraph) the writing tables of Satan: Every day Satan sits together with SAMMAEL, the Prince of Rome, and with DUBBIEL, the Prince of Persia, and they write down the sins of Israel on their writing tables, which they hand over to the Seraphim, so that the Seraphim can present them to the Holy One, blessed be He, so that He should eliminate (destroy) Israel from the world. But the Seraphim know the secrets of the Holy One, blessed be He. They know that He does not want the people Israel to perish. What do the Seraphim do about this? Every day they receive the tablets from the hand of Satan and they burn them in the burning fire, which is near the high and exalted Throne. They do this in order that the tablet should not come before the Holy One, blessed be He, when he is sitting upon the Throne of Judgment, judging the entire world in truth.

[Satan and Sammael are not allowed to approach the throne of God, but their accusations are taken by a Seraph, who destroys the tablet with the accusations against Israel and burns it. The tablet is not given to God, who 'would have to judge Israel, since the Seraph knows, God does not wish to judge or punish Israel.

Dubbiel is the guardian angel of Persia and one of the special accusers of Israel. Dubbiel is an angel who was ranked among angels who were said to act as guardians over the seventy nations. Dubbiel was counted as the protector of Persia and as such defended its interests against its enemy Israel, a role that naturally put him at odds with the Chosen People and their special patron, St. Michael the Archangel. Sammael is an angel whose name has been interpreted as meaning "angel " or Ilgod" (el) of "poison" (sam). He is the guardian angel of Ramel another enemy of Israel. He is considered in legend a member of the heavenly host who fell. He is equated with Satan and the chief of the evil spirits. He is the angel of death in this capacity he is a fallen angel but remains the Lord's semant or at least under His control. As a good angel, Sammael resided in the seventh heaven, although he is declared to be the chief angel of the fifth heaven.

Seraphim are among the highest and most splendid of the nine accepted angelic orders as developed by the sixth-century theologian Dionysius. They are the closest in all ofheaven to the throne of God.

They are said to glow as if they are on fire so brig/llly they no mortal can endure the sight.]

CHAPTER 27

RADWERIEL, the keeper of the Book of Records.

Rabbi Ishmael said: Metatron, the Angel of YHWH, the Prince of the Presence, said to me:

(1) Above the Seraphim there is one prince, exalted above all princes. He is more wonderful than all the servants. His name is RADWERIEL YHWH who is assigned to rule over the treasuries of the books.

Radweriel is appointed over the treasunJ of book of records or remembrances. (See Ma1.3:1 6). He is an angelic scribe, fluent in reading and writing. He reads the records in the Beth Din, (house/court) of justice. This is another name for the Sanhedrin.

(2) He couriers the Case of Writings, which has the Books of Records in it, and he brings it to the Holy One, blessed be He.

And he breaks the seals of the case, opens it, and takes out the books and delivers them before the Holy One, blessed be He.

And the Holy One, blessed be He, receives them out of his hand and gives them to the Scribes to see so they may read them in the Great Beth (house) Din in the height of Araboth (highest heaven) of Raqia (heaven), before the household of heaven.

(3) And why is he called RADWERIEL? Because from every word going out of his mouth an angel is created. He stands in the service of the company of the ministering angels and sings a song before the Holy One, blessed be He, as the time draws near for the recitation of the Thrice Holy One.

CHAPTER 28

The 'Irin and Qaddishin

(Watchers and Holy Ones) Rabbi Ishmael said: Metatron, the Angel, the Prince of the Presence, said to me:

(1) Above all these there are four great princes. Their names are Irin and Qaddishin. They are highly honored, revered, loved, wonderfully glorious, and greater than any of the heavenly children. There is none like them among all the princes of heaven (sky). There are none equal to them among any Servants. Each one is equal to all the rest of the heavenly servants put together.

(2) And their dwelling is near the Throne of Glory and their standing place near the Holy One, blessed be He. The brightness of their dwelling is a reflection from the brightness from the Throne of Glory. Their face is magnificent and is a reflection of the magnificence of Shekina.

(3) They are elevated by the glory of the Divince Majesty (Gebura) and praised by (through) the praise of Shekina.

(4) And not only that, but the Holy One, blessed be He, does nothing in his world without first consulting them.

Only after He consults them does He perform it. As it is written (Dan. 4: 17): "The sentence is by the decree of the Irin and the demand by the word of the Qaddishin."

(5) The Irin is two (twins) and the Qaddishin are two (twins). In what fashions standing before the Holy One, blessed be He? We should understand, that one Ir is standing on one side and the other 'Ir on the other side. Also, one Qaddish is standing on one side and the other on the other side.

(6) And they exalt the humble forever, and they humble and bring to the ground those that are proud. They exalt to the heights those that are humble.

(7) And every day, as the Holy One, blessed be He, is sitting upon the Throne of Judgment and judges the entire world, and the Books of the Living and the Books of the Dead are opened in front of Him all the children of heaven are standing before Him in fear and dread. They are in awe, and they shake. When the Holy One, blessed be He, is sitting on the Throne of Judgment to execute His judgment, His garment is white as snow, the hair on his head is like pure wool and the His entire cloak is shining with light. He is covered with righteousness all over, like He is wearing a coat of mail.

(8) And those Irin and Qaddishin (Watchers and Holy Ones) are standing before Him like court officers before the judge. And constantly they begin and argue a case and close the case that comes before the Holy One, blessed be He, in judgment, according for it is written. (Dan. 4. 17): "The sentence is by the decree of the 'Irin and the demand by the word of Qaddishin."

This section explains the function of the Irin and Qaddishin. They are two pairs of angels forming the apex of angelic po'wer. They are the holy councilors and they have authority over all things terrestrial.

They are judge and executioner. Another tradition has the Irin and Qaddishin as two classes of angels but many in number. Yet, they seem to come in sets of two each, like twins, Again, this may represent the balance of merClJ and justice always sought in hea'llen.

(9) Some of them argue the case and others pass the sentence in the Great Beth Din (Great House of the Sanhedrin) in Araboth (the highest heaven). Some of them make requests in the presence of the Divine Majesty and some close the cases before the Highest. Others finish by going down and confirming the judgement and executing the sentences on earth below, according for it is written

(Dan. 4. 13, 14): "Behold an Ir and a Qaddish came down from heaven and cried aloud and said, "Chop down the tree, and cut off his branches, shake off his leaves, and scatter his fruit: let the beasts escape from under it, and the fowls from his branches."

(10) Why are they called Irin and Qaddishin (Watchers and Holy Ones)? Because they sanctify the body and the spirit with beatings with fire on the third day of the judgment, for it is written (Has. 6: 2): After two days will he revive us: on the third he will raise us up, and we shall live before him."

[Irin and Qaddishin or ministering spirits receive men from the angel of death. They judge him with angels arguing for him. This takes two days. On the third day they pass judgment. The sentence is based on the man's character and how closely he followed the Torah. They beat them accordingly.]

CHAPTER 29

Description of a class of angels

Rabbi Ishmael said: Metatron, the Angel, the Prince of the Presence, said to me:

(1) Each one of the Angels has seventy names corresponding to the seventy languages (nations) of the world. And all of them are based upon the name of the Holy One, blessed be He. And every several name is written with a flaming pen of iron on the Fearful Crown (Kether Nora), which is on the head of the high and exalted King.

[Metatron was said to have names based upon the narnes of God. Fearful Crown refers to the crown of a sitting king, thus God.]

(2) And each one of them projects sparks and lightning. Each one of them is covered with horns of splendor all over. Lights shine from each of them, and each one is surrounded by tents of brilliance so that not even the Seraphim and the Chayoth who are greater than all the children of heaven are able to look at them.

CHAPTER 30

The 72 princes of Kingdoms and the Prince of the World are at the Great Sanhedrin.

Rabbi Ishmael said: Metatron, the Angel, the Prince of the Presence, said to me:

(1) Whenever the Great Beth Din (House of the Sanhedrin) is seated in the Araboth (highest heaven) of Raqia (heaven) there no one speaks. No mouth opens for anyone in the world except those great princes who are called YHWH by the name of the Holy One, blessed be He.

(2) How many are those Princes are there? Seventy-two princes of the kingdoms of the world besides the Prince of the World who pleads in favor of the world before the Holy One, blessed be He. Every day at the appointed hour the book with the records of all the deeds of the world is opened. For it is written (Dan. 7:10): " The judgment was set and the books were opened."

[The highest classes of angels are marked with the Tetragrammaton.

Each nation has its own angel appointed to guard and plea for its cause. What is odd about this is the equal and universal appeal to justice. There is no difference in how the court is conducted between Gentile or Jew. In this scenario, Metatron is the prince of the world.]

CHAPTER 31

The attributes of Justice, Mercy and Truth

Rabbi Ishmael said: Metatron, the Angel, the Prince of the Presence, said to me:

(1) At the time when the Holy One, blessed be He, is sitting on the Throne of Judgment, Justice is standing on His right and Mercy on His left and Truth in front of His face,

(2) then man (Some sources say "wicked man" but this is to be read as mankind) enters before Him for judgment, then , a staff comes out from the splendor of Mercy towards him and it stands in front of the man. Then man falls upon his face, and all the angels of destruction are fearful, and they shake before him. For it is written (Is. 16:5): " And with mercy shall the throne be established, and he shall sit upon it in truth."

[The fundamental balance of justice and mercy is only possible through truth, including the truth of what the real intent of the person being judged was. This is only possible with God. The angels of destruction are there to execute man, but Mercy stops them and makes the angels fear. The wording of the verse makes this point unclear.]

CHAPTER 32

The execution of judgment on the wicked. God's sword

Rabbi Ishmael said: Metatron, the Angel, the Prince of the Presence, said to me:

(1) When the Holy One, blessed be He, opens the Book, half of it is fire and half of it is flames. Then the angels of destruction go out from Him continually to execute the judgment on the wicked by His sword, which is drawn from its sheath, and it shines like magnificent lightning and pervades the world from one end to the other. For it is written (Is. 66:16): "For by fire will the Lord plead by His sword with all flesh."

(2) And all those who come into the world fear and shake before Him, when they behold His sharpened sword like lightning from one end of the world to the other, and sparks and flashes of the size of the stars of Raqia (heaven) going out from it; according for it is written (Deut. 32: 41) : If I whet the lightning of my sword."

CHAPTER 33

The angels of Mercy, of Peace, and of Destruction are by the Throne of Judgment.

Rabbi Ishmael said: Metatron, the Angel, the Prince of the Presence, said to me:

(1) At the time that the Holy One, blessed be He, is sitting on the Throne of Judgment, then the angels of Mercy are standing on His right, the angels of Peace are standing on His left and the angels of Destruction are standing in front of Him.

(2) And there is one scribe standing beneath Him, and another scribe standing above Him.

(3) And the glorious Seraphim surround the Throne on all four of its sides with walls of lightning. And the Ophannim surround them with burning staves all around the Throne of Glory. And clouds of fire and clouds of flames surround them to the right and to the left. The Holy Chayoth carry the Throne of Glory from below. Each one uses only three fingers. The length of each finger is, and times one hundred, and 66,000 parasangs.

(4) And underneath the feet of the Chayoth there are seven rivers of fire running and flowing. And the distance across of each river is thousand parasangs and its depth is thousand times ten thousand parasangs. Its length cannot be known and is immeasurable.

(5) And each river turns round in a bow in the four directions of Araboth (the highest heaven) of Raqia (heaven), and from there it falls down to Maon and is stopped, and from Maon (some sources have "Velum") to Zebul, from Zegul to Shechaqim, from Shechaqim to Raqia (heaven) to Shamayim and from Shamayim it fows on the heads of the wicked who are in Gehenna, for it is written (Jer. 23:19) : "Behold a whirlwind

of the Lord, even His fury, is gone, yes, a whirling tempest; it shall burst upon the head of the wicked."

[Maon or Velum is the name of the first heaven. The river flows down from heaven and all its levels to Gehenna, which is the burning hell. Speculation on the meaning of the numbers contained in this chapter are random. In general, 3 is the number of spiritual completeness, and 8 is the number of judgments. The number of man and his shortcomings is 6. The number 7 represents spiritual perfection. 5 represents grace and spirit.]

CHAPTER 34

The different concentric circles around the Chayoth consist of fire, water, hailstones.

Rabbi Ishmael said: Metatron; the Angel, the Prince of the Presence, said to me:

(1) The hoofs of the Chayoth are surrounded by seven clouds of burning coals. The clouds of burning coals are surrounded on the outside by seven walls of flames. The seven walls of flames are surrounded on the outside by seven walls of hailstones (stones of El-gabish, Ezek.13: 11, 13, 28: 22). The hailstones are surrounded on the outside by boulders (stones) of hail. The boulders (stones) of hail are surrounded on the outside by stones of "the wings of the tempest." The stones of "the of the winged tempest" are surrounded by the outside by flames of fire. The chambers of the whirlwind are surrounded on the outside by the fire and water.

(2) Around the fire and the water are those who sing the "Holy." Around about those who sing the "Holy" are those who sing the "Blessed." Around about those who sing the "Blessed" are the bright clouds. The bright clouds are surrounded on the outside by coals of burning juniper wood. There are thousands of camps of fire and ten thousand hosts of flames. And between every camp and every host there is a cloud, so that they may not be burned by the fire.

[The stones of hail are made of the two opposite substances of fire and ice. This, like the reference to fire and water, represent a balance of forces which, if applied within the spiritual realm, brings blessings.]

CHAPTER 35

The camps of angels in Araboth (the highest heaven) of Raqia (heaven). Angels performing the Kedushah

(Sacred Salutation of Holy, Holy, Holy)

Rabbi Ishmael said: Metatron, the Angel, the Prince of the Presence, said to me:

(1) (Other sources have 506) thousand times ten-thousand camps has the Holy One, blessed be He, in the height of Araboth (the highest heaven) of Raqia (heaven). And each camp is composed of thousand angels. [The Gematria for is "kingdom" and for it is "kingdoms. "]

(2) And every single angel is as tall as the width of the great sea; and the appearance of their face is like the appearance of lightning. Their eyes are like lamps of fire, and their arms and their feet were the color of polished brass and when they spoke words their voice roared and sounded like the voice of a multitude of them.

(3) They all stand before the Throne of Glory in four rows. And the princes of the army are standing at the beginning of each row.

(4) Some of them sing the "Holy" and others sing the "Blessed." Some run as messengers while others stand in attendance. For it is written (Dan. 7: 10): "Thousands of thousands ministered unto Him, and ten thousand times ten thousand stood before Him. The judgment was set and the books were opened."

The singing or chanting of "Holy, Holy, Holy" is returned by the phrase, "Blessed be Thou and blessed is the name of the Lord for ever and ever. "

(5) When the time nears and the hour comes to say the "Holy", first a whirlwind from before the Holy One, blessed be He, goes out and bursts on the camp of Shekina and there arises a great noise and confusion among them. For it is written (Jer. 30: 23): "Behold, the whirlwind of the Lord goes forth with fury, a continuing commotion."

(6) At that moment thousands of thousands of them are changed into sparks, thousands of thousands of them ignite into burning staves, thousands of thousands of flashes, thousands of thousands burst into flames, thousands of thousands change into males, thousands of thousands change into females, thousands of thousands burst into winds, thousands of thousands burst into burning fires, thousands of thousands burst into flames, thousands of thousands turn into sparks, thousands of thousands turn into chashmals of light; until they take upon themselves the yoke of the kingdom of heaven, the high and lifted, of the Creator of them all with fear, dread, awe, and trembling, with commotion, anguish, terror and trepidation. Then they are changed again into their former shape to have the fear of their King before them always, as they have set their hearts on saying the Song continually, for it is written (Is. 6:3): fI and one cried unto another and said Holy, Holy, Holy."

[The phrase, thousands of thousands change into males, thousands of thousands change into females . . . " is suspect and may have been added later. The idea of taking onto oneself the yoke of heaven may refers to the fact that the angels are reciting the "Holy" and Blessed" discourse, which means they understand and acknowledge the ways of heaven and the place and power of God. Judgment comes accordingly.]

CHAPTER 36

The angels bathe in the river of fire before they recite the Song

Rabbi Ishmael said: Metatron, the Angel, the Prince of Presence, said to me:

(1) At the time when the ministering angels desire to sing (the) Song, (then) Nehar di-Nur (the stream of fire) rises with many "thousand thousands and tenthousand ten-thousands" (of angels) of power and strength of fire (the intensity of the radiant fire of the angels flows) and it runs and passes under the Throne of Glory, between the camps of the ministering angels and the troops of Araboth (highest heaven).

(2) And all the ministering angels first go down into Nehar di-Nur (stream of fire), and they dip themselves in the fire and dip their tongue and their mouth seven times; (2Kings 5:14) and after that they go up and put on the garment of Machaqe Samal and cover themselves with cloaks of chashmal (the zenith of heaven) and stand in four rows over near the side of the Throne of Glory, in all the heavens.

[No meaning for the term Machaqe Samal could be found.]

CHAPTER 37

The four camps of Shekina and their surroundings Rabbi Ishmael said: Metatron, the Angel, the Prince of the Presence, said to me:

(1) In the seven Halls four chariots of Shekina are standing. Before each one stands the four camps of Shekina. Between (or behind) each camp a river of fire is continually flowing.

(2) Between (or behind) each river there are bright clouds surrounding them, and between (or behind) each cloud there are pillars of brimstone erected. Between one pillar and another there stands flaming wheels, which surround them. And between one wheel and another there are flames of fire all around. Between the flames there are storehouses of lightning. Behind the storehouses of lightning there are the wings of the Wind of the Storm. Behind the wings of the Wind of the Storm are the chambers of the tempest. Behind the chambers of the tempest there are winds, voices, thunder, and sparks emitting from sparks and earthquakes within earthquakes.

[The original intent of the verse may have been to draw a picture of the rivers running in concentric circles through the heavens and beside the river, in rows are clouds, lightning, and wind.]

CHAPTER 38

The fear in heavens at the sound of the "Holy" is appeased by the Prince of the World

Rabbi Ishmael said: Metatron, the Angel, the Prince of the Presence, said to me:

(1) At the time, when the ministering angels sing (the Thrice) Holy, then all the pillars of the heavens and their sockets shake, and the gates of the Halls of Araboth (the highest heaven) of Raqia (heaven) are shaken and the foundations of Shechaqim and the universe are moved, and the orders (secrets) of Maon and the chambers of Makon quiver, and all the orders of Raqia (heaven) and the constellations and the planets are distressed. The orbs of the sun and the moon rush away and run out of their pattens and run 12, parasangs and the wish to throw themselves down from heaven,

(2) because of the roaring voice (sound) of their song, and the noise of their praise and the sparks and lightning that proceed from their faces. For it is written (Ps. 77: 18): "'The voice of your thunder was in the heaven (the lightning illuminated the world, the earth trembled and shook)."

(3) Until the Prince of the World calls them, saying; Be quiet in your placel Do not fear because of the ministering angels who sing the Song before the Holy One, blessed be He." As it is written (Job. 38: 7): "'When the morning stars sang together and all the children of heaven shouted for joy."

[As the appointed times approached to sing the Holy, Holy, Holy, all of heaven became anxious. Metatron quieted them and gave them focus.]

CHAPTER 39

The explicit names fly from the Throne.

Rabbi Ishmael said: Metatron, the Angel, the Prince of the Presence, said to me:

(1) When the ministering angels sing the "Holy" then all the explicit names that are engraved with a flaming iron pen on the Throne of Glory go flying off like eagles, each with sixteen wings. And they surround and hover around the Holy One, blessed be He, on all four sides of the place of His Shekina.

(2) And the angels of the host, and the flaming Servants, the mighty Ophannim, the Cherubim of the Shekina, the Holy Chayoth, the Seraphim, the Er'ellim, the Taphsarim, the troops of burning fire, the armies of fire, the flaming hosts, and the holy princes, adorned with crowns, clothed in kingly majesty, wrapped in glory, tied with high honor, fall on their faces three times, saying: "Blessed be the name of His glorious kingdom for ever and ever."

[Taphsarim are the troupes of flames. Erlel, more commonly referred to in the plural as

" the Erelim", are a rank of angels in Jewish Kabbala (Cabbalah) and mythology. The name is seen to mean " the valiant/courageous. " They are generally seen as the third highest rank of divine beings/angels below God. The description in the verse seems to say that letters fly off of the Torah like eagles when it is burned.]

CHAPTER 40

The ministering angels rewarded and punished.

Rabbi Ishmael said: Metatron, the Angel, the Prince of the Presence, said to me:

(1) When the ministering angels say. "Holy" before the Holy One, blessed be He, in the proper way, then the servants of His Throne, the attendants of His Glory, go out with much happiness from under the Throne of Glory.

(2) And each one carries in their hands thousands and ten thousand times ten thousand crowns of stars, similar in appearance to the planet Venus, and put them on the ministering angels and the great prince who sing the "Holy." They place three crowns on each one of them: one crown because they say "Holy", and another crown, because they say "Holy, Holy", and a third crown because they say "Holy, Holy, Holy, is the Lord of Hosts."

(3) But in the moment that they do not sing the "Holy" in the right order, a consuming fire flashes out from the little finger of the Holy One, blessed be He, and descends into the middle of their ranks, which is divided into thousand parts corresponding to the four camps of the ministering angels, and the fire burns up in a single moment those who did not say the "Holy" correctly. For it is written (Ps.92:3): "A fire goes before him and burns up his adversaries round about."

(4) After that the Holy One, blessed be He, opens His mouth and speaks one word and create other new ones like them to replace them. And each one stands before His Throne of Glory, signing the "Holy", as it written (Lam. 12:23): "They are new every morning; great is your faithfulness."

[Here we see the full extent of the phrase, "taking on the yoke of heaven. " One is rewarded for proper worship and ceremony or annihilated if God disapproves. The text indicates that all the angels in the offending group are destroyed. Angels are created, nullifying the six days of the creation of everything.]

CHAPTER 41

Letters engraved on the Throne of Glory created everything.

Rabbi Ishmael said: Metatron, the Angel, the Prince of the Presence, said to me:

(1) Come and see the letters by which the heaven and earth were created. These are the letters by which were created the mountains and hills. These are the letters by which were created the seas and rivers, these are the letters by which were created the trees and herbs, these are the letters by which were created the planets and the constellations, these are the letters by which were created the globe of the earth and the orb of the moon and the orb of the sun, as well as Orion, the Pleiades and all the different luminaries of Raqia (heaven) were created.

(2) These are the letters by which were created the Throne of Glory and the Wheels of the Merkaba (chariot), the letters by which were created the necessities of the worlds,

(3) the letters by which were created wisdom, understanding, knowledge, prudence, meekness and righteousness by which the entire world is sustained.

(4) And I walked by his side and he took me by his hand and raised me up on his wings and showed me those letters, all of them, that are engraved with a flaming iron pen on the Throne of Glory. Sparks go out from them and cover all the chambers of Araboth (the highest heaven).

[Jewish tradition has it that God and angels spoke Hebrew, and thus all things came into existence when God spoke to them into existence in Hebrew. It is a Ven short leap of logic to assume the written word would have the same power and effect. This means within the various combinations of the 22 Hebrew letters all things were created and are sustained.]

CHAPTER 42

Opposites kept in balance by several Divine Names

Rabbi Ishmael said: Metatron, the Angel, the Prince of the Presence, said to me:

(1) Come and I will show you, where the waters are suspended in the highest place, where fire is burning in the midst of hail, where lightning flashes forth from out of the middle of snowy mountains, where thunder is roaring in the heights of the skies, where a flame is burning in the burning fire, and where voices make themselves heard within (in spite of) thunder and earthquake.

The balance indicated herein reminds one of a Zen koan - uSee the sun in the midst of the rain. Scoop clear water from the heart of the fire. This chapter reveals a fundamental truth. All things are created U in heaven by His word, sustained by His word, and reflected in the lower world where we live only after being created in heaven.

(2) Then I went to his side and he took me by his hand and lifted me up on his wings and showed me all those things. I saw the waters suspended on high in Araboth (the highest heaven) of Raqia (heaven) by the power of the name YAH. EHYE ASHER EHYE (Jah, I am that I am), and their fruits (rain) was falling down from heaven and watering the face of the world, for it is written (Ps. :13): II (He waters the mountains from his chambers:) the earth is satisfied with the fruit of your work."

(3) And I saw fire and snow and hail that were mingled together within each other and yet were undamaged. This was accomplished by the power of the name ESH OKELA (consuming fire). For it is written (Deut. 55: 24): "For the Lord, your God, is a consuming fire."

(4) And I saw lightning flashing out of mountains of snow and yet the lightning was not extinguished, by the power of the name YA SUR OLAMIM (Jah, the everlasting rock). For it is written (Is. 26: 4): "For Jah, YHWH is the everlasting rock."

(5) And I saw thunder and heard voices that were roaring within flames of fire, and they were not silenced. This is accomplished by the power of the name EL-SHADDAI RABBA (the Great God Almighty) for it is written (Gen. 17:1): "1 am God Almighty."

(6) And I saw a flame glowing in the middle of burning fire, and yet it was not devoured. This was done by the power of the name YAD AL KES YAH (the hand upon the Throne of the Lord.) For it is written (Ex. 17: 16): " And he said: for the hand is upon the Throne of the Lord."

(7) And I looked and saw rivers of fire within of rivers of water and they were not extinguished. All of this was done by the power of the name OSE SHALOM (Maker of Peace) for it is written (Job 25: 2): "He makes peace in high places." For he makes peace between fire and water, and between hail and fire, and between the wind and cloud, and between earthquakes and sparks.

CHAPTER 43

The abode of the unborn spirits and of the spirits of the righteous dead

Rabbi Ishmael said: Metatron said to me:

(1) Come and I will show you where the spirits of the righteous are that have been created and those that have returned, and the spirits of the righteous that have not yet been created (born).

(2) And he lifted me up to his side, took me by his hand and sat me near the Throne of Glory by the place of the Shekina; and he revealed the Throne of glory to me, and he showed me the spirits that have been created and had returned as well as those who were flying above the Thorne of Glory in front of the Holy One, blessed be He.

(3) After that I went to interpret the following verse of Scripture and I found what is written (Isa. 57: 16: for the spirit clothed itself before me) It refers to the II spirits that

have been created in the chamber of creation of the righteous and that have returned before the Holy One, blessed be He; (and the (His) words.) "The souls I have made" refers to the spirits of the righteous that have not yet been created in the chamber (GUPH).

[Within the entire book of 3 Enoch, this chapter could be the most important to all "Children of the book, " Jews, Christians, and Moslems. The s tory of creation has God creating evenjthing in six days. Everything must also include all of the souls that are ever to be born. These souls are housed in a chamber near the throne of God, called the Guph (Guj). This chapter tells us the souls of the righteous are housed.

The righteous souls are housed in the Guph, waiting to be clothed in flesh for their incarnation. But if the righteous souls are here, where are the unrighteous souls kept? If there were another place where the unrighteous souls are kept the distinction would indicate predestination. If the character of the soul is already determined and they are stored accordingly then how is the determination made? Are we created as righteous and unrighteous beings? Does God simply look ahead and see us as we are to be?

As the next two chapters unfold, we see hints that the Guph may not be the place where all of the souls are housed but possibly it is where the souls of the righteous are conducted to be clothed in flesh and dispatched to earth through birth. The wicked soul finds his home in Sheof. If this were true it would s till indicate predestination or foreknowledge are at work.

Mystical writings, such as the Zohar, describe God as a burning flame from where sparks fly outward. These sparks are the souls of the Jewish people. When these sparks return to the primal flame, time will come to an end. Another tradition states that when the Guph is emptied time will end.

Souls leaving the Guph are born and return to God after death.]

CHAPTER 44

Metatron shows Rabbi Ishmael the abode of the wicked and the intermediate in Shea!

Rabbi Ishmael said: Metatron, the Angel, the Prince of the Presence, said to me:

(1) Come and I will show you the spirits of the wicked and the spirits of those in between (intermediate) where they are standing, and the spirits of those in between (intermediate), where they go down, and the spirits of the wicked, where they go down.

[Now we know there are three classes of souls: the righteous, the intermediate - those in between, and the unrighteous. The obvious questions are, where were the souls of the "intermediates" kept and from where were they dispatched? Are these the souls of the "lukewarm? "]

(2) And he said to me: The spirits of the wicked g o down to Sheol by the hands of two

angels of destruction: ZAAPHIEL and SIMKIEL.

(3) SIMKIEL is assigned to rule over the intermediate to support them and purify them because of the great mercy of the Prince of the Place (The Divine Majesty). ZAAPHIEL is assigned to rule over the spirits of the wicked to cast them down from the presence of the Holy One, blessed be He, and from the magnificence of the Shekina, and he casts them into Sheot to punish them in the fire of Gehenna with rods of burning coal.

(4) And I went by his side, and he took me by his hand and pointed them all out to me.

(5) And I saw the faces of children of men and the way they looked. Their bodies were like eagles. And not only that but the colour of the complexion of the intermediate was like pale grey because of their deeds. They were stained until they become cleansed from their iniquity in the fire.

[It is interesting to note this indirect reference to Purgatory in a Jewish book written between the second and fifth centuries A.D.]

(6) And the colour of the wicked was like the bottom of a pot (burned black) because of the wickedness of their deeds.

(7) And I saw the spirits of the Patriarchs Abraham, Isaac, and Jacob and the rest of the righteous, whom they have brought up out of their graves and who have ascended to Heaven. And they were praying before the Holy One, blessed be He, saying in their prayer: "Lord of the Universe! How long will you sit upon your Throne like a mourner in the days of his mourning with your right hand behind you and not deliver your children and reveal your Kingdom in the world? And how long will you have no pity upon your children who are made slaves among the nations of the world? Your right hand is behind you. Why do you not stretch out the heavens and the earth and the heavens of the highest heavens? When will you have compassion?"

[The right hand is the symbol of power and authority. To have the right hand behind your back means you are not using the power or authority available to you.]

(8) Then the Holy One, blessed be He, answered every one of them, saying: "Since these wicked commit sins on and on, and transgress with sins again and again against Me, how could I deliver my great Right Hand when it would mean their downfall would be caused by their own hands.

[The reason God does not bring judgment upon the world is because many Jews were among the unrepentant sinners. He wishes to await their return to him before judging them. This is the ultimate mercy.]

(9) In that moment Metatron called me and spoke to me: "My servant! Take the books and read their evil deeds!" Then I took the books and read their deeds and there were transgressions to be found written down regarding each wicked one and besides that they have transgressed all the letters in Torah, for it is written (Dan. 55: 11): "Yea, all Israel have transgressed your Law." It is not written, "for they have transgressed from Aleph to Taw (A to Z) 36 (40) statutes have they transgressed for each letter?

[Some sources have "40 statues." The number " 40" is the number of severe trials and testing. The implication of the verse is that the souls have broken 40 major laws and many minor ones.]

(10) Then Abraham, Isaac and Jacob wept. Then the Holy One, blessed be He said to them: " Abraham, my beloved, Isaac, my Elect one, Jacob, my firstborn, how can I deliver them from among the nations of the world at this time?" And immediately MIKAEL (Michael), the Prince of Israel, cried and wept with a loud voice and said (Ps. 10:1): "Why stand you afar off, Lord?"

CHAPTER 45

Past and future events recorded on the Curtain of the Throne.

Rabbi Ishmael said: Metatron said to me:

(1) Come, and I will show you the Curtain of The Divine Majesty, which is spread before the Holy One, blessed be He. On it are written all the generations of the world and all their deeds (actions/ doings), both what they have done and what they will do until the end of all generations.

(2) And I came, and he showed it to me pointing it out with his fingers like a father who teaches his children the letters of Torah. And I saw each generation and within the generations I saw the rulers, the leaders, the shepherds, the oppressors (despots), the keepers, the punisher, the counsellors, the teachers, the supporters, the bosses, the presidents of academies, the magistrates, the princes, the advisors, the noblemen, and the warriors, the elders, and the guides of each generation.

[In the ancient world, these represent all major groups that have influence over the lives of people.]

(3) And I saw Adam, his generation, their deeds (actions/ doings) and their thoughts, Noah and his generation, their deeds and their thoughts, and the generation of the flood, their deeds and their thoughts, Shem and his generation, their deeds and their thoughts, Nimrod and the generation of the confusion of tongues, and his generation, their deeds and their thoughts, Abraham and his generation, their deeds and their thoughts, Isaac and his generation, their deeds and their thoughts, Ishmael and his generation, their deeds and their thoughts, Jacob and his generation, their deeds and their thoughts, Joseph and his generation , their deeds and their thoughts, the tribes and their generation, their deeds and their thoughts, Amram and his generation, their deeds and their thoughts , Moses and his generation, their deeds and their thoughts,

(4) Aaron and Mirjam their accomplishments and actions, the princes and the elders, their works and deeds, Joshua and his generation, their works and deeds, the judges and their generation, their works and deeds, Eli and his generation, their works and deeds, Phinehas, their works and deeds, Elkanah and his generation, their accomplishments and actions, Samuel and his generation, their works and deeds, the kings of Judah with their generations, their works and their doing, the kings of Israel and their generation,

their accomplishments and actions, the princes of Israel, their accomplishments and actions; the princes of the nations of the world, their accomplishments and actions, the heads of the councils of Israel, their accomplishments and actions; the heads of the councils in the nations of the world, their generations, their accomplishments and actions; the rulers of Israel and their generation, their accomplishments and actions; the noblemen of Israel and their generation, their works and their deeds; the noblemen of the nations of the world and their generations, their accomplishments and actions; the men of reputation in Israel, their generation, their accomplishments and actions; the judges of Israel, their generation, their accomplishments and actions; the judges of the nations of the world and their generation, their accomplishments and actions; the teachers of children in Israel, their generations, their accomplishments and actions: the teachers of children in the nations of the world, their generation, their accomplishments and actions; the interpreters) of Israel, their generation, their accomplishments and actions; the interpreters of the nations of the world, their generation, their accomplishments and actions;

(5) and all the fights and wars that the nations of the world worked against the people of Israel in the time of their kingdom. And I saw Messiah, the son of Joseph, and his generation and their accomplishments and actions that they will do against the nations of the world. And I saw Messiah, the son of David, and his generation, and all the fights and wars, and their accomplishments and actions that they will do with Israel both for good and evil. And I saw all the fights and wars that Gog and Magog will fight with Israel in the days of Messiah, and all that the Holy One, blessed be He, will do with them in the time to come.

[This is the first mention of two Messiahs. However, the dual functions of the Messiah can be seen as the impetus to this idea. The Messiah is seen as a peacemaker and teacher, who brings mercy. The Messiah is also seen as a warrior, destroyer, and bringer of justice.

One comes in peace and the other is determined to do war to avenge God and Israel. It appears the Messiah, son of David, is truculent compared to the son of Joseph, who will be killed for his attempt to make peace. Christians believe the same Messiah will perform both functions because he came as peacemaker and teacher but will return from heaven as the warrior of God. The text here indicates there will be two separate Messiahs.]

(6) And all the rest of all the leaders of the generations and all the works of the generations both in Israel and in the nations of the world, both what is done and what will be done hereafter to all generations until the end of time all were written on the Curtain of The Divine Majesty. And I saw all these things with my eyes; and after I had seen it, I opened my mouth in praise of The Divine Majesty saying, (Ecd. 8:4, 5): "For the King's word has power and who may say unto Him, what do you do? Whoever keeps the commandments shall know no evil thing." And I said: (Ps.: 24) "0 Lord how manifold (multi-coloured/ multifaceted) are your works!"

[Rabbi Ishmael was shown all the deeds and works of mankind for all generations. This implies predestination or foreknowledge. The reader must decide for himself or herself.]

CHAPTER 46

The place of the stars shown to Rabbi Ishmael

Rabbi Ishmael said: Metatron said to me:

(1) Come and I will show you the distance between the stars that are standing in the Raqia (heaven), for they stand there night after night in fear of the Almighty and The Divine Majesty. I will show you where they go and where they stand.

(2) I walked by his side, and he took me by his hand and pointed out all of them to me with his finger. And they were standing on sparks of flames around the Merkaba (chariot) of the Almighty, The Divine Majesty. What did Metatron do? At that moment he clapped his hands and chased them off from their place. Then they flew off on flaming wings, rose and fled from the four sides of the Throne of Merkaba (chariot), and as they flew, he told me the names of ever single one. As it is written,

(Ps. :4) "He tells the number of the stars; he gives them all their names", teaching, that the Holy One, blessed be He, has given a name to each one of them.

(3) And by the authority of RAHATIEL they enter in a numbered order to Raqia (heaven) ha-shamayim (the second of the seven heavens) to serve the world. And they go out in numbered order to praise the Holy One, blessed be He, with songs and hymns, for it is written (Ps. 19: 1): "The heavens declare the glory of God."

(4) But in the age to come the Holy One, blessed be He, will create them anew. For it is written (Lam. 52: 23): "They are new every morning." And they open their mouth and sing a song. Which is the song that they sing? "When I consider your heavens."

[Rahatiel is the angelic ruler of the stars and constellations. The Ophannim is the class of angels that move the celestial sphere. Stars 'Were considered by many cultures to be spiritual entities, or angels. This was a Babylonian concept that was absorbed. It is in this light that the stars would sing. They leave the second heaven and proceed through the heavens to the seventh heaven where they end their journey at the throne.]

CHAPTER 47

Metatron shows Rabbi Ishmael the spirits of punished angels.

Rabbi Ishmael said: Metatron said to me:

(1) Come and I will show you the souls of the angels and the spirits of the servants that served, whose bodies have been burned up in the fire of The Divine Majesty of the Almighty, that projects from his little finger. And they have been made into burning and glowing coals in the midst of the river of fire (Nehar di-Nur). But their spirits and their souls are standing behind the Shekina.

(2) Whenever the angel servants sing a song at a wrong time or they sing what was not appointed to be sung they are burned and consumed by the fire of their Creator and by a flame from their Maker from the rooms of the whirlwind. The fire blows on them and drives them into the river of fire (Nehar di-Nur). There they become mountains of burning coal. But their spirit and their soul return to their Creator, and all are standing behind their Master.

(3) And I went by his side and he took me by his hand, and he showed me all the souls of the angels and the spirits of the attending servants who were standing behind the Shekina and were standing on the wings of a whirlwind with walls of fire all around them.

(4) At that moment Metatron opened the gates of the walls within which they were standing behind the Shekina for me to see. And I raised my eyes and I saw them. I saw what of every one of the angels looked like and I saw their wings were like birds made out of flames. And it looked as if they were fashioned from burning fire. In that moment I opened my mouth in praise of The Divine Majesty and said (Ps. 92: 5): "How great are your works, 0 Lord."

[The river of fire or Nehar di-Nur is presented here as a place of resurrection of the angels since their bodies were burnt but the spirit continues and ends up again with God. However, this idea is contradicted in most Jewish mystic writings. It is possible the text here is somehow corrupted or misunderstood.]

CHAPTER 48 A

Rabbi Ishmael sees the Right Hand of the Most High

Rabbi Ishmael said: Metatron said to me:

(1) Come, and I will show you the Right Hand of The Divine Majesty, which He keeps behind Him because of the destruction of the Holy Temple; from which all kinds of splendor and light shine forth and by which the heavens were created; and whom not even the Seraphim and the Ophannim are permitted to experience until the day that salvation shall arrive.

[God became inactive because of the destruction of the temple between March and September of 70 A.D. and onward. Why God would choose the sacking of his temple to mark his quiescence might be understood by looking at the reason given for the destruction. If the Jewish people believed themselves to be the only chosen people of God, then God must be their protector. To have a heathen army come in and defeat them so soundly, looting and destroying the temple of the God that was supposed to protect them brought into question their position in the divine scheme. Since the fault could not be with God, it must have been with his people. The Jewish nation must have failed God by falling away from Him or sinning badly enough to cause God to turn them over to their enemy. Since this would be a great and grievous sin, God has chosen not to become active since that would mean having to judge His apostate people. He awaits his people to return to Him in a righteous state.]

(2) and I went by his side, and he took me by his hand and showed me the Right Hand of The Divine Majesty, with all types of praises, joyous singing. No mouth can articulate its worth, and no eye can look at it because of its greatness, and dignity and its majesty, and splendid beauty.

(3) Not only that, but all the souls of the righteous who are counted worthy to see the joy of Jerusalem are standing by it, praising and praying before it three times every day, saying (Is. 51: 9): II Awake, awake, put on strength, 0 arm of the Lord" according for it is written (Is. 63: 12): "He caused his glorious arm to go at the right hand of Moses."

(4) In that moment the Right Hand of The Divine Majesty was weeping. And there flew out from its five fingers, five rivers of tears and fell they flowed down into the great sea, and it shook the entire world. For it is written (Is. 24: 19,20): "The earth is utterly broken, the earth is totally dissolved, the earth is moved greatly, the earth shall stagger like a drunken man and shall be moved back and forth like a hut, five times corresponding to the fingers of His Great Right Hand."

(5) But when the Holy One, blessed be He, saw that there is not a righteous man in that generation, and no pious man on the entire earth, and no men doing justice, and that there is no one like Moses, and no intercessor like Samuel who could pray before The Divine Majesty for the salvation and deliverance of His Kingdom, His great Right Hand was revealed in the entire world that that He put it out from Himself again to work great salvation by it for Israel,

(6) then the Holy One, blessed be He, will remember His own justice, favor, mercy and grace, and He will deliver His great Arm by himself, and His righteousness will support Him. For it is written (Is. 59: 16): "And he saw, that there was no man" that is like Moses who prayed countless times for Israel in the desert and averted the Divine decrees from them and he wondered why there was no intercessor" - like Samuel who entreated the Holy One, blessed be He, and called unto Him and He answered him and fulfilled his desire, even if it did not fit into 4 12 the Divine plan. For it is written (I Sam. 12: 17): "Is it not wheat-harvest today? I will call unto the Lord."

(7) And not only that, but He joined fellowship with Moses in every place, for it is written (Ps. 99: 6): "Moses and Aaron among His priests." And again it is written, (Jer. 15: 1) "Though Moses and Samuel stood before Me" (Is. 63: 5): "Mine own arm brought salvation unto Me."

(8) The Holy One, blessed be He said at that time, "How long do I have to wait for the children of men to obtain salvation according to their righteousness for My power and authority? For My own sake and for the sake of My worthiness and righteousness will I deliver My power and authority and by it I will redeem my children from among the nations of the world. For it is written (Is. 48: 11): "For My own sake will I do it. For how My name should be profaned."

[At this point, God has waited as long as he wished for Israel to come back to Him in righteousness by their own power. He has decided to take them back from the heathen nations.]

(9) In that moment the Holy One, blessed be He, will reveal His Great Power and Authority (Arm) and show it to the nations of the world. Its length is the length of the entire world, and its width is the width of the world. And its splendour looks like the splendour of the sunshine in its power in the summer solstice.

(10) Then Israel will be saved from among the nations of the world. And Messiah will appear unto them, and He will bring them up to Jerusalem with great joy. And not only that but they will eat and drink for they will glorify the Kingdom of Messiah, of the house of David, in the four corners of the world.

[This is the time, not for the Messiah of the house of Joseph, but for the Messiah of the house of David. This is the time of war and leadership of the nation in a physical sense.]

And the nations of the world will not prevail against them, for it is written (Is. 52: 10): "The Lord has made bare His holy arm in the eyes of all the nations; and all the ends of the earth shall see the salvation of our God." And again (Deut. 32: 12): "The Lord alone did lead him, and there was no strange god with him." (Zech. 14: 9): "And the Lord shall be king over all the earth."

["Heaven" is the number using Gematria. The meaning seems to be that of all heavens and all worlds.]

CHAPTER 48 - B

The Divine Names that go forth from the Throne of Glory and pass through the heavens and back again to the Throne.

[Many of the names are not decipherable. Attempting to place the letters into any kind of Latinized form or alphabet made the meanings even more obscure. For this reason, the names that could be interpreted with any certainty were listed. Those that yielded only meaningless letters were marked with only a dash.]

These are the seventy-two names written on the heart of the Holy One, Blessed be He: Righteousness, -, Righteous (one) -, Lord of Host, God Almighty, God, YHWH - - - Living (one)

Riding upon the Araboth (highest heaven), - Life Giver - King of Kings, Holy One - - Holy, Holy, Holy, - - - Blessed be the Name of His glorious kingdom for ever and ever, - - Complete, King of the Universe, - - The beginning of Wisdom for the children of men, - -. Blessed be He who gives strength to the weary and increases strength to them that have no might, (Is.40:29) that go forth adorned with many flaming crowns with many flames, with innumerable crowns of chashmal (celestial substance), with many, many crowns of lightning from before the Throne of Glory. And with them there are hundreds of hundreds of powerful angels who escort them like a king with trembling and dread, with amazement and shivering, with honor and majesty and fear, terror, greatness and dignity, and with glory and power, with wisdom and knowledge and with a pillar of fire and flame and lightning - and their light is as lightning flashesof light - and with the likeness of the chashmal (the substance of heaven).

(2) And they give glory to them, and they answer and cry before them, " Holy, Holy, Holy." And they lead them in a single line through every heaven as powerful and honourable princes. And when they bring them all back to the place of the Throne of Glory, then all the Chayoth by the Merkaba (chariot) open their mouth in praise of His glorious name, saying: "Blessed be the name of His glorious kingdom for ever and ever."

CHAPTER 48 C

An Enoch-Metatron piece.

(1)"1 seized him, and 1 took him and 1 appointed him" - that is Enoch, the son of Jared, whose name is Metatron

(2) and 1 took him from among the children of men

(5) and made him a Throne over near and beside My Throne. What is the size of that Throne? Seventy thousand parasangs all of fire.

(9) committed to him 70 angels symbolizing the nations of the 4 16 world and I gave into his authority all the household above and below.

(7) And I imparted to him Wisdom and Intelligence more than all the angels. And I called his name the LESSER II YAH", whose name is by Gematria 71.

[To refresh memory, Gematria was the ancient art of numerology.

Each letter is given a number, usually determined by where it occurs in the alphabet. Numbers go from one to nine, then from ten to ninety, and, if there were enough letters, from one hundred to nine hundred. However, there are only 22 letters. Numbers are then summed. When the numbers are added they total seventy-one.]

And I arranged all the works of creation for him. And I made him more powerful than all the ministering angels.

(3) He gave Metatron - that is Enoch, the son of Jared - the authority over all the storehouses and treasuries and appointed him over all the stores (reserves) in every heaven. And I assigned the keys of each store into him.

(4) I made him the prince over all the princes and a minister of the Throne of Glory and the Halls of Araboth (the highest heaven). I appointed him over the Holy Chayoth for him to open their doors of the Throne of Glory to me, to exalt and arrange it, and I gave

to him wreathe crowns to place upon their heads. I sent him to the majestic Ophannim, to crown them with strength and glory. I sent him to the honored Cherubim, to clothe them in majesty covered with radiant sparks, to make them to shine with splendor and bright light over the flaming Seraphim, to cover them with highness. I sent him to the Chashmallim of light, to make them radiant with light and to prepare the seat for me every morning as I sit upon the Throne of Glory. I have given him the secrets above and below, which are the heavenly secrets and earthly secrets so that he can praise and magnify my glory in the height of my power).

(5) I made him higher than all. The height of his stature stood out in the midst of all who are of high of stature. I made seventy thousand parasangs. I made his Throne great by the majesty of my Throne. And I increased its glory by the honor of My glory.

(6) I transformed his flesh into torches of fire, and all the bones of his body into burning coals; and I made his eyes look like lightning, and the light of his eyebrows as a light that will never be quenched. I made his face as bright as the splendor of the sun, and his eyes like the splendor of the Throne of Glory.

[The description of Metatron is that of an angel and specifically a Seraphim, who is a fiery creature. A wreathe means victory.]

(7) I made his clothing honor and majesty, beauty and highness. I covered him with a cloak and a crown of a size of 4 18 by parasangs and this was his diadem. And I put My honor, my majesty and the splendor of My glory that is on My Throne of Glory upon him. I called him the "LESSER YHWH," the Prince of the Presence, the Knower of Secrets: I revealed every secret to him as a father and as a friend, and all mysteries I spoke to him in truth.

(8) I set up his throne at the door of My Hall that he may sit and judge the heavenly household on high. and I made every prince subject to him, so that they will receive his authority and perform his will.

(9) I took Seventy names from my names and called him by them to enhance his glory. I placed Seventy princes into his hand so that he can command them to do my laws and obey my words in every language. And the proud will be brought to the ground by his word, and by the speech of his mouth he will exalt the humble to high places. He is to strike kings by his speech, to turn kings away from their own plans, and he is to set up the rulers over their dominion for it is written (Dan. 51: 21): and he changes the times and the seasons, "and to give wisdom unto all the wise of the world and understanding and knowledge to all who understand (Dan. 51: 21): "and knowledge to them that know understanding." He is to reveal to them the secrets of my words and to teach them the command of my judgment in righteousness.

[God is the God of the universe. He is the God of all. His names are infinite. Names reveal power, authority, personality traits, and character. Metatron is given authority over the nations. There are 70 nations and Metatron has 70 names.]

(10) It is written

(Is. 55: 11): "so shall My word be that goes forth out of my mouth; it shall not return unto me void but shall accomplish that which I please." I shall accomplish that which is not written here, but " he shall accomplish. Every word and every speech that goes out from the Holy One, blessed be He, Metatron stands and carries out. And he establishes the orders of the Holy One, blessed be He.

(11) "And he shall make to prosper that which I sent." I will make to prosper what is not written here but he shall make to prosper teaching, that whatever decree proceeds from the Holy One, blessed be He, concerning a man, as soon as he makes repentance, they do not execute it upon him but they execute it upon another wicked man, for it is written (Prov. 9:8): "The righteous is delivered out of trouble, and the wicked comes in his place."

[If a man repents and is no longer wicked, the angels inflict his punishment on a person who is still wicked and has not repented.]

(12) And not only that but Metatron sits three hours every day in the high heavens, and he gathers all the souls of those dead who died in their mother's womb, and the nursing baby who died on their mother's breast, and of the scholars who died over the five books of the Law. And he brings them under the Throne of Glory and places them in companies, divisions and classes round the Presence, and there he teaches them the Law, and the books of Wisdom, and Haggada and Tradition and completes their education for them. It is written (Is. 28: 9)

"Whom will he teach knowledge? And whom will he make to understand tradition? Them that are weaned from the milk and draw from the breast."

[Ancient Jews viewed learning as one way to approach God. To study the Torah is almost as good as worship and prayer. Unborn, suckling's, those who die while studying the Torah are guiltless.]

CHAPTER 48 D

The names of Metatron. The treasuries of Wisdom opened to Moses on mount Sinai. The angels protest against Metatron for revealing the secrets to Moses and are answered and rebuked by God. The chain of tradition and the power of the transmitted mysteries to heal diseases

[The names fall into three major categories, those which are built upon the name "EI, " those that are based on the name "Metatron, " and those based on the name "Yah. " The reader will notice the letters EL, ON, and YAH or YA in the names. Although the text states there are 70 names, there are in fact 1 05 names listed. The Latinized version of the work is referenced in this list however the parsing and pronunciations are unique to this work in order to accent the holy names found within most of the name.]

(l)Seventy names has Metatron which the Holy One, blessed be He, took from His own name and put upon him. And these they are: 1 Yeho-EL Yah, 2 Yeho-EL, 3 Yofi-EL and 4 Yophphi EL, and 5 Hafifi-EL and 6 Margezi-EL, 7 Gippyu-EL, 8 Pahazi

EL, 9 Hahah, 10 Pepri-EL, 11 Tatri-EL, 12 Tabki-EL, 13 Haw, 14 YHWH, 15 Dah 16, WHYH, 17 Hebed, 18 DiburiEL, 19 Hafhapi-EL, 20 Spi-EL, 21 Paspasi-EL, 22 Senetron, 23 Metatron, 24 Sogdin, 25 HadriGon, 26 Asum, 27 Sakhpam, 28 Sakhtam, 29 Mig-on, 30 Mitt-on, 31 Mot-tron, 32 Rosfim, 33 Khinoth, 34 KhataTiah, 35 Degaz-Yah, 36 Pisf-YaH, 37 Habiskin-Yah, 38 Mixar, 39 Barad, 40 Mikirk, 41 Mispird, 42 Khishig, 43 Khishib, 44 Minret, 45 Bisyrym, 46 Mitmon, 47 Titmon 48 Piskhon, 49 SafsafYah, 50 Zirkhi, 51 ZirkhYah 52 'B', 53 Be-Yah, 54 HiBhbe-Yah, 55 Pelet, 56 Pit-Yah, 57 Rabrab-YaH, 58 Khas, 59 Khas-Yah, 60 Tafaf-Yah, 61 Tamtam-Yah, 62 SehasYah, 63 Hirhur-Yah, 64 Halhal-Yah, 65 Bazrld-Yah, 66 Satsatk Yah, 67 Sasd-Yah, 68 Razraz-Yah, 69 BaZzraz-Yah, 70 Harim Yah, 71 Sibh-Yah, 72 Sibibkh-Yah, 73 Simkam, 74 Yah-Se-Yah, 75 Sibib-Yah, 76 Sabkasbe-Yah, 77 khelil-khil-Yah, 78 Kih, 79 HHYH, 80 WH, 81 WHYH, (letters in the holy YHWH) 82 Zakik-Yah, 83 Turtis-Yah, 84 Sur-Yah, 85 Zeh, 86 Penir-Yah, 87 ZihZih, 88 Galraza-Yah, 89 Mamlik-Yah, 90 Hitt-Yah, 91 Hemekh, 92 Kham-Yah, 93 Mekaper-Yah, 94 Perish-Yah, 95 Sefam, 96 Gibir, 97 Gibor-Yah, 98 Gor, 99 Gor-Yah, Ziw, Hokbar, the LESSER YHWH, after the name of his Master, (Ex. 23: 21) "for My name is in him" , Rabibi-EL, TUMIEL, Segansakkiel, the Prince of Wisdom.

(2) And why is he called by the name Sagnesakiel? Because all the storehouses of wisdom are committed into his hand.

(3) And all of them were opened to Moses on Sinai, so that he learned them during the forty days, while he remained. He learned the Torah in the seventy ways it applies to the seventy nations, and the Prophets and the seventy application of the seventy tongues, the writings in the seventy variations of the seventy tongues, the Halakas (Jewish law and ritual) in the seventy applications of the seventy nations, the Traditions in the seventy aspects of the seventy nations, the Haggadas (Passover Seder) in the seventy aspects of the seventy tongues and the Toseftas (Secondary compilation of Jewish oral laws) in the seventy aspects of the seventy tongues.

(4) But as soon as the forty days were completed, he forgot all of them in one moment. Then the Holy One, blessed be He, called Yephiphyah, the Prince of the Law, and (through him) they were given to Moses as a gift, for it is written (Deut. 10:4): "and the Lord gave them to me." And after that it remained with him. And how do we know that it remained in his memory? Because it is written (Mal. 55: 4): "Remember the Law of Moses my servant which I commanded unto him in Horeb for all Israel, even my statues and judgments." 'The Law of Moses': that is the Torah, the Prophets and the Writings, 'statues': that is the Halakas and Traditions, 'judgments'; that is the Haggadas and the Toseftas. And all of them were given to Moses on high on Sinai.

(5) These seventy names are a reflection of the Explicit names and given to the name of Metatron: seventy Names of His by which the ministering angels call the King of the kings of kings, blessed be He, in the high heavens, and twenty-two letters (of the Hebrew alphabet) that are on the ring placed on his finger with which are sealed the destinies of the high, powerful and great princes of kingdoms and with which are sealed along with the future of the Angel of Death, and the destinies of every nation and tongue.

(6) Metatron, the Angel, the Prince of the Presence said; the Angel who is the Prince

of the Wisdom and the Angel who the Prince of the Understanding, and the Angel who the Prince of the Kings, and the Angel who the Prince of the Rulers, and the angel who is the Prince of the Glory, and the angel who is the Prince of the high ones and of the princes, all of which are the exalted, greatly honored ones in heaven and on earth:

(7) "YHWH, the God of Israel, is my witness that I revealed this secret to Moses and when I did all the host all the high heavens were enraged against me.

(8) They asked me, saying, "Why do you reveal this secret to a son of man, born of woman, who is tainted and unclean, a man of the putrefying drop? You gave him the secret by which heaven and earth, sea and land, mountains and hills, rivers and springs, Gehenna of fire and hail, the Garden of Eden and the Tree of Life were all created and by which Adam and Eve, and the cattle, and the wild beasts, the birds of the air, and the fish of the sea, and Behemoth and Leviathan, and the crawling things, the snakes, the dragons of the sea, and the creeping things of the deserts; and Torah and Wisdom and Knowledge and Thought and the imparted knowledge and the Gnosis of things above and of heaven and the fear of heaven were all created. Why did you reveal this to flesh and blood? I answered them: Because the Holy One, blessed be He, has given me authority. And furthermore, I have obtained permission from the high and exalted throne, from which all the Explicit names go forth with lightning and fire and flaming chashrnallim.

[Verse 7 makes a statement that when the complete gnosis or revealed knowledge was given to Moses (through Metatron) all the heavenly host was enraged at the act. This Knowledge was not even available to all the host of heaven but was given to a human. Verse 8 asks the question in a direct and insulting way. To slightly paraphrase, it asked, "Why did You give the secrets of creation to this human who was conceived by a woman, through the transfer of semen, which spoils and putrefies and then gives birth, when blood from birth and menses is considered unclean, as is the woman herself for a time after ritual cleansing. Considering this, all the heavenly hosts consider humans to be inferior, unclean, animals. Still, God chose to transmit to Moses the secret gnosis of creation.

Behemoth is the primal unconquerable monster of the land. Leviathan is the primal monster of the waters of the sea. Ziz is their counterpart in the sky. There is a legend that the Leviathan and tire Behemoth shall hold a battle at the end of the world. The two will finally kill each other, and the surviving men will feast on their meat. Behemoth also appears in the 1 Enoch, giving a description of this monster' s origins there mentioned as being male, as opposed to the female Leviathan.]

(9) But they (the hosts) were not appeased or satisfied, until the Holy One, blessed be He, scorned them and drove them away from Him with contempt and said to them: "I delight in him, and have set my love on him, and have entrusted to him and given unto Metatron, my Servant, and I have given to him alone, for he is Unique among all the children of heaven.

(10) And Metatron brought them out from his house and storehouses and gave these secrets to Moses, and Moses gave them to Joshua, and Joshua gave them to the elders, and the elders to give them the prophets and the men of the Great Synagogue, and

the men of the Great Synagogue gave them to Ezra and Ezra the Scribe gave them to Hillel the elder, and Hillel the elder gave them to Rabbi Abbahu and Rabbi Abbahu to Rabbi Zera, and Rabbi Zera to the men of faith, and the men of faith gave them to give warning and to heal by them all disease that ravaged the world, for it is written (Ex. 15: 26): " If you will diligently hearken to the voice of the Lord, your God, and will do that which is right in His eyes, and will give ear to His commandments, and keep all his statues, I will put none of the disease upon you, which I have put on the Egyptians, for I am the Lord that heals you."

(Ended and finished. Praise be unto the Creator of the World) Hillel was said to be one of the greatest and wisest Rabbis.

The Complete Gnostic Gospels Collection: The Gospels of Philip, Judas, Mary, Truth, and others

Micah Williams

CONTENTS

THE GOSPEL OF PHILIP

An early Greek, Valentinian collection of Jesus's sayings to his disciples. Many refer to the profound sacramental mysteries of Baptism, Anointment, the Eucharist and the Bridal Chamber.

A slave yearns to be free but he doesn't

hope to inherit his Master's house.

A boy isn't only a son, but in time

will lay claim to his father's estate.

Those who crave to be heirs of

the dead are already spiritually dead

and will inherit death.

Those who seek to be heirs of

the living are spiritually alive

and will inherit what is both

alive and dead.

The dead inherit nothing,

yet if they inherit what is living,

they'll gain Eternal Life.

A true Christian never dies

for he has not lived in vain,

to inherit spiritual death.

He who has great faith in Truth

has found the Real Life; this man

dares dying to his own Self,

to be truly alive.

Since Lord Jesus Christ came

the world has been recreated,

cities established, the dead buried.

When we were Jews we were fatherless
and had only an earthly mother.
Now, as Christians, we enjoy both
the heavenly Father and the divine Mother.
Those who sow in the hard winter
reap in glorious summer.
This world is a harsh winter;
summer is the eternal realm.
Let us sow now, in this wintry world,
so we may harvest in the splendid summer.
It is unworthy to pray
for boons in this winter.
Wait, for the summer
that will follow.
If a fool harvests in winter
he'll tear out the good he has
and be like a barren Sabbath;
Christ came to hold some in debt
and to release others from usury.
Those who were exiled,
he ransomed and made his own,
to set them apart; he pledged
them according to his Will.
When he came, he willingly
sacrificed his life, for it had
already been determined,
before this world was created.
He came first to redeem

it as it had been pledged.
It had fallen into the hands of
devilish demons and was imprisoned;
but he came to save both the
wicked and the good.
Light and darkness, life and death,
right and left, are inseparable twins.
For the good are not wholly good
nor the wicked wholly wicked,
nor is life merely life,
nor death merely death;
each will return to its primal source.
But those who transcend these
apparent opposites are eternal;
worldly names are full of deceit
and delude our minds.
They muddy the distinction
between right and wrong
with words like father, spirit, son,
life, light, resurrection and church.
In the eternal world there
are no such deceptions.
One Name is never uttered,
the Name the Father gave His Son.
For the Son couldn't have become
the Father unless he knew His Name.
Those who know this
Name never speak it.

Truth brought names into
being for our sake.
The dark powers wanted to
deceive man, to confuse his
relationship with the truly good.
They took good names and gave
them to the bad, so that with these
names they might bind them.
But through grace they remove them
from the bad and restore them to the good;
these dark forces wished to steal man's
freedom and enslave him.
These powers obstruct man's
salvation, for if man is saved,
animal sacrifice would end.
Before Christ there was no manna.
Just as Eden had many fields to feed
flocks but no wheat to feed Man.
Man used to munch like the beasts,
but Christ, the perfect Man,
brought manna from heaven so
Mankind could be fed by the spirit.
The dark powers imagine
it is by their own self will
that they do what they do;
yet the Holy Spirit secretly does
all through them, as it wills.
Truth which lives since the

beginning is sown everywhere;
many see the sowing,
few know the reaping.
Some claim that Mary's
conception was immaculate.
They're mistaken; women cannot
conceive from the Holy Spirit,
which is feminine.
It means that Mary wasn't
defiled by dark powers,
which defile themselves.
Jesus said to his disciples,
"Bring gifts to your Father's house;
don't steal from there."
Jesus is our Lord's secret name,
Christ is his revealed name.
In Syriac it is Messiah.
The Nazarene is he
who reveals the hidden.
Those who claim our Lord
first died then ascended, are wrong!
He ascended, then died.
No one hides a precious jewel
in a large container, but often
we have thrown many things into
a small worthless box.
The soul is precious, but not its flesh;
some fear they'll rise up naked

and wish to ascend fully robed,
but they don't see that those clothed
only by flesh are naked and ashamed.
In Corinthians it states:
"Flesh and blood shall
not inherit the Kingdom."
What cannot inherit is the body alone;
what will inherit is that which belongs
to Jesus and his holy communion.
In John's Gospel, Jesus says,
"He who will not eat my flesh
and drink my blood has
no life in him."
His flesh is the Word,
his blood is the Holy Spirit.
He who receives these
has real food, drink and clothes.
It is necessary to ascend
through the Word of God,
for All is contained in that.
In this world those with clothes
are better than those in rags;
in the Kingdom of Heaven
God's robes are superior
to the souls that wear them.
It is through fire and water
that the world is purified:
the visible by the invisible,

the open by the hidden.
Much is hidden in the visible:
water in flowers, fire in
baptismal oil and balsam.
Jesus won them by cunning
for he did not appear as he really was,
but in a form that they could see.
To the great he seemed great,
to the little he was little,
to the angels he was an angel,
to men he was a man.
So his Word was hidden from all;
some indeed saw him and imagined
they were seeing themselves.
When he came to his disciples
in splendid glory on the Mount
of Olives he wasn't small;
he became great and made his
disciples great so they could
see him in his greatness.
On that day he said in gratitude,
"You who have united perfect light
with holy spirit, unite us with the
angels as well.
Don't scorn the Lamb; without him
it's impossible to know the King.
No one may visit the King without
robes of light.

The Heavenly Man has many
more sons than the earthly;
Adam's sons soon die,
but the sons of the Perfect Man
don't die, and are ever reborn.
The Father creates a son,
but the son hasn't the power
to create another.
He who has been reborn is
unable to bestow regeneration,
so the son wins brothers but not sons.
All men and women in this world
are born naturally, but those reborn
in God are nurtured by heaven.
It is by the divine kiss of grace
that the Perfect are reborn;
we also embrace each other to aid
conception by one another's grace."
Three walked with Christ:
Mary, his mother;
her sister, also Mary;
and Mary Magdalene.
All three were called Mary.
Father and son are single names,
omnipresent, above and below;
in the concealed and the revealed
the Holy Spirit is dual:
it is in the revealed below and

in the concealed above.
Some holy men are
served by sinister powers,
deceived by a spirit into the belief
that they're serving an ordinary man.
A disciple asked Jesus for something
from this world. He answered,
"Ask your mother. She'll bring you
things which belong to another."
The apostles said to the disciples,
"May our sacrifices contain salt!"
They called Sophia, the
Divine Wisdom, "salt".
Without "the savour of salt",
no sacrifice will be acceptable.
Sophia is childless, so she is
termed a "grain of salt".
Wherever they manifest in their
own path, the Holy Spirit and her
offspring will be fecund.
What the Father owns,
He gives to the son when
he arrives at manhood.
Those who've fallen away
yet are reborn by the spirit
may drift because of the spirit.
So by the same exhalation,
fire blazes and is extinguished.

Echamoth means wisdom of death;
one who knows death is termed
"the lesser wisdom".
There are tame beasts like cattle,
mules, dogs and sheep, but wild beasts
live mainly in the desert.
Man ploughs his field with
the aid of the ox, and from
tame beasts he's fed.
The Perfect Man ploughs
through his subdued powers,
preparing for all to come into Being.
Thus the world is established
through good and evil, right and left.
The Holy Spirit shepherds
us and rules all powers:
tame, wild and unique.
He hedges us in so we cannot stray.
Adam was created to be beautiful,
but Cain was not worthy.
Adultery followed murder;
he was the snake's child.
God is a Master Dyer,
His good and true dyes
dissolve with the robes they dye.
His dyes are immortal
by means of His colours;
first, He dips with water.

It's impossible to see what exists,
unless one becomes similar.
But the worldly man sees
the sun without being a sun;
the same with heaven and earth.
If you know the Spirit
you become the Spirit;
if you know Christ
you become Christ-like;
if you know the Father
you become as the Father.
The worldly see the All but
fail to know their own Self;
through Truth you learn
to know your Self;
what you know you become.
Faith accepts, love bestows.
None can receive without great faith.
No one can truly give without love;
he doesn't seek gain from what he gives.
He who has received something
other than our Lord remains a Jew.
The apostles prior to
ourselves had names for him.
Jesus was first the Nazarean,
then Christ, and then the Messiah.
Messiah means both Christ
and "the measured";

Jesus means “redemption”,
Nazarene “the truthful”.
Both the Nazarene and Jesus
have been justly measured.
If a pearl falls into mud
it becomes dirty and spoiled,
but if it is washed in balsam oil
it becomes precious;
yet it is always valued
in the sight of its owner.
The Sons of God,
wherever they may be,
are also valued by their Father.
If you say “I’m a Jew,”
no one’s impressed;
if you say “I’m a Roman,”
no one’s depressed.
If you say you’re a Greek,
a barbarian, a slave or a freeman,
no one’s worried.
But if you say “I’m a Christian,”
people will quake with fear.
Would I were like that person
whose name they cannot bear to hear.
God consumes man,
egos are sacrificed before Him;
animals were sacrificed
to those who weren’t God.

Glass goblets and pottery jugs
are both formed by fire;
if glass breaks it can be re-moulded,
but clay vessels are shattered,
for they came into being without breath.
A mule that turned a mill stone
walked a hundred leagues,
but when released it was still
on the same spot!
There are folk who make
pilgrimages without progress.
When dusk falls they see
neither city nor town,
man-made monuments
nor sights of nature,
powers nor angels;
fools suffer in vanity.
Jesus is the Eucharist;
in Syriac he's called Pharisatha,
"the one who is stretched out";
Jesus came to nail this world
to the Cross!
Jesus entered Levi's dye works;
he took seventy-two dyes and
threw them in the vat.
The cloths all emerged pure white.
He said, "The Son of Man
comes as a dyer."

The childless Wisdom
is mother of angels.
Of all his disciples he loved
his companion, Mary Magdalene,
the most, and kissed her.
The disciples asked,
"Why do you love her most?"
He answered, "When a blind and
sighted man are both in darkness,
they are equal.
When light dawns, he who can
see will know the light;
he who is blind will stay in the dark."
Jesus said, "Blessed be he who IS,
before he came into being,
for he who IS has always been
and always shall be."
Man's mastery is invisible,
and lies in the concealed.
So he controls animals who
are stronger in terms of the visible;
thus they survive.
But when he leaves,
they quarrel and fight,
kill one another and
become cannibals.
Now they can all eat because a
superior man has tilled the ground.

If someone dives deep into
the well of living water and
surfaces empty handed, saying,
"I am a Christian,"
he has only borrowed the
name with interest.
If he receives the Holy Spirit,
His Name is the gift.
He who accepts this gift
doesn't have to give it back,
but from those who borrow at interest,
payment is demanded.
This is the way this
mystery is experienced.
Marriage is also a great mystery!
Without it our world couldn't continue;
contemplate this relationship.
Marriage in imagination
and fantasy is a defilement.
Forms of demonic spirits
are male and female;
males unite with souls that dwell
in the female form of those
who are disobedient.
None can escape them,
for they delay those who do not
receive the male and female powers
of bride and groom.

They are received from the
reflected light of the bridal chamber.
When a loose woman sees a lone
man, she leaps on him to defile him.
Similarly, lechers, when they see
a lone beauty, they seduce, to defile.
But if man and wife are seen together,
the female cannot seize the man
nor can the man enter the woman.
So if this symbol and an angel
are united, nothing harmful
can penetrate man or woman.
He who is no longer "of the world"
cannot be delayed on the grounds
that "he was once in the world".
He is obviously beyond
the plagues of lust and fear;
he masters the mind and senses
and is above jealousy.
If the enemy comes to attack,
he'll be defeated by a higher power.
There are some who claim
to be faithful, just to vanquish
impure thoughts and feelings.
But if they're firm in the Holy Spirit,
nothing unclean can ever touch them.
Don't be afraid of the body,
but don't adore it.

If you fear, it will gain mastery;
if you adore, it will render you helpless.
So the pilgrim lives in the world,
in regeneration, or in between.
God prevent me from falling
in between two places;
there is spiritual death.
In the world there's good and evil;
its goodness is not wholly good,
nor is its evil wholly evil.
But there's an evil that is diabolic,
this "in betweenness".
While in the world, it is worthy
to seek and find regeneration,
so that when we leave the body
we are at peace and not left hanging
in the middle.
Many stray from the straight path;
be wise and don't "be of this world"
before you sin.
There are some who are impotent
in their will to act and procrastinate;
they miss the mark.
An apostle, in a vision,
saw many folk trapped in a fire.
The voice of the Lord
offered to save them;
they disbelieved, hesitated,

and all perished in the flames.
It's from fire and water that
spirit and soul come into Being.
It is from these elements,
and light, that the groom of
the bridal chamber comes to be.
The fire is the baptismal
anointing oil.
The light's form is white,
bright and beautiful.
Truth does not come
into the world without robes;
it enters through words and pictures.
Truth cannot be received
by the world in any other way.
There is rebirth and
an image of rebirth.
We are born again through
the image of "Resurrection".
The bridal chamber is the
image of "Regeneration".
Those who speak the names
of the Father, the Son and the
Holy Spirit, do so for you.
If we do not know them in the heart,
the name "Christian" will be removed.
But we receive the boundless
grace of the power of his cross.

This power the apostles
called right and left;
it transforms men from
mere Christians into a Christ.
The Lord performed all his
acts in mystery: baptism,
communion, redemption,
and in the bridal chamber.
He said, “I came to make
the below as the above,
the outside as the inside,
and to unite them all through
the Word and the symbol.”
Those who claim,
“There’s the heavenly man,
and one above him” are wrong.
There are two heavenly men:
one revealed, who is below,
and one who owns the hidden,
who is above.
It is better to say “internal and external
and what’s outside the external”.
That is the reason our Lord called
destruction the “outer darkness”.
He said, “Enter the chamber of
your heart, seal the door then pray
to your Father who is in secret.”
The Father is the one within

them all and is the perfection.
There's nothing else
beyond "That I am".
Before Christ, some came from
where they couldn't enter;
if they did go in, they couldn't exit.
Those who entered, Christ released;
those who came out, he returned.
When Adam was still with Eve
there was no death;
after separation death appeared.
If a man or woman regains
his or her former Self,
there'll be an end to death.
"My God, my God. Oh Lord,
why have you forsaken me?"
Jesus pronounced these words
on the cross as a mystery,
quoting from King David's Psalms.
The bridal chamber is not fit
for beasts, slaves and loose women.
It is for free men and the virginal.
By the Holy Spirit and Christ,
we're born again, through both;
we're baptised by the Spirit and,
when reborn, made One.
You cannot see your reflection
in a glass or pool without light.

Nor can you see reflected light
without a mirror or water,
so it is right to baptise
in light and water.
The light is the oil.
In Jerusalem there were
three temples for the sacrifice.
The one facing west
was named “Holy”,
the south-facing temple
was the “Holy of the Holy”,
the east-facing one
the “Holy of Holies”,
where only the High Priest
was allowed.
Baptism is the Holy,
Redemption is the
Holy of the Holy;
the Holy of the Holies
is the bridal chamber.
Baptism contains
redemption and resurrection;
redemption happens
in the bridal chamber.
The veil was lifted so some
below could rise above.
Dark powers cannot see
those robed in Perfect Light.

They cannot be impeded by them.
We are enrobed sacramently
in this light by atonement.
If the female did not divorce the male
she would not die with the male;
his exile is the advent of death.
Christ came to heal this alienation.
The bride is reunited with her
groom in the bridal chamber and
can never be divorced again.
Eve separated from Adam
because they were not united
in the bridal chamber at the heart's core.
Adam's soul came into Being
through the breath of the spirit.
The mother was given,
his soul was taken and the spirit granted;
linked to spirit he spoke words
beyond comprehension.
Dark powers were envious for they
had missed the chance to enter
the wedding chamber.
Jesus came to the River Jordan
in the perfection of the
Kingdom of Heaven,
conceived before the All
and reborn anew.
Anointed, he anointed afresh;

redeemed, he redeemed his flock.
I must speak about the great mystery;
The Father of All married a virgin,
who descended, and fire glowed
upon their wedding day.
His visible body, the whole universe,
came into Being on that day.
He left the bridal chamber
as one who came into being
from groom and bride.
So Jesus established all
through these miracles.
It is best for each disciple
to abide in his peace.
Adam came into being
from two virgins:
the Spirit and the Earth.
Christ's birth came to heal
the evil from the Fall.
Two trees grow in Eden:
one bears beasts, the other mankind.
Adam ate from the tree of beasts.
He became like an animal,
so his offspring worshiped them.
Men make gods
and praise their creation.
What a man achieves
depends on his talents,

and his children.
They commence in ease,
but man is made in the image of
strength yet has children with ease.
In this world slaves serve the free;
in heaven, the free will minister to slaves.
Children of the bridal
chamber minister to the
children of their marriage.
The name of these offspring is peace.
They don't need form
because they have meditation;
they are abundant in their Glory.
Those who enter living waters
will bless them in his Name.
Jesus said, "So we shall
fulfil all righteousness."
Those who say they'll die first
and then rise again are mistaken.
If they do not receive
resurrection while alive,
they'll receive nothing when they die.
I, Philip the Apostle, said,
"Joseph planted a forest
because he needed wood.
He made a cross from his trees;
his son was crucified on that cross.
But the Tree of Life is at

the heart of that forest.
We press baptismal oil
from the olive,
and resurrection follows.
The world is a corpse eater
consuming dead animals;
all who eat that meat also die.
Truth is a Life consumer;
no one who feeds upon it will die.
Jesus brought such food.
The Garden of Eden is the
place where angels say,
'Eat this and don't eat that,
as you so desire.'
Where I eat, all is from
the Tree of Knowledge.
It destroyed Adam but can
now bring men back from death.
The Tree is the Law.
It's empowered to give
knowledge of good and evil.
It neither removes evil
nor establishes good,
but kills those who choose
disobediently.
God said, 'Eat this,
don't eat that,'
and death was begun.

The chrism, the oil of holy unction,
is superior to the ceremony
of baptism itself.
The word Christian is derived
from chrism and the name Christ.
The Father anointed the Son;
the Son anointed the apostles,
who anointed us.
He who has been anointed
owns the resurrection,
the light, the cross
and the Holy Spirit.
The Father anointed the Son
in the bridal chamber
of the heart's core;
the Son surrendered his will.
The Father was in the Son
and the Son in the Father.
This is the Kingdom."
Jesus said, "Some have entered
baptism and the kingdom laughing,
as if it was of little worth,
so, out they come."
The world came through error,
for the Creator wished it to be
immutable and immortal.
It failed to reach His aim;
things cannot be immutable

but His Sons are; no one can become
immutable without first becoming
His Son. But he who is unable
to receive cannot give.
The grail contains water and wine,
consecrated as His blood,
for which we give thanks.
It is filled with Holy Spirit
and is from the perfect man;
when we drink we receive
His perfection.
The living water is His body.
We must don the living man;
before we bathe in the living waters
we must strip bare so we can
wear the perfect man.
Horses sire horses, men sire men,
God sires a god.
Compare that with groom and bride
who come from the chamber.
There's no real Jew, but from
Judaism came Christianity;
these are the Chosen, the sons of man,
known in the world as the children
of the bridal chamber so they may
endure for life everlasting!
In this life, marriage between
husband and wife shows strength

offset by physical frailty;
in the eternal sphere
the form is not the same.
They are not separate;
both come from the one
strong enough to rise above
the heart of flesh.
It is needed to own the All,
to know one's Self.
If one doesn't know one's Self
it's impossible to enjoy what's owned;
those who've come to know
themselves enjoy what they own.
The ignorant will be unable
to delay the perfect man or see him.
To attain the right to enter the Kingdom
one must be adorned with his Light.
The true priest is totally holy,
for he has consecrated the bread;
by enlivening the water of baptism
Jesus rid man of death.
If we descend to those living waters,
we do not descend to death;
then we will not be recycled
into the world's spirit.
When this spirit blows
it brings a harsh winter;
when the Holy Sprit breathes,

glorious summer blooms.
He who knows the Truth
is free from sin,
but he who sins is its slave.
Truth is the mother,
knowledge the father;
those whom the world believes
to be sinless are free.
Knowledge of Truth
can make people proud;
real freedom is being free
from arrogance.
Love builds, but he who
is free often becomes her servant,
through love, of slaves,
unable to reach Truth.
Love never controls;
it doesn't claim this is "yours"
and this is "mine" but says,
"All is yours!"
Spiritual love is wine and perfume;
if those anointed come with
bad smelling ointment,
then they should leave.
The good Samaritan gave
wine and oil to the weak man;
his ointment healed because
love cures a multitude of sins.

A mother's child looks like her husband,
if he truly loves her; if he or she cheats,
the child resembles one of their defilers.
If the wife sleeps with her husband
but thinks only of her lover,
the child will look like him.
You who dwell with God's Son,
don't adore the world but love the Lord
so your offspring will be like Him
and not the world.
Man enjoys sex with a woman,
the stallion with a mare,
the bull with a cow;
so spirit mingles with spirit,
reason weds reason, light shares light.
If you're born a man or a woman,
a human being will love you;
if you become truly spiritual,
the spirit will love you.
If you become one with
He who dwells above,
saints in heaven will
kneel down before you.
If you become a beast, outside
and below the spiritual realm,
neither human, spirit, reason
nor light will love you;
the Spirit within, and above,

won't dwell in you;
you'll lose your Friend.
He who subdues his personal
will shall become free.
He who becomes free
by grace of his master,
but then barters himself back
to hard slavery of his personal will,
won't ever be free again.
If you're a farmer you need
earth, rain, wind and sun;
God as your Farmer requires you
to cultivate faith, hope, love
and Self Knowledge.
Faith is our fertile ground;
hope, our gentle rain;
love, the soft breeze;
Self Knowledge, the sunshine!
Grace descends to earth from heaven.
Blessed is the one who saved souls;
that one is Christ.
He came to earth and unburdened all
who had faith in him, the perfect man.
The Word of God tells us the
Saviour is beyond description;
No one else can achieve
so much, or comfort so many.
He comforts all, never causing sorrow

to those who take refuge in Him alone;
wickedness and guile cause distress.
The perfect man brings peace and love,
yet some are stressed by that notion.
There was once a farmer who
owned sons, slaves, cattle, dogs,
swine, corn, barley, grass and nuts.
He was a caring man;
he gave bread to children,
corn meal to slaves,
bones to dogs, acorns to pigs.
So it is with God's disciples;
bodily appearances won't mislead them.
They'll scrutinise each other's spiritual
condition and advise appropriately.
There are animals in human form;
when He sees what they are
He feeds them the right diet.
To slaves He gives basic lessons,
to children, detailed guidance.
Our Lord is the Son of Man and
his son is he who creates through Him;
The Son of Man can also give birth;
to create a creature,
to give birth to offspring.
He who creates strives for all to see;
He who brings rebirth toils in private
and is concealed.

Only a man and wife can
tell when they enjoy sex.
Marriage is a mystery;
if there's mystery in the
wedlock of impurity,
how much more mystery is there
in the purity of the bridal chamber?
The sacred marriage is not carnal;
it is without desire and subject
to God's will, not from darkest night
but from brightest light.
When sex goes public, it's prostitution.
The bride can play the whore,
to be defiled by a lecher if she leaves
the bedroom and is seen.
Let the true wife confide only in
her parents, and friends and family
of the groom; they are permitted
to enter the bridal chamber.
The rest must pray only to hear
her voice and enjoy the perfume
of her ointment; let them feed from
table crumbs like puppies.
Brides and grooms belong
to the chamber;
no one should see them together
until they're like them.
Abraham was circumcised,

teaching that it is right to
admonish the flesh.
Providing man's inner parts are
protected, they'll labour and live;
once exposed, they'll stop!
If a man's intestines are opened up,
he'll die.
The same with a tree.
While the root is covered,
it will shoot and grow;
if it's exposed, the tree will wither.
It is so with all birth in this world.
If the root of wickedness
lies hidden in the dark
it waxes strongly;
when exposed to the light
of awareness it perishes.
That is why Matthew writes,
"Already the axe is laid
at the root of the trees";
it will not only cut the trunk
but also sever the root.
Jesus pulled up the root
of worldly sinfulness;
prophets partly did his work.
Each one of us must dig down deep
within ourselves and find the root
of this evil egotism in the heart,

so it will perish.
If we ignore this root,
more poisonous fruit
is produced in the heart;
it becomes our task master
and enslaves us, forcing us
to do what it desires.
It is powerful until seen and is active;
ignorance is the mother of all evil;
It will end in death!
For those who come from this,
iniquity will cease to exist.
When all the Truth is revealed
then man may be perfected.
Truth, unlike ignorance, while latent
is at rest, but when revealed
is stronger than the foe.
It brings freedom!
John wrote, “Truth
will set you free.”
Ignorance is slavery,
Self knowledge is liberation.
If we know Truth,
its blossom will flower in
our hearts and bring salvation;
at the moment we’re a mere
appearance in creation.
We say that the strong are held in

respect as great people and the
reviled are the weak, who are despised;
but the truth is different
and revealed in a symbol.
The bridal chamber is concealed;
it is the holy in the Holy.
The bridal veil hides how
God commands His work;
when unveiled, this house
will be destroyed.
The Godhead will retire,
not to the Holy of Holies
for it will not mingle
with the pure light
and flawless perfection.
It will rest beneath the
arms of the cross;
an ark will be their refuge
when the deluge descends.
The true priests may
enter within the veil
with the high priest;
the veil was not open only
at the top for then it would be
closed to those below.
It was not open only at
the bottom for then it would
be closed to those above.

It was open from top to bottom.
Those above revealed to
those below, so we could know
the mysteries of Truth.
Truth is what is held in great
respect and is really strong!
We enter bowed in weakness;
we are humble compared with
God's great power and glory.
His power and glory surpass
all power and glory.
Divine perfection is revealed
with the concealed secrets of Truth.
The Holy of Holies opens;
we are invited to the bridal chamber.
Hidden wickedness is now
less effective, but not cleansed
from the seed of the Spirit;
many may still be slaves of evil.
When revealed, the perfect light
will shine on all; all those within
its rays will be anointed and receive
baptism of the chrism.
The slaves shall be free
and the prisoners redeemed!
Matthew wrote, "Every plant
my Father in Heaven has not
planted shall be plucked."

The exiled will return to
unity and be fulfilled.
All who enter the bridal
chamber will light the light
as at night weddings.
But the mysteries of the
marriage are perfected by day,
not at night; an eternal day
that never sets.
All who become sons of the
bridal chamber will receive the light;
they'll be invisible and free
from torment, even in this world.
When he departs,
he'll have known Truth
through these symbols;
The world has become Eternal,
and is perfect for him.
This is how truth is given;
not hidden in darkest night
but revealed in brightest day
of holy light!

THE GOSPEL OF MARY MAGDALENE

Originally written in Greek, the Gospel of Mary Magdalene tells the disciples about Mary's unique revelations through her relationship with Jesus. Andrew and Peter question her veracity and ask why a woman should become a favourite disciple. They are admonished by Levi.

Mary questioned her Master,

"At the end of an aeon,

will all matter be destroyed?"

Jesus answered,

"All of nature, its forms and

creatures are interrelated;

all will be returned to their

original source.

The essence of matter also returns

to the source of its own nature.

He who has ears, let him comprehend!"

Peter said, "As you've told us

almost everything, tell us this also:

what is the world's sin?"

Jesus replied,

"There is no sin in reality!

It is you who create sin,

when you do deeds, such as adultery,

that are called sinful.

That's why Good enters your heart

to return you back to your source.

This is why you get ill

and eventually die;

he who understands,

let him understand.
Matter caused powerful passions
to enter into you, forces which
come from its opposites in nature.
Then a sickness arises in the body;
so be of strong faith!
If you're weak, gather strength
in the presence of Nature;
he who has ears to hear,
let him hear!"
Then Jesus greeted them saying,
"Peace be with you all.
Take my peace into your Selves;
be watchful so nobody leads
you astray claiming 'Look there,
look here for the son of man.'
I tell you that the son of man
is within you all!
Seek him inside; those who
search diligently and earnestly
shall surely find him.
Then leave and preach the truth
of the Kingdom to those with
ears to hear; don't invent rules
beyond those I've given.
Don't make laws like law-makers do
or else you'll be held back."
After he had said this he left.

The disciples were upset.
They complained,
"How can we go to the Gentiles
and preach the truth of the
Kingdom of the Son of Man?
If they won't save him,
how will they save us?"
The Mary rose and said,
"Don't grieve! Be brave;
his grace is always with you
to guard you.
Let's praise his magnitude;
he's prepared us and turned us
into real men and women!"
When Mary said this
she lifted their hearts up to the Good;
they started to study his words.
Peter said to Mary, "Dear sister,
we know our Saviour loves
you more than the rest of women.
Tell us his words that you remember,
those we've never heard before."
Mary answered,
"What's concealed from you I'll tell;
I saw him in a vision and I told him.
He said, 'Blessed are you that
your strength wasn't shaken by
my appearance, for where the

heart is lies buried treasure.'
I asked, 'Lord, does he or she
who sees the vision perceive
it through soul or spirit?'
He answered, 'One perceives
through neither soul nor spirit
but by mind, which mediates
between both; visions are mental.'
I pondered. 'I never saw you descend,
now I see you ascend.
Why does my mind deceive me
since you are part of me?'
My soul answered,
'But you didn't recognise me;
I serve you as your robe
but you don't know me.'
When the voice ended
I rejoiced inwardly.
When I came to ponder on ignorance,
the third dark power,
it questioned my soul saying,
'Where are you heading?
You're enslaved by evil,
so don't judge me.'
My soul replied,
'Why judge me; I haven't
judged you. I was imprisoned,
although I never imprisoned.

I wasn't recognised, but I've known
that All is being destroyed,
both in earth and heaven.'
When my soul had conquered ignorance
it rose up and saw the fourth power,
which assumes seven forms.
The first is darkness, the second
desire, then ignorance, fear of death,
power of the flesh, foolish reason,
and self-righteous pedantry.
These are the powers of anger
and doubt; they ask, 'From where
did you come, killer of men;
where are you heading,
slayer of space?'
My soul replied,
'What bound me is dead,
what enveloped me has been
vanquished; my desires are over
and ignorance is no more.
In this life I was freed from the
world and the chains of forgetfulness.
From now on I will rest
in the eternal now; for this age,
this aeon, and in stillness.'"
Then Mary was silent, for this was
the truth Jesus had revealed.
Andrew then spoke,

"Say what you like about
what Mary has said, but I
don't believe Jesus would tell
us such strange notions!"
Peter said, "Did he really speak
with Mary, a woman, without our
knowing? Are we to listen to her?
Did he favour her more than us?"
Then Mary cried to Peter,
"My brother, do you believe
I made this up, or that I would
lie about Jesus?"
Levi admonished Peter,
"You've always been
quick to anger;
now I see you doubting
a woman as worthy as Mary.
Who do you think you are
to dispute her testimony,
like an enemy?
If Jesus made her upright,
who are we to disown her?
Jesus knew her well; that's
why he loved her more than us.
Let's be penitent and don the robe
of the perfect man and make him
one with ourselves, as he taught.
Let's proclaim his word,

not make more laws beyond

those he ordered!”

The disciples then disbanded

and began to teach his Gospel.

THE GOSPEL OF JUDAS

A Cainite Gnostic Gospel, AD c150, composed in Greek, translated into Coptic, and recently rediscovered. Condemned by Irenaeus as heretical, it redeems Judas. He is portrayed not as a villainous traitor but, radically, as the complicit, preordained instrument for Christ's Passion.

At a solemn, momentous,

most awesome hour,

the blessed Son of God,

the Divine Logos,

Lord Jesus Christ,

descended on Earth:

he came to save our fallen, sinful world,

he performed many miracles,

and executed wondrous marvels.

He transformed water into wine,

fed the hungry multitudes,

with fine loaves and fresh fishes,

he raised Lazarus from the dead.

He mercifully healed the sick,

the halt, leprous, lame and blind;

he cast out Satanic devils,

walked on the blue sea of Galilee.

I Judas, in this my testament,

tell all he revealed to me,

over one long week,

three days before we observed Passover;

when we sup on unleavened bread,

and sip the sacramental wine.

During his ministry,

some journeyed joyfully
on the sacred way of
pure righteousness,
but many fell down
on the slippery path
tempted by the evil inclination.
To further his work,
he gathered together
twelve trusted disciples,
among whom I was included.
He taught us Gnosis,
about the unseen,
unknown mysteries,
beyond the mind,
and this world.
He prophesied all
that would happen,
The Great Apocalypse,
at the end of time.
He lived in Judaea among us;
we'd chosen a lush green pasture
beneath Mount Tabor to pitch our
tents, in a grove of Lebanon Cedars.
The cooing of doves sounded
like hymns of praise.
A nearby lake of still waters
quenched our thirst.
The place reminded us of

David's famed Shepherd Psalm;
our souls were restored.
Surprisingly, he often failed
to appear as a man,
but came as a youth!
Once he discovered us
deep in meditation.
He chanted the grace
before breaking bread,
then heartily laughed.
We were shocked, and asked him
"Why mock us when we're prayerful?"
The Lord answered, "I'm not
laughing at your good selves,
you, who imagine you're worshipping
of your own free will; but through
God's will, he shall be praised."
"Master", we exclaimed,
"You must be the Son of God!"
He said, "Do you truly think you
know who I really am?
Nobody from any nation will
ever know my True Nature!"
When we heard his admonition,
anger rose up in us, wicked
thoughts were felt in our hearts.
When he witnessed our folly,
he said, "Why let anger disturb you?

God, the divine light, within you,
has caused that displeasure
to arise in your minds.
Allow any man or woman
who's mature enough,
to bring a Perfect Being,
and come face to face with me!"
The other disciples replied,
"We're all brave,
but none among us has
the strength to stand up to you,
except Judas, the Essene,
and even he can't gaze in your eyes,
he turns his look away"
I fell silent, and then said,
"Lord, I know who you truly are!
and from where you emerge,
the Kingdom of Barbello,
the Mother Divine!
She's known from the Gnostic Triad,
Mother, Father and Son;
the incomprehensible womb,
God the Infinite Formless Spirit,
and Autogenes, the Christ.
The perfect glory, immeasurable,
hidden, invisible.
Yet, oh Lord, I'm unfit
to pronounce the Name

of that One, who sent you!"
Jesus knew well that
I'd realised Gnostic Secrets.
He said to me,
"Leave them! I shall reveal
to you more hidden secrets of
the Kingdom of Heaven.
It is probable that you'll
reach that holy place,
but you must first suffer
great tribulation and sorrow.
You'll be replaced by Matthias
so the disciples might be complete
as the essential number twelve."
Astonished, I replied,
"When will you inform me
of these great mysteries?
When shall the Great Festival of Light
dawn for all imprisoned humanity?"
Then Jesus departed from us.
Next morning he returned to
the remaining disciples.
They told me that they asked him,
"Lord, where did you go?
What did you do after you left us?"
He said, "I visited a noble, sacred
people beyond your world."
We were amazed and enquired of him,

“What beings are there higher and holier
than us, and not of this world?”
He laughed once more!
“Why are you thinking about them?
I tell you! nobody on this Earth
will ever know them, nor human children
ever belong to them.
Nor will any angelic force of
luminaries reign over them.
They don’t come from this aeon.
Humanity comes from a lower region.
They come from another power,
not from that force which governs you.”
When they heard these cryptic
utterances, they were confounded
and struck dumb!
Once more Jesus came;
the disciples told him,
“We all saw you in a strange
dream last night.
What’s the meaning of
such mysterious visions?”
Jesus said, “Why conceal
your experiences, speak!”
“We saw a large temple in
which there was a huge altar,
and twelve men who claimed
to be priests, namely Levites.

There was a crowd pressing us,
at the altar, until we stopped
taking sacrificial offerings.
We were pressing on them too."
Jesus interrupted, "What manner
of priests were they?"
"Some are celibate for a fortnight,
others sacrifice their children,
others, even, their wives!
Meanwhile they're flattering
each other, and acting meekly.
Some even lie with men,
others are slaughterers,
committing every sin in the book!
Yet these priests call on your name,
while in the task of preparing
their foul sacrifices, their altar remains
filled with obscenities."
Then the disciples fell silent,
and were deeply perturbed.
Jesus said, "Why be perplexed?
I tell you that they write my name
on stellar powers, through the
medium of humans.
In my name they plant trees
which are barren!
Now I'll interpret your dream.
You're the suppliants receiving

sacrifices at that hideous altar!
They're the false Gods of the lower
mind, to whom you pay obeisance!
You're the twelve priests,
the so-called Levites, you saw!
The beasts you watched being
slaughtered are the herds of
people you're leading astray.
That's how the King of
Anarchy sets himself up,
assuming my name!
Generations of hypocrites
will cling to him!
Then another imposter will
defend the adulterers,
perverts and child murderers;
those who feign fasting
and all such wicked sinfulness.
Those who claim to be like
angels are the omens written in
the stars that bring about destruction.
For humanity has been told
'The Lord received your sacrifice
from priests of falsehood!'
But it's Almighty God,
that One who rules the entire universe,
who'll ordain their disgrace,
at the end of time.

Stop sacrificing in this way!
It's on that altar you sin.
Then these things are beyond your fate,
you'll become like angels and
enjoy everlasting life.
Stop contending with me,
each one of you has his own destiny.
I have come to refresh
God's beautiful Eden Garden.
I'm the fountain that waters
the Tree of Life, and the righteous
generations that endure.
Sinners cannot defile the devout
way of life for ever and ever."
Later I encountered Jesus;
he was alone and I asked him,
"Master, what is that special fruit
the righteous will bear?"
He answered and said, "The souls
of all humans will eventually perish,
but those who are righteous, when they have
completed an era in heaven's kingdom,
their flesh will perish, but their souls shall
live and they'll be resurrected!"
I then asked, "What about
the rest of humanity?"
He replied, "It's impossible to
sew seeds on rocky ground

and then harvest luscious fruits.
This is the stony path of the corrupt,
with their perverse knowledge.
The right hand of God created
humanity that their souls may ascend.
Not even angelic power can know
that place which righteous men
and women inherit."
"Rabbi, you've heard the
dream of the other disciples.
Pray listen to mine."
Jesus laughed!
"Why are you disturbed?
Now you're my thirteenth disciple,
tell me, and I'll support you."
"The twelve were stoning me,
abusing me harshly.
I came also to that same place,
but I saw a temple booth and
my eyes failed to measure its scope.
Elder Sages with grave presence,
encircled the booth,
roofed with green branches,
thick, leafy, scented, sappy,
gleaming with emerald light,
as at the Feast of Tabernacles.
Inside the house was a
fervent congregation.

Oh Master, let me be
included among them."
Jesus said, "Your guiding star
led you astray, Judas;
no mortal is worthy to enter
that sacred tabernacle you saw.
That place is reserved for holy ones,
a place where neither Sun nor Moon
shall rule over them.
They shall stay steadfast for eternity
in that Kingdom of saintly hosts.
Look, now I've enlightened you
about that Kingdom's Mystery,
and the mistake of your guiding star,
deceived by the rulers of the twelve aeons."
"Master, surely my soul isn't governed
by the Archons of the twelve aeons?"
"Alas, Judas, you'll mourn deeply,
when you see all the realms
and peoples dwelling there."
"Then, what good have I gained
now you've released me
to join a nobler race?"
"You'll become my thirteenth disciple,
but you'll be cursed by humanity,
yet eventually reign over them
and ascend to my holy generation.
Come unto me, and I'll teach you

about mysteries beyond mortal sight.
There's a magnificent kingdom, infinite,
whose limits no angel has ever reached.
Inside dwells the Great Invisible Spirit.
No angelic eye has seen, nor heartfelt
intuition grasped, its immensity,
nor can it ever be Named.
An illuminated cloud,
the Supernal Shekinah,
covers that blessed habitation.
The Great Invisible Spirit commanded
'May an angel be generated to act
as my attendant!'
Then a beautiful divine form,
the luminary, Autogenes,
manifested from the shining cloud.
Four higher angels came forth, through
Autogenes, from a second cloud,
they came to attend on him.
Autogenes proclaimed, 'Let Adamas,
the Archetypal Man, be!'
He appointed the first luminary
to reign over the sanctuary.
'Now!' he said, 'send angels
to praise and worship here!'
A host of Angels came to be.
He did the same with the second
luminary, and the same again till

the rest of the realms of Light
were autogenously created.
Adamas lived in the primal cloud,
yet none of the godlike angels
could see that luminous cloud.
After the semblance of an angel
he created the progeny of Seth.
By his will he generated
seventy-two luminaries to shine
in that imperishable race.
Then, by his will, the seventy-two
created three hundred and sixty,
so each luminary possessed five.
Their Father is the twelve kingdoms,
of the twelve luminaries.
Each kingdom has six heavens,
so seventy-two heavens can be.
The seventy-two luminaries,
each with five firmaments,
were given power, with an army,
a myriad of angels for adoration;
as well as virgin spirits, to worship
the Kingdoms and Aeons of Heaven.
It's that host of immortal ones,
who're called 'Cosmos' or that
which destroys to cleanse.
It was by the will of the Father,
the seventy-two luminaries,

with Autogenes and his kingdoms,
that primordial man, with humanity,
came into being.
They inhabited the Cosmos
with immortal powers.
Their kingdom contained
the cloud of Gnosis and
the great archangel named El."
Autogenes then said,
"Allow twelve angels, to come into
being so they may reign
over chaos and obliteration."
A flaming angel appeared from
the cloud, exhaling fire;
his face streaming with blood.
He was named Nebro the Apostate,
also called Yaldebaoth.
Then another angel came,
named Saklas.
Nebro ordered six angels,
with Saklas, to wait upon him.
They fostered twelve more angels
in the celestial realms.
Each received a kingdom to rule.
These twelve sovereigns with
their twelve angels said,
"Each one of you must guard
and protect these generations.

Firstly Seth, also called Christ,
secondly Harmathoth,
thirdly Falila, fourthly Yobel,
finally Adonaios.
These are the Five, to govern
Extinction and Anarchy."
Saklas addressed his angels,
"We shall form two human
beings in the divine image,
to be named Adam and Eve.
In the luminous cloud,
Eve will be called Zoe, or life.
In her name all the generations
shall seek after life."
Saklas ordained that they
and their offspring shall endure
for an entire season of time.
I then asked Jesus,
"What then was the longest time
a human being could live?"
He answered, "Why be astonished
that the days of Adam and his
offspring are counted?
It's there that he was given his realm
with its ruler, for a limited time."
I then asked,
"Does the human soul perish?"
He replied, "Almighty God

ordered Archangel Michael
to lend souls to human beings
so they might praise him.
He commanded Gabriel to give
the soul to the spirits of a great
unconquered generation, so that these
souls shall seek after the kingdom
of heaven within them, and is created
to dwell among the spirits of the angels.
For God ordained Gnosis to be
granted to Adam and his followers,
so that the Monarchs of Anarchy and
Obliteration could not reign over them."
I asked Jesus,
"What shall these peoples do?"
He answered, "It's the power
of the constellations that controls
the fate of everything.
When Saklas finishes the work
ordained for him, the first star
will be born along with the
generations to come, and all
that's prophesied will manifest.
They shall multiply their seed
in my name, and oversee the
death of their children. But Judas
in my name, your star of destiny
shall reign over my thirteenth realm."

Then Jesus laughed heartily.
I asked him why he mocked me so.
He replied, "It's not you I'm scorning
but the mistakes inherent in the stars!
These stars float adrift with five
opponents, all of them will eventually
be destroyed with their works.
I tell you, Judas, that those who make
offerings to Saklas are evil: you shall
overtake them, for it's your destiny to
sacrifice this body which bears me!
Then the realm of Adam's auspicious
generation shall be elevated on high.
Now all has been revealed to you,
lift up your eyes unto the hills,
see the holy Shekinah and its light
of glory, with her diadem,
the suns that shine about her.
That star which leads is yours!"
I raised my eyes,
I saw that luminous cloud,
I became part of her.
Those standing on the Earth below
heard a voice speaking from the cloud
saying "A great new generation has
been formed in my image!"
Then the high priests among those
people on the ground muttered, because

Jesus had come into the temple vestibule,
to pray and meditate.
They were terrified of him because
the congregations believed he was
indeed a mighty Prophet.
They approached me, Judas, and asked,
"Why are you here? You're a disciple
of that Jesus aren't you?"
Then Jesus answered them
according to their expectations.
They handed me some silver shekels,
as was preordained by my Master;
I delivered him to the High Priests,
according to God's Almighty Will.
Amen.

THE GOSPEL OF TRUTH

This powerful early Greek Gnostic Treatise covers topics such as "The Quest for the Father", the "Hope of Salvation" and the "Need for a Saviour". All will help to redeem the Soul from its ignorance.

The Gospel of Truth is sheer

perfection and holy joy!

For all those who've received

their Father's grace by knowing

who He really IS.

Through the force of His Word,

which issued from the fullness

of the Godhead.

That is Christ,

who is in the heart of his Father,

with the sacred task he's been set,

to save and enlighten those in ignorance.

This gospel gives hope of certainty

for all who diligently enquire.

When the Whole went

seeking for the One

from whom All come,

the All was found to

be the Divine Self,

Almighty God, inscrutable,

indescribable, supreme.

Nescience had caused

anxiety and fear,

a smutty fog that made

people feel blind.
Error became potent
and, through folly, began
creating with force and beauty
a falsity of truth.
This wasn’t an embarrassment
for the inscrutable, indescribable
Supreme; it was as nothing,
this angst, forgetfulness and guile,
for Real Truth is unchanging perfection.
From this fact, learn to hate error,
which lacked knowledge of the
source and dropped into dense mist,
regarding the Father,
forming illusion to frighten and
seize those beings existing in
the intermediate realm.
The Father didn’t cause this error,
although all emanates from Him.
Knowledge came from Him,
that forgetfulness which causes error
might be destroyed.
The Gospel of Christ, when sought,
reveals the secret mysteries to those
purified through His grace,
enlightening all encased in darkness
through forgetfulness.
He pointed out the Way of Truth,

which he preached.
Error became enraged,
persecuted and attacked him,
but was nullified by his sacrifice.
Crucified, he became
a source of Knowledge
concerning his Father.
It didn't lead to annihilation
because his Way was practised.
Those who practised rejoiced,
discovering Him in themselves.
As for the inscrutable, unknowable
One, the Father, the Flawless One,
who created the All and contains the
All and whom the All always needs,
He held flawlessness within himself,
which He didn't pass on to the All;
He wasn't envious;
what envy could there possibly be
between Himself and the All?
For if the Age had received
His flawlessness, the All
wouldn't have returned
to the Father.
He holds their flawlessness,
granting it as a boon to those
who return to Him with perfect
knowledge of the Unity.

It is He who created the All;
in Him dwells the All;
All have great need of Him.
Our Father wills that the nescient
will eventually know and love Him.
Christ was teacher of All,
peaceful and at ease.
In houses of devotion he came
and spoke His Word.
Philosophers, wise in their
own opinion, tried to refute Him.
He defeated them for they
were ignorant, and in their folly
they came to hate him.
Children came, those to
whom knowledge of their Father
hadn't been forgotten,
and he strengthened them.
They learned about, they knew,
they worshiped the Father.
The living gospel of the Father was
inscribed on their hearts' splendour!
That which pre-existed in the
Father's will before His creation,
within His inscrutability.
That secret tome which
nobody could steal, for anyone
who stole it would perish.

Nobody among the faithful
would have been saved unless
this tome had been revealed.
The all-loving Christ was
long-suffering in bearing
the suffering of others,
until he received that tome,
since he knew his own death
would bring new life for the multitude.
When a rich householder dies
there's often a secret clause
in his will revealing his fortune.
So it was with the All
which dwelled secretly,
while our Father of the All,
from whom all space emanated,
remained unseen.
When Christ came,
he became the Gnosis
of that secret tome
and was crucified.
He revealed the tome of his
Father by his death on the cross.
Such a magnificent teaching!
He attracts his own death,
although Life Everlasting
is his robe of glory.
Having thrown off transient tatters,

he donned the cloak of durability,
which nobody could steal.
Having come to the vale of fear,
he walked through it.
Those who were naked and
unclothed through forgetfulness
gained understanding and flawlessness.
Then they taught the
truth from their hearts,
to those open to receive.
Those who were willing to learn
his doctrine are alive and are
inscribed in the book of life.
It is about their own Real Self
that they hear teaching,
receiving it from their Father
and turning inwards towards Him.
It is necessary that the All
shall aspire towards Him,
for the flawlessness
of the All is in Him.
If the aspirant has understanding,
the Father takes him back to Himself.
For he who is trapped in necsience
lacks, and what he lacks is crucial.
He needs that Self Knowledge
which will make him flawless.
For the flawlessness of the

All dwells in the Father;
they must turn inwards towards Him.
He chose them beforehand and
matured those who came from Him.
Those whose names He knew in
advance were summoned for the end.
Thus the names the Father
has uttered have understanding;
the names of the uncalled
remain nescient.
Those who stay in nescience
until the end are people of
forgetfulness and will vanish.
Why are these wretched ones
nameless and not summoned?
Only he who has the understanding
that descends through grace is called.
He listens, responds, turns within
and cleaves towards Him.
He acknowledges His call and
yearns to perform his Father's will;
he wishes to please Him and
is rewarded with peace.
Each name comes before Him,
knowing from where he came
and where he is going.
The Chosen knows, like a drunkard
who has returned to sobriety.

Christ has rescued
many from falsehood;
he has visited their hearts,
from which they had strayed.
Because of an abyss
they fell into falsehood,
the void which encloses a space
in which nothing is enclosed.
It was a miracle:
they were within the Father
while not recognising Him,
and they were able to walk on,
for they failed to understand or to
know the One in whom they dwelled.
If His will hadn't issued from Him
as revelation, the knowledge of
how His various rays harmonise
would have stayed in nescience.
This is the Knowledge of
the Book of Life He gave to
twenty-three Aeons at the end.
He showed how His sacred
letters are neither vowels
nor consonants, so that one
could read them and think
they were unwise.
Yet they are letters of Truth
to those who know how to read.

Each letter is a total conception,
like a whole volume, for they are
letters inscribed by the One!
Our Father composed them for
all Aeons so they would know Him.
His wisdom meditates
on His Word, His doctrine
unveils His knowledge.
Patience is its crown;
joy is in perfect concord.
His splendour uplifts that
which His will has unveiled.
His peace has taken it into itself,
His love has enrobed it,
His faithfulness has taken it to heart.
In this way the Word of
Almighty God the Father
advances into the All,
as the fruit of His heart's core
and the seal of His will.
It maintains the All, elects
them and absorbs its effect.
It purifies, leading them back to
Him and into the Divine Mother,
also to the Christ of infinite sublimity.
The Father unveils His heart,
the Holy Spirit.
He reveals what is secret,

His son, so through His grace
the aeons may know Him
and cease toiling in seeking Him,
but abide in Him,
knowing that is true peace.
Having remedied the lack
He destroyed the form,
the sphere in which He worked.
For where there's jealousy
and conflict, it's lacking;
but where there's Oneness,
there lies flawlessness.
The lack manifests because
our Father was unknown;
when He's known,
that will vanish.
It's like a man in nescience;
when knowledge comes,
nescience is dissolved.
Night disappears when dawn breaks;
lack dissolves in the flawlessness.
From that time on, form is
invisible and disappears in
mingling with the One.
Now its works lie
fragmented in time;
Oneness will become
flawless and in time make

all space the same.

He creates whomever and whatever;

He wills by bestowing name and form

and causes those that are born

to be unaware of their Creator.

Those yet to be born are as nothing,

but are in Him and wish to be born

when He wills; like in the time to come.

Before all manifests, He knows

what He'll create and destroy.

But His unborn fruit are ignorant

and can do nothing without His grace.

All space in our Father is

from the One, who created it

from nonexistence.

He who has no root has no shoot,

and although he imagines he has come

into existence, he will cease.

For he who doesn't truly exist

can never come into fullness

of flawless Being.

How then did he regard himself?

As one who comes into existence

like night-time shadows and ghosts.

But when the Light shines on his

fright he sees that he is as nothing.

So they were in ignorance

of their Father,

He being invisible to them.
Since through fear, turmoil,
imbalance, doubt and strife,
there were myriad delusions.
Imaginary souls lost in heavy torpor,
full of agonising dreams.
Either they're trying to escape
without help or they come
hunting after others.
Striking blows or receiving them,
falling from heights or flying in air.
Being slain without a slayer or
slaying their friends, covered in blood.
When those that suffer
these nightmares wake up,
they see them as nothing
for they themselves are nothing.
Such is the path of those who've
shed their nescience, like a dream
without substance.
The knowledge of their Father
comes as something of great worth,
like a glorious sunrise.
Each one lived as if in a deep
sleep when ignorant, and awoke
on realisation of the Good
when he returned to the Father.
Blessed is he who restores

the sight of the spiritually blind!
The Holy Spirit chased them
with great haste, to wake them up!
Holding out his hand to those lying
helpless on the earth, he pulled up
those that were not yet awakened!
He told them how to know
their Father and His Son.
When they'd seen and heard Jesus,
he showed them how to savour
and feel him, the beloved one.
When Christ came teaching
about their Father, the unknowable,
inscrutable one, he breathed into
them meaning, action and will,
revealing the Light to very many.
Instantly they turned
inwards towards him.
The materialists were exiles
and failed to see his similitude,
and couldn't know him.
He came in bodily form
without obstacles,
for purity is unconquerable.
He again revealed new doctrine
about what's in our Father's heart,
having revealed His perfect Word!
When the Light had shone,

through his lips as well as his voice,
all Life was given new birth.
He passed on to them his
apperception of comprehension,
compassion and redemption.
Energy of spirit
flowed from our Father's
boundlessness and sublimity,
ending chastisement and torment,
for some had been led astray
from the light of His countenance.
Those in need of mercy had
fallen into falsehood and bondage.
He vanquished these foes
by his strength and enlightened
them with his teaching.
He became the Way for sheep
who had strayed from knowledge
into nescience.
He was a great find for seekers,
a foundation for those toppling,
flawlessness for those corrupted.
He was the good shepherd
who deserted the ninety-nine
that were safe and searched for
that one that had strayed.
He celebrated when he found
the lost sheep, for ninety-nine

is a number held in the left hand.
When one more is found,
one hundred is a number
held by the right.
It attracts what was
lacking in the left
and places it in the right.
One hundred signifies soundness;
it is our Father's number.
Even on the Sabbath day
he laboured for the sheep
fallen into the ditch.
He breathed new life into them
so they might know the Truth
inwardly and become sons
of inner knowledge.
What kind of Sabbath
is it that forbids salvation
to work so you may live?
From daylight above
which knows no night,
and from that sun which never
sets because it is flawless.
Utter from the heart
"I am the perfect day!
And in me dwells that light
which never sets."
Teach the Truth to those that

seek, and knowledge to those
fallen into the pit through falsehood.
Steady the stance of all who've
slipped and reach out with open arms
to all those who are sick at heart.
Feed the famished,
grant peace to the fatigued,
raise up all who wish to arise,
awaken all who wish to awaken!
For you are the
comprehension that has
been brought forward into light.
If power acts, it becomes
more powerful!
Pay attention to your own Real Self!
Don't spend time on that which
you've rejected from your petty self.
Don't return to the vomit
you've thrown up.
Don't be like moths or
worms that cause decay,
for you've already cast them out.
Don't make a home for Satan;
you've already vanquished that fiend!
Don't hold up those that form
barriers which have nearly fallen.
The lawless are the ones to scorch,
rather than the just.

The lawless work alone;
the righteous work amongst their flock.
Do the will of our Father;
we all come from Him!
Our Father is sublime;
His will is beneficent.
He has watched over you
so you may find peace.
He takes notice of your
works because His children
are His incense,
the grace of His Face.
Our Father loves His fragrance
and reveals it everywhere.
It combines with matter
and bestows perfume
on His light and peace;
He makes it superior
to shape and sound.
It's not the senses that smell
the perfume but the breath,
which attracts His fragrance
to itself and is subsumed.
He preserves and transfers
it back to its original home,
from where it first emerged,
the primary fragrance
that has grown cold.

It is a subtle form, like ice
which once was liquid,
but when breathed on, heats up.
Cold fragrance comes from duality,
so faith comes and dissolves division!
And brings forward the intense heat
of the Godhead that lives in Christ,
the Pleroma of Love.
So frigidity will never return,
and there'll be Oneness
and flawless thought.
This is the promise of the
Pleroma, for those who wait
for salvation from above.
While the hope
on which they are waiting
lies in the waiting.
For those whose similitude
is light without shadow,
the Pleroma is on its way.
The lack isn't because of the
boundlessness of our Father,
who allows time for the lack
to be healed.
Although no one says,
"The Flawless One
must come this way."
But the deepening of our

Father's Love is extensive
and the concept of falsehood
is nonexistent in Him.
It is faith which may fall
but can again stand up
in the knowing of Him,
and he who has been chosen
and who shall return;
this is metanoia.
So flawlessness breathed,
and chased away the sins of those
who'd fallen, to find repose.
Forgiveness is the light in
the lack, the Word of the Pleroma.
The doctor rushes to where
the disease is rampant
because it is his will.
He who bears a lack
does not conceal it
because someone possesses
what the other lacks.
So the Pleroma,
which is not lacking,
fills any lack in what it
provides for itself to fulfil.
So we might receive grace,
for when we lacked,
grace was deficient.

That causes our contraction
to smallness in a graceless place.
When this contraction was
received, He unveiled that which
was lacking, the Pleroma.
The finding of the Light of Truth,
which arose because it is constant.
This is why Jesus is referred
to as being "in their midst".
So those in perplexity might
receive a turning inwards,
and he might anoint them
with his precious salve.
The salve is our Father's
infinite compassion
and unconditional love,
which He hands to them.
Those whom He's anointed
have become flawless;
full jars receive ointment.
The jar empties of ointment
because there was a lack,
and the salve was applied.
His breath attracts healing,
by its own power;
for those without lack,
no seal need be broken
nor salve used.

What they lack our
flawless Father refills.
He is good;
He knows his plants,
because it is He who planted
them in His own garden.
Now His Eden
is a haven of peace.
This is the flawlessness
in the will of our Father
and these are the words
of His contemplation.
Each one of His words
comes from His will,
in the unveiling of His Word.
While they were at peace through
the depth of His meditation,
which was the First,
there issued a mind that spoke
the one Word of silent grace.
This was termed "thought",
for they were held in it
before it was unveiled.
It was the First,
when the will of Him
who willed, so willed it.
His will is what our Father
lives in, and is satisfied.

Nothing ever happens
without Him,
nor can anything happen
without His will,
which is inscrutable.
His mark is the will
that no one can know Him.
Nor is it possible to investigate
Him so as to know Him.
What He wills is “that”,
even if it displeases those
in the way, seeking God,
desiring our Father.
For He knows all their
beginnings and their ends.
At their end He’ll enquire
of them, directly.
The end is the final receipt of
knowledge about He who is
concealed and is our Father.
From whom the genesis issued
and to whom all shall return.
They have issued from the
splendour and rejoicing
of His Holy Name.
The name of our Father is the Son.
It is He who first named the One
who came from Him and is Himself.

He is that One to whom belongs
all that exists around Him,
and that is our Father.
His is the Name;
His is the Son;
He can be known.
The Name is unseen because
it is the enigma of the unseen,
which comes to ears that
are full of Him.
Our Father's name is unutterable,
but known through His Son.
The Name is Great.
Who will be capable
of uttering His holy Name?
Only our Father,
who owns the Name,
and his sons, in whom
the Name lives.
Since our Father is unborn,
He alone is the One who
created for Himself the Name,
before He created the Aeons,
so that His Name as Father
might rule as Lord.
That is His Name in Truth,
stable in control,
through His flawless force.

His Name is wordless.
Nor does His Name consist of
mere names; it is unseen.
He gave the Name to Himself alone,
for only He can know Himself
and has the power to give a Name.
For the nonexistent is nameless,
but the One who exists lives
with a name and He alone knows it.
The Father,
the Son,
is His Name!
He never concealed it in matter,
but it lived as for the Son;
He alone gives a Name.
The Name is Father,
for that Name is also the Son.
Where indeed would
Divine mercy find a Name
except in our Father?
A man will ask his neighbour,
"Who is it who can give a Name
to Him who existed before Himself?"
As if children never received
a name from their parents.
First we must pursue
the enquiry, "What does
the Name mean?"

It is the Name in Truth,
not the Name from our Father
but the Real Name!
He didn't receive the Name
on credit, as others might,
according to the way
that each name is given.
But this is the Real Name;
there's no one there to give it
to Him, for He's unnameable,
inscrutable, unknowable.
Until that time when He who
is flawless speaks of Him alone,
it is He who has authority
to utter the Name and know it.
When it pleased Him that
His Name, which is beloved,
should be His Son,
He named him "He who
came from the deep".
Christ spoke about concealed secrets,
knowing our Father is the Supreme
Being without wickedness.
So he brought himself to teach
about where He came from
and where He rests.
And to preach about the splendour
of the Pleroma, the magnitude of

his Father and His Divine sublimity.
About the place from where he came
and the realm where he was confirmed.
He'll be quick to return,
receiving manna and growth,
and his dwelling in the Pleroma.
All the rays from our Father are
Pleromas, and the source is the One
who created them in His own Self.
He designated their fate;
each is created so through their
own will they may return.
For where they place their will,
their source, He lifts them to the
great spiritual heights of their Father.
They rest their burden on
His head and they're maintained,
welcoming Him as if they'd
greeted His face with kisses.
Yet they don't always act this way
for they are not so exalted,
yet they are not deficient
in their Father's splendour.
They didn't regard their
Father as diminutive or severe,
or liable to anger, but knew
that He was without evil,
unshakeable and sublime,

knowing all space before
they originated and without
need to be taught.
This is the way of those who
already have some taste from
above of His boundless magnitude.
As they attend on the flawless One
who waits for them with open arms,
they won't descend to hell,
nor suffer envy, pain and death.
They will rest in peace, neither toiling
nor being twisted around the Truth.
For they are Truth; their Father is within,
they are in Him, who is flawless!
Undivided in His beneficence,
lacking nothing, at perfect peace,
rejuvenated in Spirit.
They'll be attentive to
finding their own source and
not endure loss to their soul.
This is the isle of the blessed,
this is their golden land.
The rest must understand
that it's inappropriate for me,
being in His place,
to speak about anything else.
It is from there that I come
to be and it is right to attend

all the time to our Father of All
and our real brothers,
those who benefit from
His unconditional love,
which is constantly poured out,
for He dwells in their midst.
They demonstrate in Truth
and dwell in Life Everlasting
and witness His Flawless Light
filled with their father's seed,
which lives in His heart and
the Pleroma, while His Holy Spirit
celebrates and magnifies
the One in whom He lives.
He is goodness;
His offspring are flawless,
fit to bear His Name.
He is our Father;
we are His children
whom He loves!

THE GREATEST HUMAN EVIL IS FORGETFULNESS OF GOD

An early Gnostic text warning of the grave spiritual dangers should the Soul lose hold of its essential Self. It stresses the need for Recollection and Self Remembering leading to eventual salvation.

FROM *Corpus Hermeticum VII*

Dear fellows, where are you

rushing to like drunkards, tipsy

and staggering on the rich wine

of reason, forgetful of God?

You cannot stomach it;

already you're about to vomit!

Halt! Sober up!

Elevate yourself by mental power.

Maybe not all of you can do that,

but some of you can!

For the degeneration that flows

from forgetfulness is drowning

the earth, infecting soul and body,

veiling the soul like a cloak and

stopping you from abiding in the heart.

So don't be swept away

by this mad flood!

Find the way into your heart!

Look for a good teacher

to show you the path

to the gates of remembrance.

Where there's a light,

radiant and bright,

free from darkness.

Where nobody is drunk,

but keeps their mental eye

on that Great Being who

wills to be known in their heart.

That Great Being cannot

be seen or heard, or spoken

or thought about,

only by a higher subtle

intellect that transcends

normal matters of the mind.

But first strip off the

soiled cloak you wear,

the foul mantle of forgetfulness,

the base of wickedness,

the link with evil,

the black pit,

the spiritual death,

the walking corpse,

the moving coffin,

the domestic rogue who

feeds on guile, which he relishes,

and conspires to cause your downfall.

Such is the habit;

the filthy coat you've put on,

that is your foe!

It suffocates you and drags you

down to its cruel self, into the gutter.
Otherwise, through aspiration
and seeing the beauty of Truth
and the Good that dwells in you,
you will come to despise this
vile enemy who plots to destroy you.
It ruins the mind and pollutes
the senses by muddying them
with gross materialism,
filling them with disgusting
lust for inane pleasure,
to prevent you from understanding
what you should understand!
And, what is worse,
it will stop you from seeing
forever what you should really see!

THE SECRET BOOK ACCORDING TO ST JOHN I, II & III

Introductory extracts from the "Apocryphon of John", son of Zebedee, outlining Gnostic mythology. They see Almighty God as the Source of all Being and describe the structure of the Divine Cosmology before Genesis. Probably composed around AD 180.

One day John,

brother of James,

a son of Zebedee,

was going to synagogue.

A Pharisee called Arimanios

met him and said,

"Where is your teacher,

the one you followed?"

John replied, "He's gone back

to the place he came from."

Arimanios said, "That

Nazarene has confused you.

He lied and closed your mind

and put you off the teachings

of our fathers!"

When I heard this

I left the synagogue

and went into the desert.

I was upset and said to myself,

"How was our Saviour chosen?

Why did he enter this world,

and who sent him?

And what is that place

that we'll all go to?"
While I was musing,
suddenly the heavens opened!
All creation glowed with light.
I was very frightened,
when I saw in the brilliant light
a boy, standing upright.
Then he changed into an old person,
then a young one, all in bright light,
so that there appeared, as it were,
three beings in one form.
Then this multiformed image
addressed me and said,
"John, why do you doubt?
Why are you terrified?
Are you a stranger to visions?
Don't be frightened.
It is I who am with you forever,
It is I who am the Father,
Mother and Son.
I am uncorrupted and pure.
I've come to enlighten you
on what exists, what is to come,
and what is to be.
So you may know about
the spiritual and the material realm,
the invisible and the visible,
and all about the Perfect Man.

Pay attention so you can
pass this on to others like you,
from the inheritance of this Perfect Man,
so they might know Truth.
This is my book on the
teachings of Jesus, my Messiah,
and the unveiling of God's mysteries,
which he taught, and his great
teachings secreted in silence."
I asked this triadic figure
if I might hear this Truth.
He proclaimed and answered:
"There is nothing that
can rule over the One.
It is that One which is God
and Father of the All.
The transcendent, immanent,
deathless Self, shining as pure light,
which nobody can see.
This absolute spirit is
more than a God,
for nothing is above Him
and all is in Him.
He rests alone
and is independent.
He is perfect; He needs nothing
and lacks for nothing.
He is boundless,

unsearchable,
immeasurable,
invisible.
External,
internal,
eternal,
ineffable,
unnameable.
He is flawless,
impeccable,
incorporeal;
neither great
nor small.
He has no quantity,
quality or attributes.
He is inscrutable
and beyond time.
He is King of Kings,
bestowing life,
knowledge, goodness,
mercy and salvation.
He is at rest, in silence,
as primordial Being
and pure Light.
He looks at himself
alone in perfect peace,
the fount of living waters
exercising divine will.

This complete totality,
the Aeon above Aeons,
the power and glory,
the virgin spirit,
the womb for creation,
Mother-father,
archetypal Man,
macrocosm and microcosm.
He gazed at the Whole,
in the pure light of
Absolute Consciousness,
and conceived its sole offspring,
a luminous spark.
He was granted a cooperative spirit,
which was clairvoyant intellect.
That spirit rested with
the anointed one, the Christ,
and wished to create by the Word,
from its Will.
By the grace of the spirit,
out of the light of the anointed,
all powers originated.
Beauty, as the first angel, Harmozel,
and with this eternal realm,
loveliness, truth and form.
Oroiael is the second,
angelic light, reflection,
cognisance and memory,

Daueithal was third,
intelligence, love
and archetypal ideal form.
Eleleth was fourth,
perfection, peace and wisdom.
From his will the first
manifestation was named:
the Primordial Man, the Adam.
His son Seth was placed
in the second realm,
with the souls of Saints.
In the fourth realm were
placed unrepentant souls,
unacquainted
with the Perfection.
They later repented and
inhabited the fourth light,
to glorify the invisible spirit.
Wisdom conceived an idea
derived from herself,
to show an image.
But her consort did not agree,
so she conceived alone.
Her birth was imperfect
for it lacked her consort's will
and had a misshapen form;
it was named Ialtabaoth.
It was snake-like,

with a leonine face,
and from its eyes
flashed lightning.
She cast it out so none of
the immortals might know it,
and enveloped it in a glowing cloud.
She put a throne in the middle
of the cloud so it would be invisible,
except to the Mother Of All Living.
Then the Primal Creator, Almighty God,
ordered all things in Perfection."*

*The two final verses commence a new development of ideas and are omitted.

THUNDER

A unique Gnostic revelation by a mysterious Female Deity, stressing the importance of the essential "I Am-ness". Also known as the "Perfect Mind", it contains parallels with ancient Indian literature which refers to the I AM form.

I have issued from a Great Power

and visit all who contemplate me;

I have been discovered

by those who search diligently.

Pay attention, those that meditate

upon me, and listen well!

All of you who are patiently waiting,

take me to your Self!

Don't dismiss me from your mind

and don't let your inner voices

despise me; don't forget me at any

time or place; be watchful!

I am the first and the last,

I am both respected and ignored,

I am both harlot and holy.

I am wife and virgin,

mother and daughter,

organs of my mother,

barren, yet many are my sons.

I am She whose marriage

is auspicious, but I am husbandless.

I am the midwife who doesn't

carry the balm of birth pains.

I am bride and groom

sired by my spouse;
I am mother of my father,
sister of my husband,
and he's my son.
I am slave of He who anointed me.
I am ruler of my children, but
He is the One from whom I was born.
He shall be my Son in time;
my strength is from Him!
I am the rod of His potency
in His youthful virility,
and He is the staff of my old age.
Whatever He wills, happens.
I am the unfathomable silence
and the thought that comes often,
the voice of many sounds,
and the word that appears frequently.
I am the meaning of my Name.
Why am I despised?
Do you love me and hate
those who love me too?
If you deny me then admit me,
You, who pretend to tell the truth
about me, really lie.
Yet you who've lied about me
also tell the Truth.
If you know me, forget me,
and those who don't know me,

let them know!

I am knowledge and ignorance.

I am embarrassment and effrontery,

shameless and ashamed.

I am courage and fright.

I am war and peace. Listen!

I am disgraced yet almighty.

Notice my poverty and richness.

Don't be unkind to me when I'm

thrown out upon the ground.

You'll find me hidden in those

yet to come; don't peer at me

when I'm on the dung heap.

Don't desert me or cast me out;

you'll find me in the Kingdom.

Don't gaze at me when I'm ejected

in disgrace, nor mock me.

Don't hurl me amongst those

who are slain violently.

I am merciful and cruel.

Be vigilant!

Don't despise my servitude.

Don't admire my self-control;

don't forsake me in my ineptitude.

Never fear my power;

don't hate my timidity

or pour scorn on my arrogance.

I am She who dwells in all terror,

the strength and the trembling.
I am She who is pathetic and
pleased in a pleasant place.
I am stupid and I am wise.
Why do you despise me
in your councils?
I'll be quiet among the quiet.
I shall manifest and speak,
yet why do Greeks hate me?
I am a Philistine among Philistines,
yet have the wisdom of Athens
and craftiness of the barbarians.
My image is great in ancient Egypt,
but is nothing amongst Philistines.
I've been hated everywhere,
but also adored.
I am that which people call
life and you call death.
I am called the Law
and lawlessness.
I am the hunted
and the captured.
I am the dispersed
and the collected.
I don't keep festivals,
but have many feasts.
I am both godless and
She who knows God is Great!

I am the One you've
contemplated and mocked.
I am ignorant, yet I teach.
I am despised, yet admired.
I am the One who conceals
and then reveals her Self.
But when you conceal
your Self, I shall appear.
When you appear I'll hide.
Hold me to your Self
from comprehension and regret.
Take me to your Self
in ugly and ruined places.
Rob those who are good,
even in their ugliness.
Ashamed, take me to
your Self shamelessly;
scold my organs in yourself.
Advance, all that know
me and my organs;
establish high creatures
amongst the lowly.
March onto childhood;
don't hate that state
because it appears tiny.
Don't reject greatness
in smallness.
My nature is peace,

but war comes from me.
I am an exile
and a subject;
I am substance
and unsubstantial.
Those who do not cling
to me are ignoramuses,
but those who dwell in
my substance know me.
Those who are close
don't know me.
When you are near,
I'm distant.
On the day you're distant,
I am close.
I am within, in your heart;
I am your true nature,
the creativity of your Self.

THE GOSPEL OF THOMAS

A primary scripture of the Early Eastern Church, recorded by Jude Thomas the Apostle, relating intimate Gnostic sayings of Jesus to his disciples, many of which do not appear in the New Testament. Originally written in Greek before AD 200.

These are the secret words

of Almighty God,

which Lord Jesus Christ

uttered and were scribed by

his disciple Thomas.

He said, "He who comprehends

the inner meaning of these words

will be immortal.

Permit whoever seeks

never to cease from seeking

until he finds.

When he succeeds

he will be turned around;

when he's so turned

he'll be amazed and shall

rule over the All.

If those who lead you

say 'God's Kingdom's in Heaven,'

then birds will fly there first.

If they say 'It's in the sea,'

the fish will swim there first.

For God's Kingdom dwells in

your heart and all around you;

when you know your Self

you too shall be known!
You'll be aware that you're
the sons and daughters of
our living Father.
But if you fail to know
your own Self
you're in hardship
and are that hardship."
His disciples enquired,
"Should we fast?
How should we pray?
Should we give to charity?
What should we eat?"
Lord Jesus replied,
"Don't lie!
Don't do what you hate!
All's seen by Heaven.
There's nothing hidden
that won't be made known.
There's nothing secret
that will stay concealed
without first being shown.
Happy is the lion
that a man will eat;
the lion will become a man.
Cursed is the man whom
the lion eats for that lion
will become a man.

Man is like a skilled
angler who casts his net
and draws it up, full of fish.
Among them he finds
big and small fish.
He throws back the small
and keeps the large.
He who has his ears wide open,
let him hear!
A sower went to sow.
He filled his hand with seeds
and scattered them on the field.
Some fell on the path,
rooks flew down and ate them;
some fell on rocks and failed to root.
Others fell on thorns that choked
them, and worms ate them up.
Some fell on good soil
and grew good fruit,
sixty times the measure
and even double.
I've set fire to this world,
to keep it blazing until
it burns away.
Heaven will pass away;
that which is above heaven
will also pass away.
Dead souls don't live,

live souls don't die;
yet when you treat dead souls
you bring them alive.
When you're in the Light
what will you do?
At birth you were One,
then you made two.
What will you do?"
The disciples asked,
"We know you'll leave us.
Who'll then rule over us?"
Jesus replied,
"Wherever you arrive,
go to James who is righteous,
because of whom, even heaven
and earth came into existence;
now tell me whom I resemble."
Simon Peter answered him first,
"You're like a righteous angel."
Matthew said, "You're like
A sage or lover of wisdom."
Thomas said, "My lips won't let
me say you're like anyone."
Jesus replied,
"I'm no longer your Master
because you've drunk
from living water.
You're enlivened

by the bubbling source
which I've caused to flow."
He took Thomas on one side
and addressed three sayings
of Almighty God to him.
When Thomas returned
they enquired, "What did
Jesus say?"
Thomas replied,
"If I tell you what he said
you'll pick up stones
and hurl them at me;
fire will rise up from them
and burn you all up!"
Lord Jesus then said,
"If you fast you'll get into sin;
if you pray for boons
you'll be condemned;
when you give alms
you may wound your spirit.
When you go to other lands,
into their countryside,
if they welcome you,
eat what they provide
and heal their sick.
What enters your sight won't
harm you, but what comes out
of your mouth can defile you.

When you see He who's
unborn from a womb,
prostrate and worship,
for He's your Father.
Men believe I've come to
bring peace to this world,
but they don't understand
that I've come to bring
divisions on earth,
fire, struggle and strife.
If there are five in a house,
three will fight two,
two will fight three.
Father versus son,
son against father;
they'll stand up better
being alone.
I'll show you what
no eye has seen,
no ear has heard,
no hand has touched,
and what is not yet risen
in men's hearts."
The disciples then said,
"Tell us what our end will be."
He answered,
"Have you seen the beginning
that you may know the end?

Where there's a beginning
there's no end.
Happy is the man or woman
who can stand bravely
at the beginning.
He or she shall know the
end and won't taste death."
The disciples then enquired
about the Kingdom of Heaven.
Jesus replied, "It's like a
grain of mustard, smaller than
other seeds, but when it falls
on ploughed ground it grows
a large stem and shelters the birds."
Mary asked Lord Jesus,
"Whom are your disciples like?"
He replied, "Like small children
living in a field which isn't theirs.
When the owners return
they'll demand their land back;
the disciples have to strip off
their outer pretensions
and pay back their loan.
So if the landlord of the house
knows a burglar is coming
he'll stay awake before he breaks in.
He'll not allow the rogue
to steal his goods.

So, watch this world;
get ready for deeds
with great strength,
otherwise thieves will
find a way to break into you,
and the reward you expect,
they'll get.
In your heart let there be
a man of understanding!
When the corn ripens
he comes in haste,
sickle in hand, and reaps!
He who has his ears wide open,
let him hear!"
Lord Jesus saw babies
being breast fed.
He said to his disciples,
"These infants being suckled
are like those who enter
my Father's House."
They answered,
"Shall we, being as children,
come into His Kingdom?"
Jesus replied,
"Make the two into One
and the inner as the outer
and the outer as the inner,
the above as below,

the male and female
into a single One.
So the male isn't male and
the female isn't female any more.
When you make two eyes
into a single eye,
a hand into a hand,
a foot into a foot,
a picture into a picture,
then you'll enter the Kingdom.
I'll choose you,
as one from a thousand;
you'll stand bravely,
being a single One."
His disciples said, "Show us
that place where you are;
we need to search for it."
He answered, "If you have ears
then pay attention and listen!
There's perfect Light
at the heart of a Man of Light;
he lights up the whole world.
If he fails to shine there's darkness.
If you don't give up the world
you won't find the Kingdom.
If you don't keep the Sabbath
as a real Sabbath,
you won't know my Father.

I stood bravely
in the middle of the world;
I came in a body.
I found them drunk!
None were thirsty.
My soul was afflicted for
mankind, for they are blind
at heart and do not see.
Empty, they enter this world,
empty they'll leave!
But now they're drunk!
When they sober up they'll
change their Knowledge.
A fortified city built on a
high mountain will not fall,
nor is it a secret.
What you hear clearly
between your two ears,
shout from the roof tops.
Nobody lights a lamp and
hides it; instead they put it
on a stand so everyone can
enjoy its light.
If a blind man guides the blind,
they'll both slip into a ditch.
It's impossible to enter
the house of a strong man
and win it by force.

One must bind his hands,
then one can enter.
Have no cares from dawn
until night for what you try."
His disciples asked,
"On which day will you
make yourself known to us?"
Lord Jesus replied,
"When you rid yourselves
of guilt and shame and tear off
your old rags and trample them
beneath your feet like children.
Then you'll see the Son of
He who is the living God,
and you'll never need fear again.
Many years you've yearned to hear
these words of God which I give you.
You've no one else
from whom to hear them;
there'll be days when you
look for me and fail to find me.
To he who holds the Truth
in his hand, more shall be handed;
he who doesn't hold the Truth,
even the little he has shall be taken away.
Be your Self, especially when
you're approaching death."
His disciples enquired,

"Who are you that you can say
these words to us?"
Lord Jesus answered,
"From what I say
can't you see who I am?
But you're like those Jews
who love the tree and shun its fruit,
or love the fruit and shun the tree.
He who blasphemes against
my father shall be forgiven,
but he who blasphemes
against the holy Spirit
shall not be forgiven,
in earth or in heaven.
Grapes aren't picked
from thorn bushes,
nor are figs found on thistles.
A good man brings
virtue out of his barn;
a bad man brings ill will
from the evil stored in his heart.
He spreads guile from his heart's
plenty and spreads wickedness.
From Adam until John the Baptist,
among children of the womb
there's none higher than he.
John has a vision
that won't be blurred.

But as I've said, he among you
who becomes like a small child
shall know the kingdom
and be greater than John.
If two make peace in their one house,
they'll say with faith to the mountain
'Move!' and it will move.
Happy are the solitary
and those chosen, for they
shall find God's Kingdom.
If you seek it in your heart
you shall enter again."
His disciples asked,
"On which day will peace
for the dead come about?
When will a new world come?"
Jesus replied,
"What you desire
has already come,
but you don't realise it."
His disciples said,
"Two dozen prophets
spoke to Israel;
they all prophesied
your true nature."
Jesus replied,
"You've ignored
he who lives with you,

and you've spoken
about the dead.
He who knows this world
has found a corpse;
he who has found a corpse,
this world finds unworthy.
The Kingdom of heaven is like
a farmer who bought good seed;
his foe came one night, stole his
seeds and then sowed weeds.
The farmer forbade his
workmen to hoe the weeds,
saying, 'In pulling the weeds
you may ruin the wheat too.'
But I say, at harvest time
the weeds will crop;
they must all be hoed
and burnt!"
Jesus and his disciples
saw a Samaritan
travelling to Judea
carrying a lamb.
Jesus said, "Why does
he bear that lamb?"
They answered,
"To kill and eat it.
While it's alive he can't eat it,
only when it's dead can he dine."

Jesus then said,
"You yourselves, find the
place of peace within,
or you too will be like
dead lambs and be eaten!
I tell my cryptic parables
to those worthy to hear them.
Whatever effort your right side
may attempt, don't let your left
know what it tries.
There was a rich man who
said, 'I'll use my wealth
to sow, reap and plant
and fill up my barns
so I lack nothing.'
That night he died.
He who has ears wide open,
let him hear!
A man planned a feast;
when he'd prepared the food
he sent his servant to invite the guests.
The servant met the first
and said, 'My master
asks you to dinner.'
The man answered,
'I've got money ready
for some merchants;
they'll come this evening,

and I wish to place some orders,
so I'm sorry, I can't come.'
He went to another and said,
'My master invites you to dinner.'
The man answered,
'I've just bought a farm.
I must collect the rents,
so I'm sorry, I can't come.'
The servant went back and
told his master that those
he'd invited couldn't come.
The master told his servant,
'Go out on the street and
bring any you can find
so they may come and eat.'
So you see, busy business people
will not enter the house of my Father.
Show me the stone
that the builders have rejected;
that one shall be my corner stone.
He who understands all
but lacks Self Knowledge lacks all.
Be happy when you're
reviled and harassed;
but peace won't be found
if your mind harasses you at heart."
A man said to Jesus,
"Please tell my brothers to share

my father's goods with me."

Jesus answered,

"Oh man, who made me to be

a divider; is that who I am?

The harvest is great,

the labourers are few and sluggish;

pray to the Lord to send good workmen.

There are many looking down the well,

but few are diving deeply.

I am the Light above them all;

I am the All; the All issues from me

and reaches me.

Cut wood, I am there;

lift stone, I am there.

Why did you come here

to my countryside?

To see a reed shaken by the wind,

or a man clothed in soft garments?

Your kings and nobles wear fine

robes but do not know Truth!"

A woman from the mob

that had gathered said,

"Blessed is the womb

that gave birth to you,

my Lord, and the breasts

that suckled you."

He answered,

"Happy are all those

who’ve heard my words,
the hidden secrets of my
Father, The Living God, and
have kept them in good Faith.
For there may come a
time when you’ll say,
‘Happy is the womb
that didn’t give birth,
and the breasts that didn’t feed.’
He that loves the world,
identifies with his body,
and he who does so,
the world is unworthy of him.
He who’s become rich,
let him be king,
and he who has power,
let him abandon it.
He who is near to me
is close to the fire,
and he who is distant
is far from my Kingdom.
Pictures are seen by men,
but that pure Light which
reveals them lies veiled.
In the reflection
of my Father’s Light
His Light will be seen;
but His image will be

hidden by His Light.
On the day you see the
Light of your own true Self,
you'll rejoice!
But if you only see forms
which from the beginning
were in you, and don't die
to them or know them,
how can you stand the Light?
Adam was created from a vast
power and great fecundity.
He wasn't fit for you
for had he been worthy
he wouldn't have known
spiritual death.
Foxes have holes,
birds boast nests;
the Son of Man has
no den where he can
lay down his head and rest.
Decadent is the soul
that depends on the body;
miserable is the man
attached to the flesh.
Angels and Prophets will
visit you and hand you
what is truly yours.
You must give back

what’s in your keeping.
Pray to your Self and ask,
‘When will they come
to collect what’s theirs?’
Why do you clean only
the lip of a cup when
He who made the inner
also made the outer?
Follow me!
My yoke is easy,
my lordship is gentle;
you’ll find peace.”
The disciples asked,
“Who are you?
So that we may trust you.”
Lord Jesus replied,
“You merely contemplate
the surface of heaven and earth,
but he who stands before you
you don’t know; nor do you
know how to find out.
Search and you shall find!
But what you’ve asked me
I held from telling you;
now I wish to speak.
But you do not seek
after Self Knowledge.
Don’t waste good food on dogs;

they leave it on a dung heap.
Don't hand pearls to pigs;
they'll pollute them.
He who earnestly and
persistently seeks, shall find!
To him who knocks hard,
the door will be opened.
If you have money,
don't lend just for interest,
but give it to him who needs it.
The Kingdom of Heaven
is like a good woman who
takes leaven, hides it in dough
and bakes loaves.
Those that have ears to hear,
let them hear!
The Kingdom of Heaven is
also like a foolish woman carrying
a load of flour on a long road;
the sack splits and flour pours out,
but she doesn't realise.
Because she doesn't see what
has happened, she isn't worried,
but when she gets home her sack is empty.
The Kingdom of Heaven
is like a brave soldier
wishing to slay a giant;
he draws his sword at home

and strikes through the wall
to test his confidence.
Then he goes and kills the giant."
His disciples said,
"Your mother and brothers
are waiting outside."
He replied, "All those here
who do the will of my Father
are my mother and brothers;
they're the ones who will enter
the Kingdom of Heaven."
The disciples showed Jesus
a gold shekel, saying,
"Caesar's collectors
demand taxes from us."
Jesus replied, "Hand to
Caesar what is Caesar's,
to God what is God's,
and what is mine hand to me.
He who doesn't reject
his mother and father
because of my teaching
won't become my disciple,
for my mother gave me birth
but my real Mother gave me life.
Pity the Pharisees;
they're like dogs
sleeping in an ox's shed.

They neither eat nor
let the ox eat.
Blessed is the man who
knows when thieves will
break into his house.
He can get up, collect himself, and
be ready to act before they come."
The disciples said,
"Let's pray and fast today."
Jesus answered, "What sin
have I committed or by what
have I been conquered?
When the bridegroom leaves
the bridal chamber, then
we'll fast and pray.
He who knows his real
Mother and Father, can he
be called the son of a whore?
When you make two into
One you'll be sons of Man,
and if you command a
mountain to move, it will move.
The Kingdom of Heaven
is like the good shepherd
who owned a hundred sheep.
When the fattest was lost he
left all the others until he found it.
He told his flock, 'I loved that one

more than the rest.'
He who drinks my words with
understanding shall be like me,
and I shall become him and the
secret things will be revealed.
The Kingdom of Heaven
is like the farmer who owned
a field with buried treasure
that he did not know was there.
When he died he left the land
to his son, who, also being
ignorant, sold the field.
The man who bought it found
the gold while ploughing and
was able to grant loans at a
fair rate of interest.
He who has known this
world and become wealthy,
let him disown it.
The earth and heavens
may turn back before you,
but he who is truly alive
won't know fear or death.
He who finds himself
to be of this world is unfit.
Pity the body that
leans upon the soul;
pity the soul that

leans upon the flesh."
His disciples enquired,
"On what day will
the Kingdom come?"
Lord Jesus replied, "It won't
come through anticipation;
they won't say, 'Look, it's here,
or look over there.'
The Kingdom of Heaven
covers the Earth with glory,
but mankind fails to see it!"
Simon Peter said to the
Lord and his disciples,
"Let Mary leave us, because women
are unfit for the Life Everlasting."
Jesus replied,
"Wait, I'll guide her soul,
to make her as a real man,
in that place which transcends
the differences between the sexes,
so she'll become a living spirit.
For each woman who makes
herself male in this way
and overcomes all differences
will enter the Kingdom of Heaven!"

THE GOSPEL OF PETER

But of the Jews no man washed his hands, neither did Herod nor any one of his judges: and whereas they would not wash, Pilate rose up. And then Herod the king commanded that the Lord should be taken into their hands, saying unto them: "All that I commanded you to do unto him, do ye."

Now there stood there Joseph the friend of Pilate and of the Lord, and he, knowing that they were about to crucify him, came unto Pilate and begged the body of Jesus for burial. And Pilate sending unto Herod, begged his body. And Herod said: "Brother Pilate, even if none had begged for him, we should have buried him, since also the Sabbath dawneth; for it is written in the law that the sun should not set upon one that hath been slain (murdered)."

And he delivered him unto the people before the first day of (or on the day before the unleavened bread, even their feast. And they having taken the Lord pushed him as they ran, and said: Let us hale the Son of God, now that we have gotten authority over him. And they put on him a purple robe, and made him sit upon the seat of judgement, saying: "Give righteous judgement, thou King of Israel." And one of them brought a crown of thorns and set it upon the Lord's head; and others stood and did spit in his eyes, and others buffeted his cheeks; and others did prick him with a reed, and some of them scourged him, saying With this honour let us honour (or at this price let us valuethe son of God.

1And they brought two malefactors, and crucified the Lord between them. But he kept silence, as one feeling no pain. And when they set the cross upright, they wrote thereon: "This is the King of Israel." And they laid his garments before him, and divided them among themselves and 1cast the lot upon them. But one of those malefactors reproached them, saying: "We have thus suffered for the evils which we have done; but this man which hath become the saviour of men, wherein hath he injured you?" And they were wroth with him, and commanded that his legs should not be broken, that so he might die in torment.

Now it was noonday, and darkness prevailed over all Judaea: and they were troubled and in an agony lest the sun should have set, for that he yet lived: for it is written for them that the sun should not set upon him that hath been slain (murdered). And one of them said: "Give ye him to drink gall with vinegar": and they mingled it and gave him to drink: and they fulfilled all things and accomplished 1their sins upon their own heads. And many went about with lamps, supposing that it was night: and some fell. And the Lord cried out aloud saying: "My power, my power, thou hast forsaken me." And when he had so said, he was taken up.

And in the same hour was the veil of the temple of Jerusalem rent in two.

And then they plucked the nails from the hands of the Lord and laid him upon the earth: and the whole earth was shaken, and there came a great fear on all.

Then the sun shone forth, and it was found to be the ninth hour. And the Jews rejoiced, and gave his body unto Joseph to bury it, because he had beheld all the good things which he did. And he took the Lord and washed him and wrapped him in linen and brought him unto his own sepulchre, which is called the Garden of Joseph.

Then the Jews and the elders and the priests, when they perceived how great evil they had done themselves, began to lament and to say: "Woe unto our sins: the judgement and the end of Jerusalem is drawn nigh."

But I with my fellows was in grief, and we were wounded in our minds and would have hid ourselves; for we were sought after by them as malefactors, and as thinking to set the temple on fire. And beside all these things we were fasting, and we sat mourning and weeping night and day until the Sabbath.

But the scribes and Pharisees and elders gathered one with another, for they had heard that all the people were murmuring and beating their breasts, saying: "If these very great signs have come to pass at his death, behold how righteous he was." And the elders were afraid and came unto Pilate, entreating him and saying: "Give us soldiers that we (or they may watch his sepulchre for three days, lest his disciples come and steal him away and the people suppose that he is risen from the dead, and do us hurt." And Pilate gave them Petronius the centurion with soldiers to watch the sepulchre; and the elders and scribes came with them unto the tomb, and when they had rolled a great stone to keep out (al. together withthe centurion and the soldiers, then all 3that were there together set it upon the door of the tomb; and plastered thereon seven seals; and they pitched a tent there and kept watch.

3And early in the morning as the Sabbath dawned, there came a multitude from Jerusalem and the region roundabout to see the sepulchre that had been sealed.

3Now in the night whereon the Lord's day dawned, as the soldiers were keeping guard two by two in every watch, 3there came a great sound in the heaven, and they saw the heavens opened and two men descend thence, shining with (lit. havinga great light, and drawing near unto the sepulchre. 3And that stone which had been set on the door rolled away of itself and went back to the side, and the sepulchre was

X.

3opened and both of the young men entered in. When therefore those soldiers saw that, they waked up the centurion and the elders (for they also were there keeping 3watch); and while they were yet telling them the things which they had seen, they saw again three men come out of the sepulchre, and two of them sustaining the other (lit. the 4one), and a cross following, after them. And of the two they saw that their heads reached unto heaven, but of him that 4was led by them that it overpassed the heavens. And they 4heard a voice out of the heavens saying: Hast thou (or Thou hastpreached unto them that sleep? And an answer was heard from the cross, saying: Yea.

XI.

4Those men therefore took counsel one with another to go and report these things unto Pilate. And while they yet thought thereabout, again the heavens were opened and a 4man descended and entered into the tomb. And they that were with the centurion (or the centurion and they that were with himwhen they saw that, hasted to go by night unto Pilate and left the sepulchre whereon they were keeping watch, and told all that they had seen, and were in great agony, saying: Of a truth he was the son of God.

4Pilate answered and said: I am clear from the blood of 4the son of God, but thus it seemed good unto you. Then all they came and besought him and exhorted him to charge the centurion and the soldiers to tell nothing of that they had 4seen: For, said they, it is expedient for us to incur the greatest sin before God, rather than to (and not tofall into 4the hands of the people of the Jews and to be stoned. Pilate therefore charged the centurion and the soldiers that they should say nothing.

XII.

5Now early on the Lord's day Mary Magdalene, a disciple (fem.of the Lord-which, being afraid because of the Jews, for they were inflamed with anger, had not performed at the sepulchre of the Lord those things which women are accustomed to do unto them that die and are 5beloved of them-took with her the women her friends and 5came unto the tomb where he was laid. And they feared lest the Jews should see them, and said: Even if we were not able to weep and lament him on that day whereon he was 5crucified, yet let us now do so at his tomb. But who will roll away for us the stone also that is set upon the door of the tomb, that we may enter in and sit beside him and perform 5that which is due? for the stone was great, and we fear lest any man see us. And if we cannot do so, yet let us cast down at the door these things which we bring for a memorial of him, and we will weep and lament until we come unto our house.

XIII.

5And they went and found the sepulchre open : and they drew near and looked in there, and saw there a young man sitting in the midst of the sepulchre, of a fair countenance and clad in very bright raiment, which said unto them: 5Wherefore are ye come? whom seek ye? not him that was crucified? He is risen and is departed; but if ye believe it not, look in and see the place where he lay, that he is not here: for he is risen and is departed thither whence he was sent. 5Then the women were affrighted and fled.

XIV.

5Now it was the last day of unleavened bread, and many were coming forth of the city and returning unto their 5own homes because the feast was at an end. But we, the twelve disciples of the Lord, were weeping and were in sorrow, and each one being grieved for that which had befallen 6departed unto his own house. But I, Simon Peter, and Andrew my brother, took our nets and went unto the sea: and there was with us Levi the son of Alphaeus, whom the Lord (For Fragment II see Apocalypse of Peter.)

INFANCY GOSPEL OF THOMAS

The following translation is based on the Greek text printed in Ronald F. Hock's The Infancy Gospels of James and Thomas. The text is a slightly modified version of Tischendorf A. Chapters and verses are divided as in the "Scholars Version" translation.

CHAPTER 1

(1) I, Thomas the Israelite, am reporting to you, all my brothers from the nations, to reveal the childhood and the greatness of our Lord Jesus Christ, what he did in my country after he was born. This is the beginning of it.

CHAPTER 2

(1) When the boy Jesus was five years old, he was playing in a narrow part of a rushing stream. (2) He was gathering the flowing waters into ponds, and immediately they were made clean, and he ordered these things with a single word. (3) And after he made clay, he molded twelve sparrows from it. And it was the Sabbath when he did these things. But there were also many other children playing with him.

(4) Then, a certain Jew saw what Jesus was doing while playing on the Sabbath. Immediately, he departed and reported to Jesus' father, Joseph, "Look, your child is in the stream and he took clay and formed twelve birds and profaned the Sabbath?"

(5) And Joseph went to the area and when he saw him, he shouted, "Why are you doing these things that are not permitted on the Sabbath?"

(6) Jesus, however, clapped his hands and shouted to the sparrows, "Depart, fly, and remember me now that you are alive." And the sparrows departed shrieking.

(7) When the Jews saw this, they were amazed. After they had gone away, they described to their leaders what they had seen Jesus do.

CHAPTER 3

(1) The son of Annas the scribe was standing there with Jesus. Taking a branch from a willow tree, he dispersed the waters which Jesus had gathered. (2) When Jesus saw what had happened, he became angry and said to him, "You godless, brainless moron, what did the ponds and waters do to you? Watch this now: you are going to dry up like

a tree and you will never produce leaves or roots or fruit."

(3) And immediately, this child withered up completely. Then, Jesus departed and returned to Joseph's house. (4) The parents of the one who had been withered up, however, wailed for their young child as they took his remains away. Then, they went to Joseph and accused him, "You are responsible for the child who did this."

CHAPTER 4

(1) Next, he was going through the village again and a running child bumped his shoulder. Becoming bitter, Jesus said to him, "You will not complete your journey." (2) Immediately, he fell down and died.

(3) Then, some of the people who had seen what had happened said, "Where has this child come from so that his every word is a completed deed?"

(4) And going to Joseph, the parents of the one who had died found fault with him. They said, "Because you have such a child, you are not allowed to live with us in the village, or at least teach him to bless and not curse. For our children are dead!"

CHAPTER 5

(1) And taking his child aside, he warned him, saying, "Why are you doing these things? These people are suffering and they hate us and cause trouble for us."

(2) Then, Jesus said, "I know that the words I speak are not mine. Nevertheless, I will be silent for your sake, but these people will bear their punishment." And immediately his accusers became blind.

(3) When they saw what he had done, they were extremely afraid and did not know what to do. And they talked about him, saying, "Every word he speaks, good or evil, is an event and becomes a miracle."

(4) When Joseph saw that Jesus had done this, however, he was outraged and took his ear and pulled it extremely hard. (5) Then, the child became angry and said to him, "It is enough for you to seek and not find, but too much for you to act so unwisely. (6) Do you not know that I am not yours? Do not trouble me."

CHAPTER 6

(1) A teacher named Zacchaeus overheard everything Jesus said to Joseph and marveled, saying to himself, "As just a child, he utters these things." And taking Joseph aside, he said to him, "You have a wise child; he has a good mind, but give him to me that he may learn letters. I will teach him all knowledge so that he will not be rebellious."

(3) Replying, Joseph said to him, "Nobody except God can subordinate this child. Do not consider him to be a small cross, brother."

(4) As Jesus heard Joseph saying this, he laughed and said to Zacchaeus, "Really, teacher, what my father has said to you is true. (5) I am the Lord of this people and am here in your presence and have been born among you and am with you. (6) I know where you are from and how many years there will be in your lives. I am telling you the truth, teacher, when you were born, I existed. And if you want to be a perfect teacher, listen to me and I will teach you wisdom which nobody knows except me and the one who sent me to you. (7) For you are my disciple and I know you, how old you are and how old you will live to be. (8) And when you see the cross my father has described, you will believe that everything I have said to you is true."

(9) Then, the Jews who were present and heard Jesus were amazed and said, "What a strange and remarkable event. The child is only five years old and already he says such things. For we never heard anyone who speaks words like this child does."

(10) Replying to them, Jesus said, "Are you so amazed? Then you should believe more of what I said to you. I really also know when you and your parents were born and I will tell you this remarkable fact: even when the world was created, I and the one who sent me to you existed."

(11) When the Jews heard the child say this, however, it made them angry, even though they were not able to reply to his speech. (12) Then, the child came forward and leaping toward them, he said, "I taunted you! For I know that you are amazed by little things and have minuscule minds."

(13) Since they thought they were being consoled by the child's exhortation, the teacher said to Joseph, "Lead him to the school and I will teach him letters."

(14) So Joseph took him by the hand and led him into the classroom. (15) And the teacher wrote the alphabet for him and began to practice it many times, but the child said nothing and did not answer him for a long time. (16) Becoming outraged, the teacher hit him on the head. After enduring this stoically, the child said to him, "I am teaching you more than being taught by you because I know the letters you are teaching me and your judgment is great. These things are to you like a copper pitcher or a clashing cymbal which do not offer glory or wisdom through sound. (17) Nobody understands the power of my wisdom." (18) Then, when his rage was finished, he said the alphabet from alpha to omega very quickly.

(19) Looking the teacher in the face, he told him, "Since you do not know the nature of the alpha, how are going to teach me the beta? (20) Hypocrite, if you know, first teach me the alpha then I will believe what you say about the beta." (21) Then, he began

to tell the teacher about the first letter. And the teacher was not strong enough to say anything.

(22) Then, while many were listening, he said to Zacchaeus, "Listen, teacher, and observe the structure of the first letter, (23) how it has two standard lines and impresses coming to a point in the middle and remaining there, coming together, lifting up, dancing, having three corners, having two corners, without strokes, of one family, well-balanced, as long as the alpha has equal lines."

CHAPTER 7

(1) When Zacchaeus heard such great words and allegories of this sort about the first letter from the child, he was at a loss over what his defense and teaching could be. (2) And he said to those present, "Oh me, I am suffering and at a loss and am ashamed of myself because I took this child. (3) So take him, I urge you, brother Joseph. I am not able to bear his stare or his direct speech. (4) This child was not born of the earth; he is even able to subdue fire. Perhaps, he was born before the creation of the world. (5) What womb bore him, what sort of mother brought him up, I know not. (6) Oh me, friends, I am going out of my mind. (7) I deceived myself and am suffering unimaginably. I struggled to have a student and I have found that I have a teacher. (8) Brothers, consider the shame: an experienced leader has been conquered by a child! (9) And I may have to lose heart and die because of this child. For at this very hour, I am not able to look him in the eye. (10) When everyone says that I have been conquered by a child, what can I say? And what more is there to say about the lines of the first letter than what he already told me? I do not know. (11) So I beg you, brother Joseph, take him to your house. Whether I should call him a god or an angel or something else, I do not know."

CHAPTER 8

(1) While the Jews were advising Zacchaeus, the child had a great laugh and said, "Now, the fruitless bear fruit and the blind see and the deaf in the understanding of the heart hear. (2) I am here from above that I may rescue those below and call them to higher things, just as the one who sent me to you commanded me."

(3) And when the child completed his speech, those who were under his curse were immediately saved, (4) but from then on, nobody dared to make him angry because they did not want to be cursed or crippled.

CHAPTER 9

(1) And after a few days passed, Jesus was up on a roof of a house. And one of the children playing with him died after falling off the roof. And when the other children saw, they fled and Jesus was left standing alone.

(2) When the parents of the one who had died came, they accused Jesus, "Troublemaker, you threw him down."

(3) But Jesus replied, "I did not throw him down, rather he threw himself down. When he was not acting carefully, he leaped off the roof and died."

(4) Jesus leaped off the roof and stood by the corpse of the boy and cried out with a loud voice and said, "Zeno," - for that was his name - "rise up, talk to me: did I throw you down?"

(5) And rising up immediately, he said, "No, Lord, you did not throw me down, but you did raise me up."

(6) And when they saw this, they were overwhelmed. The parents of the child glorified God on account of the sign which had happened and they worshipped Jesus.

CHAPTER 10

(1) A short number of days later, when a certain young man was splitting wood in the neighborhood, his ax fell and cut through the bottom of his foot. As it became bloodless, he was dying.

(2) Then, there was a great clamor and a crowd formed and the child Jesus ran there. And forcing his way through the crowd, he went and seized the young man's wounded foot. Immediately, it was healed.

(3) Then, he said to the young man, "Get up now, chop the wood and remember me."

(4) When the crowd saw what had happened, they worshipped the child, saying, "Truly, the spirit of God dwells in this child."

CHAPTER 11

(1) When Jesus was six years old, his mother sent him to draw water to carry into the house. But he accidentally let the water go in the crowd, (2) and crashing, the water jar broke. (3) But unfolding the cloak which was thrown around him, he filled it with water and carried it to his mother.

(4) When his mother saw the sign he had done, she kissed him and treasured in her heart the mysterious things she had seen him do.

CHAPTER 12

(1) Then again, in the season of sowing, the child went with his father to sow grain in their field. And as his father was sowing, the child Jesus also sowed one measure of grain. (2) And after he harvested and threshed it, it produced one hundred measures. (3) And calling all the poor of the village to the threshing floor, he gave them grain freely. And Joseph carried the remaining grain away. (4) Jesus was eight years old when he did this sign.

CHAPTER 13

(1) Since his father was a carpenter, he was making plows and yokes in that season. (2) An order for a bed was given to him from a rich man, (3) but one of the boards, the one called the crossbeam, was shorter than the other. And since Joseph had no idea what to do, the child Jesus said to his father Joseph, "Put the two pieces of wood down and line up the ends."

(3) And Joseph did just as the child told him. Then, Jesus stood at the other end and grasped the shorter piece of wood and stretching it, he made it equal with the other.

(4) And his father Joseph saw and was amazed and, taking the child, he kissed him, saying, "I am blessed because God gave me this child."

CHAPTER 14

(1) When Joseph saw the child's willingness and age and that his mind was also ready, he again wanted him to become accustomed to letters. So, taking him, he gave him to another teacher. (2) The teacher said to Joseph, "First I will teach him Greek, then Hebrew." For the teacher knew about the child's earlier attempt and was afraid. Nonetheless, after writing the alphabet, he instructed the boy for many hours, even though he did not reply to him.

(3) Then, Jesus said to him, "If you are really a teacher and if you know the letters so well, tell me the meaning of the alpha and I will tell you the meaning of the beta."

(4) As he was growing frustrated, the teacher struck him on the head. Then, Jesus became angry and cursed him. Immediately, he fainted and fell on his face.

(5) Then, Jesus turned back to Joseph's house, but Joseph was distressed. He instructed the boy's mother, "Do not let him out the door because the people who anger him will die."

CHAPTER 15

(1) After some time had passed, again another teacher, a close friend of Joseph, said to him, "Send the child to me in my classroom. Perhaps with flattery, I will be able to teach him the letters."

(2) And Joseph said to him, "If you are sure, brother, take him with you." And while he took him along with much fear and anxiety, the child went along gladly.

(3) And coming boldly into the classroom, he found a book lying on the desk and taking it, he read the letters in it. Opening his mouth, he spoke in the Holy Spirit and taught the law to those standing there.

(4) A large multitude came and stood around, listening to him. And they marveled at the fullness of his teaching and the readiness of his speech, saying, "This is a child saying such things."

(5) When Joseph heard what was going on, he was afraid and ran to the classroom, thinking, "This teacher is not accustomed to him."

(6) The teacher, however, said to Joseph, "Brother, I want you to know that I received the child as a student, but since he is full of grace and wisdom, I am asking you, brother, take him to your house."

(7) When the child heard these things, he immediately smiled at him and said, "Since you have spoken and witnessed correctly, for your sake the one who was wounded will be healed." And at once, the other teacher was healed. Then, Joseph took the child and went back to his house.

CHAPTER 16

(1) Then, Joseph sent his son James to tie up wood and bring it into his house, but the child Jesus also followed him. And while James was collecting the bushes, a viper bit his hand. (2) And as he lay on the ground dying, Jesus approached and blew on the bite. And immediately, his anguish ceased and the animal broke apart and at once James was healthy.

CHAPTER 17

(1) After these things happened, an infant in Joseph's neighborhood died and his mother mourned greatly. When Jesus heard that she was extremely sad and was making an uproar, he ran there frantically.

(2) And finding the child dead, he touched his stomach and said, "I say to you, infant, do not die, but live and be with your mother."

(3) Immediately, he was resurrected and laughed. Then, Jesus said to the woman, "Take the child, give him your breast, and remember me."

(4) And when the crowd standing around saw this, they were amazed and said, "Truly, this child either was God or an angel of God because all his words are completed deeds." And Jesus departed from there playing with other children.

CHAPTER 18

(1) Another year later, a man building a house died after falling from the full height of it. And after a great commotion began, Jesus stood up and went there. (2) And seeing the dead man lying there, he grabbed his hand and said, "I say to you, man, arise, do your work." And rising up immediately, he worshipped him.

(3) When the crowd saw, they were amazed and said, "This child is a heavenly being. For he has saved many souls from death and has the power to continue saving souls throughout his whole life."

CHAPTER 19

(1) When he was twelve years old, his parents went to Jerusalem with a caravan for the festival of Passover, as was their custom. (2) And after the Passover, they returned to their home. When they departed, however, the child Jesus returned to Jerusalem, although his parents thought he was in the caravan. (3) After traveling along the road for one day, they sought him among their relatives. When they did not find him, they grieved. And they turned back to the city, searching for him.

(4) And after three days, they found him in the temple, sitting in the middle of the teachers and listening to the law and questioning them. (5) Everyone paid attention to him and was amazed at how this child was questioning the elders and teachers of the people so closely, interpreting the chief points of the law and parables of the prophets. (6) Then, his mother Mary came to him and said, "Why did you do this to us, child? See how we are troubled as we search for you."

(7) And Jesus said to them, "Why are you searching for me? Do you not know that I must be in my father's house?"

(8) Then, the scribes and Pharisees said, "Are you the mother of this child?"

(9) She said, "I am."

(10) And they said to her, "Blessed are you among women because God has blessed the fruit of your womb. For we have never seen or heard such glory or virtue or wisdom."

(11) When Jesus got up, he followed his mother and submitted to his parents. And his mother treasured everything that had happened. (12) And Jesus continued to grow in wisdom and age and grace.

(13) To him be the glory forever and ever, amen.

INFANCY GOSPEL OF JAMES

CHAPTER 1: JOACHIM'S PLIGHT

(1) In the histories of the twelve tribes of Israel, Joachim was a very rich man. And he doubled the gifts he offered to the Lord, saying to himself, "One is from my surplus for all the people, and the other is to the Lord God for forgiveness, to atone for me."

(2) Now the great day of the Lord was approaching, and the people of Israel were offering their gifts. But Reubel stood before him and said, "It's not right for you to offer your gifts first, since you haven't had a child in Israel."

(3) And Joachim was very grieved and went to the (history) of the twelve tribes of the people, saying to himself, "I'll look in the (history) of the twelve tribes of Israel to see whether I'm the only one who hasn't had a child in Israel." And he searched, and found that all the just people in Israel had raised children. And he remembered that in the last days of the patriarch Abraham, the Lord God gave him a son, Isaac.

(4) And Joachim was very grieved, and didn't go to his wife, but gave himself to the wilderness and pitched his tent there. And Joachim fasted forty days and forty nights, saying to himself, "I won't go down for food or drink until the Lord my God considers me. Prayer will be my food and drink."

CHAPTER 2: ANNA'S PLIGHT

(1) Now his wife, Anna, mourned and lamented for two reasons. She said, "I lament that I'm a widow and that I don't have a child."

(2) Now the great day of the Lord was approaching, and her servant Juthine said to her, "How long are you going to humiliate your soul? Look, the great day of the Lord has approached, and it's not right for you to grieve. But take this headband which the leader of the workplace gave me. It's not right for me to wear it, since I'm your servant, and it has a royal mark."

(3) And Anna said, "Get away from me! I won't do this. The Lord God has greatly humiliated me. Maybe a trickster gave this to you, and you've come to get me to share in your sin."

And Juthine the servant said, "Why should I curse you, since you haven't heard my voice? The Lord God has made your womb infertile, to give you no fruit in Israel."

(4) And Anna was very grieved, and removed her garment of mourning, washed her head, and put on her wedding garment. And at about the ninth hour she went down

into her garden to walk around. She saw a laurel tree and sat down under it. And after resting, she petitioned the Lord. She said, "God of my ancestors, bless me and hear my prayer, as you blessed our mother Sarah and gave her a son, Isaac."

CHAPTER 3: ANNA'S LAMENT

(1) Anna looked intently to heaven and saw a nest of sparrows in the laurel tree. And Anna lamented, saying to herself,

"Woe is me! Who gave birth to me? What womb bore me? I was born as a curse before the people of Israel and have been despised; they've mocked me and banished me from the Temple of the Lord my God.

(2) "Woe is me! What am I like? I'm not like the birds of heaven, because even the birds of heaven are fruitful before you, Lord.

"Woe is me! What am I like? I'm not like the animals, because even the animals are fruitful before you, Lord.

"Woe is me! What am I like? I'm not like the wild beasts of the earth, because even the wild beasts of the earth are fruitful before you, Lord.

(3) "Woe is me! What am I like? I'm not like these waters, because even these waters are serene yet churn, and their fish bless you, Lord.

"Woe is me! What am I like? I'm not like this earth, because the earth produces her fruits when it's time and blesses you, Lord."

CHAPTER 4: THE LORD'S PROMISE

(1) And look! An angel of the Lord stood nearby, saying to her, "Anna, Anna, the Lord has heard your prayer. You'll conceive and give birth, and your offspring will be spoken of through the whole world."

And Anna said, "As the Lord God lives, whether I give birth to a boy or a girl, I'll bring it as a gift to the Lord my God, and it will minister to him all the days of its life."

(2) And look! Two angels came, saying to her, "Look, Joachim, your husband, is coming with his flocks." For an angel of the Lord had gone down to Joachim, saying, "Joachim, Joachim, the Lord God has heard your prayer. Go down from here. Look, your wife, Anna, has conceived in her womb."

(3) And immediately Joachim went down and called the shepherds, saying to them, "Bring here to me ten lambs without spot or blemish, and the ten lambs will be for

the Lord God. And bring me twelve tender calves for the priests and the elders. And a hundred male goats for all the people."

(4) And look! Joachim came with his flocks, and Anna stood at the gate. And she saw Joachim coming with his flocks, and immediately ran and flung herself around his neck, saying, "Now I know that the Lord God has greatly blessed me. For look! The widow is no longer a widow, and look! The one without a child in her womb has conceived."

And Joachim rested for the first day in his house.

CHAPTER 5: MARY'S BIRTH

(1) And the next day, he was offering his gifts, saying to himself, "If the Lord God is reconciled to me, the plate worn by the priest will make it clear to me." And Joachim offered his gifts and paid attention to the priest's plate as he went up to the altar of the Lord. And he didn't see sin in it. And Joachim said, "Now I know that the Lord God has been reconciled to me and has sent all my sins away from me." And he went down from the Temple of the Lord justified and went into his house.

(2) And about six months were completed, and in the seventh month she gave birth. And Anna said to her midwife, "What is it?"

And the midwife said, "It's a girl!"

And Anna said, "My soul is magnified this day!" And she laid down her child.

And when her days were completed, Anna cleansed her flow of blood. And she gave her breast to the child, and gave her the name Mary.

CHAPTER 6: MARY'S FIRST YEAR

(1) And day by day, the child grew stronger. When she was six months old, her mother stood her on the ground to test whether she could stand. And walking seven steps, she came to her mother's breast, and her mother caught her up, saying, "As the Lord my God lives, you won't walk on this ground again until I bring you into the Temple of the Lord."

And she made a sanctuary in her bedroom and didn't allow anything sacrilegious or impure to pass through it. And she called the pure daughters of the Hebrews, and they played with her.

(2) And when the child grew to be a year old, Joachim made a great feast, and called the chief priests, and the priests, and the scribes, and the elders, and all the people of

Israel. And Joachim brought the child to the priests, and they blessed her, saying, "God of our ancestors, bless this child and give her a name that'll be spoken forever among all generations."

And all the people said, "So be it. Amen!"

And they brought her to the chief priests, and they blessed her, saying, "Most High God, look upon this child, and bless her with a final blessing which can't be surpassed."

(3) And her mother took her up to the sanctuary of her bedroom and gave her breast to the child. And Anna made a song to the Lord God, saying:

"I'll sing a holy song to the Lord my God, because God has visited me, and has removed the criticism of my enemies.

"And the Lord God has given me the fruit of God's justice, singular yet manifold before God.

"Who will report to Reubel's people that Anna nurses a child? 'Listen, listen, twelve tribes of Israel: Anna nurses a child!'"

And Anna rested in the sanctuary of her bedroom. And she went and ministered to them. When dinner was finished, they went down rejoicing and glorifying the God of Israel.

CHAPTER 7: MARY GOES TO THE TEMPLE

(1) And she cared for her child through the months. When she was two years old, Joachim said, "Let's take her to the Temple of the Lord, so that we may keep the promise we made, so that the Lord won't be angry with us and find our gift unacceptable."

But Anna said, "Let's wait until her third year, so that she won't seek her father or mother."

And Joachim said, "Let's wait."

(2) And the child became three years old, and Joachim said, "Let's call the pure daughters of the Hebrews. And let them take their lamps, and let them be lit, so that the child won't turn back, and her heart won't be drawn away from the Temple of the Lord." And they did so until they went up to the Temple of the Lord.

And the priest welcomed her, kissed her, and said, "The Lord God has magnified your name among all the generations. Through you, the Lord will reveal his redemption of the people of Israel in the last days."

(3) And he sat her down on the third step of the altar, and the Lord God poured grace upon her. And she danced on her feet, and all the house of Israel loved her.

CHAPTER 8: MARY TURNS TWELVE

(1) And her parents went down, marveling and praising and glorifying the Lord God that the child hadn't turned back. And Mary was in the Temple of the Lord. She was nurtured like a dove, and received food from the hand of an angel.

(2) And when she became twelve years old, there was a council of the priests, saying, "Look, Mary has been in the Temple of the Lord twelve years. What should we do about her so that she won't pollute the sanctuary of the Lord our God?" And they said to the chief priest, "You stand at the altar of the Lord. Go in and pray about her, and if the Lord God reveals anything to you, we'll do it."

(3) And the chief priest went in, taking the robe with twelve bells into the Holy of Holies, and prayed about her. And look! An angel of the Lord stood nearby, saying, "Zechariah, Zechariah, go out and assemble the widowers of the people, and let them each bear a staff. And whomever the Lord God points out with a sign, she'll be his wife."

And the heralds went down through the whole surrounding area of Judea, and sounded the trumpet of the Lord. And look! All the men rushed in.

CHAPTER 9: JOSEPH PROTECTS MARY

(1) And Joseph threw down his axe, and went to their meeting. And when they had all gathered, they went to the priest with their staffs. And having taken all their staffs, he went into the Temple and prayed. And when he had finished the prayer, he took the staffs, went out, and gave them back. But there wasn't a sign among them. And Joseph took his staff last, and look! A dove went from the staff, and flew upon Joseph's head. And the priest said to Joseph, "You've been chosen to welcome the virgin of the Lord into your own care."

(2) But Joseph refused, saying, "I have sons and am an old man, but she's young. I won't be a laughingstock among the people of Israel."

And the priest said, "Joseph, fear the Lord your God, and remember what God did to Dathan, Abiron, and Kore; how the earth opened and swallowed them all because of their rebellion. And now fear, Joseph, so that these things won't happen in your house."

(3) And being afraid, Joseph welcomed her into his care, and said to her, "Mary, I've taken you from the Temple of the Lord, and now I bring you to my house. I'm going away to build houses, but I'll come back to you. The Lord will protect you."

CHAPTER 10: THE VEIL OF THE TEMPLE

(1) And there was a council of the priests, saying, "Let's make a veil for the Temple of the Lord."

And the priest said, "Call the pure virgins from the tribe of David to me." And the officers went out and searched and found seven. And the priest remembered that the child Mary was from the tribe of David and pure before God. And the officers went out and brought her.

(2) And they brought them into the Temple of the Lord, and the priest said, "Cast lots for me to see who will spin the gold and the white and the linen and the silk and the violet and the scarlet and the true purple."

And the lot for the true purple and scarlet fell to Mary. And she took them into her house. This was the time that Zechariah fell silent, and Samuel took his place until Zechariah could speak. And Mary took the scarlet and was spinning it.

CHAPTER 11: THE ANNUNCIATION

(1) And she took the pitcher and went to fill it with water, and look! A voice was saying to her, "Rejoice, blessed one! The Lord is with you. Blessed are you among women."

And Mary looked around to the right and the left, to see where the voice might be coming from. And she became terrified and went into her house. And setting down the pitcher, she took up the purple and sat upon her throne and spun the purple.

(2) And look! An angel of the Lord stood before her, saying, "Don't fear, Mary, because you've found grace before the Lord of All. You'll conceive from God's word."

And hearing this, Mary questioned herself, saying, "Will I conceive from the Lord, the living God, and give birth like all women give birth?"

(3) And the angel of the Lord said to her, "Not like that, Mary, because the power of God will overshadow you, so the holy one who will be born from you will be called the Son of the Most High. And you'll call his name Jesus, because he'll save his people from their sins.

And Mary said, "Look, I'm the servant of the Lord. May it be to me according to your word."

CHAPTER 12: MARY VISITS ELIZABETH

(1) And she made the purple and the scarlet, and she took it to the priest. And taking it, the priest blessed her and said, "Mary, the Lord God has magnified your name, and you'll be blessed among all the generations of the earth."

(2) And Mary rejoiced and went to her cousin Elizabeth. And she knocked at the door. And Elizabeth heard, flung down the scarlet, and rushed to the door. And she opened it and blessed her and said, "How is it that the mother of my Lord should come to me? Because look, the one in me leaped and blessed you!"

But Mary forgot the mysteries which Gabriel the angel had told her. And she looked intently into heaven and said, "Lord, who am I, that all the women of the earth will bless me?"

(3) And she spent three months with Elizabeth. And day by day, her womb grew larger, and Mary was afraid. She went to her house and hid herself from the people of Israel. She was sixteen years old when these mysteries happened to her.

CHAPTER 13: JOSEPH QUESTIONS MARY

(1) And she was in her sixth month. And look! Joseph came from his building, and came into the house, and found her pregnant. And he struck his face and flung himself on the ground in sackcloth and wept bitterly, saying, "How can I look to the Lord God? What prayer can I say about this young girl, since I took her as a virgin from the Temple of the Lord God and didn't protect her? Who has set this trap for me? Who has done this evil thing in my house? Who has defiled the virgin? Aren't I reliving the story of Adam? For as Adam was glorifying in the hour of prayer, the serpent came, found Eve alone, and deceived her, and now it's happened to me!"

(2) And Joseph stood from the sackcloth and called her and said to her, "God cared for you. Why have you done this? You've forgotten the Lord your God. Why have you humiliated your soul? You were nourished in the Holy of Holies and received food from the hand of an angel!"

(3) And she wept bitterly, saying, "I'm pure, and I haven't known a man!"

And Joseph said to her, "Where then did this thing in your womb come from?"

And she said, "As the Lord my God lives, I don't know where it came from!"

CHAPTER 14: JOSEPH'S DREAM

(1) And Joseph was very afraid and kept quiet about her, considering what to do about her. And Joseph said, "If I hide her sin, I'll be found resisting the law of the Lord, but if I reveal her to the people of Israel, I'm afraid that what's inside her might be angelic, and I'll be found handing over innocent blood to the judgment of death. So what will I do about her? I'll secretly set her free from me."

And night overtook him. (2) And look! An angel of the Lord appeared to him in a dream, saying, "Don't fear this child, for the one in her is from the Holy Spirit. And she'll give birth to a son, and you'll call his name 'Jesus,' because he'll save his people from their sins."

And Joseph arose from his sleep and glorified the God of Israel, who had given grace to him. And he protected her.

Chapter 15: THE CHIEF PRIEST QUESTIONS MARY AND JOSEPH

(1) And Annas the scribe came to him and said to him, "Joseph, why haven't you appeared among our traveling group?"

And he said to him, "Because I was weary from the trip and rested the first day back."

And Annas turned and saw Mary pregnant.

(2) And he quickly went to the priest and said to him, "Joseph, about whom you bore witness, has acted very lawlessly."

And the priest said, "What's this?"

And he said, "The virgin that Joseph took from the Temple of the Lord, he's defiled her and has stolen her wedding and hasn't revealed it to the people of Israel."

And in response the priest said, "Has Joseph done this?"

And Annas the scribe said to him, "Send officers, and you'll find the virgin pregnant."

And the officers went and found her just as he said. And they led her together with Joseph to the court.

(3) And the chief priest said to her, "Mary, why have you done this? Why have you humiliated your soul and forgotten the Lord your God? You were raised in the Holy of Holies, and received food from the hand of an angel, and you heard its hymns and danced before it. What is this that you've done?"

And she wept bitterly, saying, "As the Lord God lives, I'm pure before God, and I haven't known a man!"

(4) And the priest said, "Joseph, what is this that you've done?"

And Joseph said, "As the Lord my God lives, and the witness of God's truth, I'm pure toward her."

And the priest said, "Don't bear false witness, but tell the truth. You stole her wedding and didn't reveal it to the people of Israel, and you haven't bowed your head under the mighty hand that should bless your offspring."

And Joseph fell silent.

CHAPTER 16: THE TEST

(1) And the priest said, "Return the virgin you took from the Temple of the Lord."

And Joseph was tearful.

And the chief priest said, "I'll give you the water of the Lord's rebuke to drink, and it'll reveal your sin in your eyes."

(2) And taking (the water), the priest gave it to Joseph and sent him into the wilderness. And Joseph returned unharmed.

And he gave it to Mary and sent her into the wilderness. And she returned unharmed.

And all the people were amazed that their sin wasn't revealed.

(3) And the priest said, "If the Lord God hasn't revealed your sin to you, neither do I judge you." And he set them free.

And Joseph took Mary and went to his house, rejoicing and glorifying the God of Israel.

CHAPTER 17: THE CENSUS

(1) Now an order went out from Augustus the king to register how many people were in Bethlehem of Judea.

And Joseph said, "I'll register my sons. But what should I do about this child? How will I register her? As my wife? I'm ashamed. As my daughter? But the people of Israel know she's not my daughter. This is the day of the Lord; I'll do whatever the Lord wants."

(2) And he saddled the donkey, and sat her on it, and his son led it, and Samuel followed.

And as they neared the third mile, Joseph turned and saw that she was sad. And he was saying, "Likely the one inside her is troubling her."

And again Joseph turned and saw her laughing, and he said to her, "Mary, why are you like this, that I see your face laughing at one time, but then sad?"

And she said to him, "It's because I see two people in my eyes. One is crying and mourning, and one is rejoicing and exulting."

(3) And they came to the middle of the journey, and Mary said to him, "Joseph, take me down from the donkey, because the one who's inside me is pushing to come out."

And he took her down from the donkey and said to her, "Where will I take you and shelter you in your awkwardness? This place is a wilderness."

CHAPTER 18: TIME STANDS STILL

(1) And he found a cave there, brought her (to it), and stationed his sons with her and went to look for a Hebrew midwife in the region of Bethlehem.

(2) Now I, Joseph, was wandering but not wandering. And I looked up to the dome of heaven and saw it standing still, and into the sky, and I was astonished to see that even the birds of heaven were still. And I looked at the ground and saw a bowl lying there, and workers reclining, and their hands were in the bowl, and they were chewing but not chewing, and they were picking up food but not picking up food, and they were bringing it to their mouths but not bringing it to their mouths. Rather, all their faces were looking up.

And I saw sheep being driven, but the sheep stood still. And the shepherd lifted his hand to strike them, but his hand was raised. And I looked into the torrent of the river and saw young goats, and their mouths were in the water but not drinking.

And suddenly, everything resumed its course.

CHAPTER 19: JESUS' BIRTH

(1) And look! A woman was coming down from the mountain, and she said to me, "Man, where are you going?"

And I said, "I'm seeking a Hebrew midwife."

And in reply she said to me, "Are you from Israel?"

And I said to her, "Yes."

Then she said, "And who's the one giving birth in the cave?"

And I said, "My betrothed."

And she said to me, "She's not your wife?"

And I said to her, "Mary was nurtured in the Temple of the Lord, and it was decided by lot that she would be my wife, yet she's not my wife; but she's conceived from the Holy Spirit."

And the midwife said, "Really?"

And Joseph said to her, "Come and see."

And the midwife went with him. (2) And they stood in front of the cave, and a bright cloud overshadowed the cave. And the midwife said, "My soul is magnified today, because my eyes have seen something wonderful. Salvation has been born to Israel!"

And immediately the cloud withdrew from the cave, and a great light appeared in the cave, so that their eyes couldn't bear it. And a little later, the light withdrew until an infant appeared. And he came and took the breast of his mother, Mary.

And the midwife cried out and said, "How great today is for me, that I've seen this new miracle!"

(3) And the midwife went out from the cave, and Salome met her.

And she said to her, "Salome, Salome, I have to describe a new sight to you. A virgin has given birth, which is against her nature!"

And Salome said, "As the Lord my God lives, unless I examine her condition, I won't believe that the virgin has given birth."

CHAPTER 20: SALOME'S EXAMINATION

(1) And the midwife went in and said, "Mary, position yourself, because there's no small test coming concerning you."

And Salome examined her. And Salome cried out and said, "Woe because of my lawlessness and my unbelief! Because I've tested the living God, and look! My hand is on fire and falling away from me!"

(2) And she dropped to her knees before the Lord, saying, "God of my ancestors, remember me, that I've descended from Abraham, Isaac, and Jacob. Don't make an example of me to the people of Israel, but give me the back to the poor, because you know, Lord, that in your name I've healed people, and I've received my wages from

you."

(3) And look! An angel of the Lord appeared, saying to her, "Salome, Salome, the Lord of All has heard your prayer. Bring your hand to the child and lift him up, and you'll receive salvation and joy."

(4) And Salome joyfully went to the child and lifted him up, saying, "I worship him, because a great king has been born to Israel." And immediately Salome was healed, and she left the cave justified.

And look! A voice was saying, "Salome, Salome, don't report the wonderful things you've seen until the child comes into Jerusalem."

CHAPTER 21: THE MAGI

(1) And look! Joseph prepared to go out into Judea when a great commotion arose in Bethlehem of Judea. For magi came, saying, "Where is the king of the Jews? For we saw his star in the East and have come to worship him."

(2) And when Herod heard, he was disturbed, and he sent officers to the magi, and sent for the chief priests and questioned them in his palace, saying to them, "What has been written about the Christ? Where will he be born?"

They said to him, "In Bethlehem of Judea, for this is what's written." And he set them (the chief priests) free.

And he questioned the magi, saying to them, "What sign did you see about the one who's been born king?"

And the magi said, "We saw an immense star shining among the other stars and dimming them so much that they weren't even visible. And so we knew that a king had been born for Israel, and we came to worship him."

And Herod said to them, "Go and search, and if you find him, report to me so that I can also come and worship him."

(3) And the magi went, and look! The star they had seen in the East led them until they came to the cave, and it stood over the head of the cave. And when they saw him with his mother Mary, the magi took gifts from their bags: gold, and frankincense, and myrrh.

And having been warned by the angel not to go into Judea, they returned to their country by another way.

CHAPTER 22: THE SLAUGHTER OF THE INFANTS

(1) When Herod saw that he had been tricked by the magi, he was angry. He sent out his killers, telling them to kill all the infants two years old and younger.

(2) And when Mary heard that the infants were being killed, she was afraid. She took her child, wrapped him in cloths, and put him in a manger for cows.

(3) And when Elizabeth heard that John was sought, she took him up into the hills and looked around for somewhere to hide him, but there wasn't a hiding place. Then Elizabeth groaned and said, "Mountain of God, take a mother with her child," because Elizabeth was unable to go up higher. And immediately, the mountain split and took her, and a light shone through the mountain for her. For an angel of the Lord was with them, protecting them.

CHAPTER 23: THE MURDER OF ZECHARIAH

(1) But Herod asked for John and sent officers to Zechariah, saying to him, "Where are you hiding your son?"

But he replied, saying to them, "I'm a minister of God, and I sit in God's Temple. How should I know where my son is?"

(2) And his officers went away and reported all these things to Herod. And Herod was angry, and said, "His son is about to be king over Israel!"

And he sent his officers again, to say to him, "Tell me the truth. Where's your son? You know that your life is in my hand."

And the officers went away and reported these things to him.

(3) And Zechariah said, "I'm a martyr of God if you shed my blood, because the Lord will receive my spirit, since you'll be spilling innocent blood at the entrance of the Temple of the Lord."

And around daybreak, Zechariah was murdered, and the people of Israel didn't know that he was murdered.

CHAPTER 24: MOURNING FOR ZECHARIAH

(1) But at the hour of greeting, the priests came, and Zechariah didn't meet them to bless them as was customary. And the priests stood around for Zechariah, waiting to greet him with a blessing and to glorify the Most High God.

(2) But when he delayed, they were all afraid. But one of them gathered the courage to go into the sanctuary and saw blood clotted beside the altar of the Lord. And a voice was saying, "Zechariah has been murdered, and his blood won't be wiped away until his avenger comes!"

When he heard this saying, he was afraid, and he went and reported to the priests what he had seen and heard. (3) And they gathered their courage and went and saw what had taken place. And the panels of the Temple cried out, and they (the priests) ripped their clothes from top to bottom. And they didn't find his corpse, but they found his blood had turned to stone. And they were afraid, and they went out and reported to all the people that Zechariah had been murdered. And when all the tribes of the people heard, they mourned him and wept three days and three nights.

(4) And after three days, the priests held a council about who should replace Zechariah. And the lot fell to Simeon, for he was told by the Holy Spirit that he wouldn't see death until he saw the Christ in the flesh.

CHAPTER 25: CONCLUSION

(1) Now I, James, wrote this history in Jerusalem when there was a commotion over Herod's death. I went into the wilderness until the commotion in Jerusalem had died down. I was glorifying the Lord God, who gave me the wisdom to write this history.

(2) And grace will be with all who fear the Lord. Amen.

Enjoyed your Christian reading?

Don't end your introduction to Christian literature here.

Send a blank email to

thegoodchristian10@gmail.com

for access to Christian audiobooks.